Women Sailors AND SAILORS' Women

Women Sailors and Sailors' Women

An Untold Maritime History

DAVID CORDINGLY

RANDOM HOUSE NEW YORK

RANDOM HOUSE and colophon are registered trademarks of
Random House, Inc.

Library of Congress Cataloging-in-Publication Data

Cordingly, David.

Women sailors and sailors' women: an untold maritime history /
David Cordingly.

p.   cm.

Includes index.

ISBN 0-375-50041-3

1. Women and the sea. I. Title.

G540.C685   2001

910.4'5—dc21   00-062762

Random House website address: www.atrandom.com

Printed in the United States of America on acid-free paper

98765432   24689753   23456789

First Edition

BOOK DESIGN BY MERCEDES EVERETT

For Shirley

CONTENTS

INTRODUCTION

From earliest times the sea has been regarded as a male domain. Fishermen labored around the coasts with nets and lines while their wives stayed on shore to mind their homes and bring up their children. Later explorers and adventurers set sail across the oceans in search of new lands hoping to make their names and their fortunes from their discoveries. The crews of their ships, as well as the crews of the hundreds of thousands of merchant ships and warships that would follow in their wake, were always male. Or were they?

Recent studies have shown that a surprising number of women went to sea. Some traveled as the wives or mistresses of captains. A few were smuggled aboard by officers or by seamen of the lower deck. An increasing number of cases have come to light of young women dressing in men's clothes and working alongside the sailors for months and sometimes years on end. In 1807, Lieutenant William Berry of HMS *Hazard* was charged with committing "the unnatural and detestable sin of sodomy" with a boy in the crew.[1] One of the principal witnesses at the court-martial was a fourteen-year-old girl from Cornwall named Elizabeth Bowden. She was listed on the books of the *Hazard* as a boy of the third class and appeared in court dressed in a long jacket and blue trousers. It had taken her shipmates six weeks to discover her sex, and when they did so, the captain of the *Hazard* gave her a separate apartment to sleep in and allowed her to remain on board as an attendant to the officers. Hannah Snell, the most famous of the female sailors, spent four and a half years serving in the army and the navy as a man in the 1740s and astonished her companions when she finally decided to reveal that she was a woman.

It is equally surprising to find that it was common practice in the British Navy and not unusual in the United States Navy for the wives of boatswains, carpenters, and cooks to go to sea on warships. They acted as mothers to the boys in the crew, and when the ship went into action, they assisted the gun crews and nursed the wounded. Exactly how many ships had warrant officers' wives on board we shall never know, because their presence was not officially acknowledged, but every now and again we learn of their presence in an old seaman's memoirs or in the transcripts of a court-martial. The journals of ships' surgeons are a particularly valuable source of information because they note whether a woman on board has given birth to a baby beside the guns, or whether visiting prostitutes have caused an outbreak of venereal disease among the crew. Captain John Fyffe, commander of HMS *Indefatigable,* took the unusual step of including women in the set of orders that he drew up for his crew in 1812: "The women belonging to the ship are to be permitted to go on shore twice a week on market days. Should they go on any other day, or in any respect act contrary to the regulations of the ship, they are not to be suffered to come on board again."[2]

In the nineteenth century, a number of the captains of merchant ships took their wives to sea with them, and in several cases the wives had to take charge of the ship when the captain fell ill. Some of these women proved to be truly heroic. Mary Patten was nineteen years old and four months pregnant when her husband collapsed in a storm as they approached Cape Horn. Since no other member of the crew could navigate, she took command of the vessel, a clipper ship the size of the *Cutty Sark,* and sailed her around the Horn to San Francisco. Equally heroic were the women who looked after the lighthouses. The most famous was probably Grace Darling, who in 1838 helped her father row an open boat through a winter gale to rescue the survivors of a shipwrecked paddle steamer from a rocky outcrop off the coast of Northumberland. She became a national heroine, but her exploits pale into insignificance beside the achievements of the American lighthouse keeper Ida Lewis, who for thirty years looked after Lime Rock light in the harbor of Newport, Rhode Island. During that time she rescued eighteen lives, on several occasions risking death to do so. The U.S. Life Saving Service presented her with its highest award for her "unquestionable nerve, presence of mind, and dashing courage."[3]

This book began as a study of seafaring heroines like Mary Patten and Hannah Snell, but it soon became apparent that there was scope for a wider study. The women's lives were defined by their role in a traditionally male world, so it seemed logical to question the role of the men in that world. What did the sailors think of their women? Did they simply love them and leave them and forget all about them when their ship sailed over the horizon? To what extent did sailors live up to their reputation for having a wife in every port? How does one reconcile the sailor's love of women with the superstition that a woman at sea brings bad luck? And what about all those sailors' stories about mermaids?

This proved to be a vast subject and some of the findings have been unexpected. The usual view of the seafaring man is that once he heads out to sea, he is far too busy to concern himself with women. Mariners' journals are mostly filled with observations on the weather, navigational notes, and the behavior of the ship and the crew. If the mariner is of an inquiring mind, he records unusual birds and sea creatures and the appearance of islands and harbors overseas. We imagine that when he has any spare time at sea, the sailor spends it mending sails, tying knots, making ship models, gambling, drinking, smoking, dancing the hornpipe, or singing sea chanties. In fact, sailors spent, and no doubt still do spend, a great deal of time thinking about women. Many, if not most, of their songs and sea chanties featured women; they decorated their arms and chests with tattoos dedicated to their mothers or sweethearts; they collected souvenirs to take home to their women; and above all they wrote letters to their women. These letters are often heartrending to read and show that the happy-go-lucky sailor was often desperately homesick and wanted nothing more than for the voyage to end so that he could return to his loved ones at home.

There were of course many who reveled in the freedom and opportunities that a sailor's life gave them. Captain Augustus Hervey took full advantage of his aristocratic connections, and his dashing image as the commander of a 74-gun warship, to bed every attractive woman he met during his voyages around the Mediterranean. Most of the young, unmarried sailors in the navy and the merchant service lost no time in seeking out women in the brothels and dance halls of the waterfront whenever they were given permission to go ashore in a foreign port. There is nothing surprising in this, but it is interesting to learn from the evidence of prostitutes and policemen operating in the sailors' district of London in the nineteenth century that sailors frequently sought out the same prostitutes each time they came ashore, entrusted them with their wages, and in general treated them as if they were married to them for as long as they remained in port.

And what about the women who were left behind? It has to be said that the lot of a sailor's woman was not a happy one. "I wish you had been a parson or anything but a sailor," wrote Jenny, wife of Captain George Rodney, in 1756. "Then I had not known the uneasiness of being parted from him I love better than life."[4] For some it was the loneliness that was the worst thing. For others it was the prolonged separation and the constant, gnawing anxiety that their husband and the father of their children might be lost at sea. This applied to the wife of an admiral as well as to the wife of an ordinary seaman, or a Scottish fisherman, or a deckhand on a whaling ship. And all too often there were tragedies that left a widow and orphans grieving their loss.

With a few exceptions the scope of the book has been limited to the seafarers and their women on both sides of the North Atlantic and in particular to those based on the principal ports of Britain and the United States. Occasional forays into the Pacific have been limited to the voyages of the American whaling ships and a brief glimpse at the lovely women of Tahiti, who became a legendary attraction for sailors following the visits of Captain Cook and Captain Bligh to an island that was seen as an earthly paradise.

The subject matter has been set out in the form of a voyage, beginning with the ships at anchor and looking at the life of sailors' women in the seaports. We move on to observe the press gangs rounding up men to fill the ships before they set sail, and then follow the ships to sea. Out at sea we find that among the apparently all-male crew are a number of women disguised as cabin boys or marines, and we find out which of the stories of female sailors are true and which are fictitious. We also follow the lives of the wives of warrant officers and captains of merchantmen and whaling ships who accompanied their husbands on their voyages. The chapter on men without women begins with a look at homosexuality on board naval ships as revealed in some of the courts-martial of the eighteenth century. The transcripts of these trials are extraordinarily graphic in their description of what took place and reveal the draconian punishments that the Royal Navy inflicted on those found guilty of the crime punishable by the 29th Article of War.

The ambivalent attitude of sailors toward women at sea is examined in the chapter on women and water. The old adage that women brought bad luck is entirely contradicted by the centuries-old belief that women had mystical powers over the oceans. In the era before Christ, sailors in distress would appeal to an appropriate goddess, and in Christian times, they prayed to the Virgin Mary for a safe voyage and deliverance from the perils of the sea. On the other hand, we find the conventional belief that most ships' figureheads depicted women to be far from the case. The predominance of female figureheads was a nineteenth-century phenomenon, and it is only because so many more of these have survived than the earlier lions, dragons, and warriors that we assume that women were more popular on the bows of ships.

From figureheads, sirens, and mermaids, we move on to the behavior of sailors in foreign ports, and then as the ships return home, we look at the lighthouses that guarded the coast and the stories of some of the women who looked after the lights. We end with the sailors' return and see how the women fared in their absence. We are back in the seaport where the voyage began.

Women Sailors
AND SAILORS' Women

Women on the Waterfront

THE ENGLISH ARTIST THOMAS ROWLANDSON WAS AN ASTUTE OBSERVER of sailors and their women, and his engravings provide a vivid picture of life in the waterfront taverns of London around 1800. The faces of his sailors are gnarled and weather-beaten, and their expressions are drunkenly happy or leery and lustful. They are dressed in short blue jackets, loose white shirts, and either baggy trousers or the distinctive garments known as petticoat-breeches. They have brightly colored handkerchiefs knotted around their necks and curiously shapeless black hats jammed on their heads. In one cartoon, entitled *Despatch, or Jack preparing for sea,* a sailor sits on the knee of one young woman while he gropes her companion's breast. In his spare hand he has a drink, and he is shouting encouragement to two musicians who stand beside him scraping away on their fiddles. In another cartoon a sailor and his woman dance an energetic hornpipe while their companions drink and smoke and look on with approval. A couple can be seen making love on the floor, and the whole atmosphere of the tavern reeks of tobacco smoke and strong liquor.

The women in Rowlandson's pictures are young and pretty and buxom. They wear little caps with feathers and ribbons on their heads, necklaces around their shapely necks, and low-cut, high-waisted dresses that emphasize their generous figures. Some of the women are barmaids and others are sailors' wives or sweethearts or whores. All of them appear to be having a good time.

These tavern scenes provide a stark contrast with the descriptions of life in London's East End some fifty years later. Bracebridge Hemyng contributed a chapter on sailors' women to Henry Mayhew's great work *London Labour and the London Poor,* first published in 1851. Among the women Hemyng met during his forays into the sailors' districts of Wapping and Limehouse was China Emma. She was short and rather stout with a pale face and a vacant expression. She lived in Bluegate Fields, a narrow street off the Ratcliffe Highway, and she was looked after by an eccentric Irishwoman who endeavored to stop her from drinking herself to death. China Emma had acquired her nickname because she lived with a Chinese sailor, but she was not Chinese herself. She was born on Goswell Street to parents who kept a grocery. Her mother died when she was twelve years old and her father took to drink. Within three years he was dead, and Emma went to stay with her sister, who soon went off with a man, leaving Emma to fend for herself. She was unable to get any work and things looked bad until she met a sailor. She moved in with him, and they lived as man and wife for six years. Unhappily, like thousands of other sailors, he contracted yellow fever in the West Indies and died. One of his shipmates gave her the news and brought her back the silver snuffbox that her sailor had kept his tobacco quids in.

China Emma moved from street to street and kept herself going by working as a prostitute. Sometime after she moved to Bluegate Fields, she met a Chinese sailor named Apoo, who became her regular partner. He sent her money when he was away, but by now Emma had become an incurable drunkard. Apoo had no patience with her drinking and sometimes resorted to drastic measures. He used to tie her arms and legs together and take her outside into the street: "He'd throw me into the gutter, and then he'd throw buckets of water over me till I was wet through; but that didn't cure; I don't believe anything would; I'd die for a drink; I must have it, and I don't care what I does to get it."[1]

Emma sometimes had melancholy fits when she wished she were dead. Several times she attempted suicide by throwing herself into the

Thames, but her attempts were always foiled. On one occasion she leapt out of the first-floor window of a waterfront house in Jamaica Place, but a passing boatman fished her out of the water with a boat hook. As she explained to her interviewer, "I've no luck; I never had since I was a child."

China Emma and Rowlandson's buxom wenches represent two stereotypes of sailors' women. The former is a pathetic example of the downtrodden victims who attracted the attention of Victorian clergymen and social reformers; the latter are in the tradition of the charming girls with names like Pretty Nancy and Sweet Poll of Plymouth who appear in so many sailors' songs and ballads. Both these stereotypes existed and were typical of their times, but they were only the most visible of the sailors' women to be found in every port.

The women we hear least about are the close relatives of sailors and in particular their mothers and sisters. We catch glimpses here and there. Captain John Cremer, more familiarly known as Ramblin' Jack, came from a seafaring family in the East End of London and left a journal describing his adventures at sea. He was born around 1700 on East Lane, Bermondsey, on the south bank of the Thames a mile or so downstream from the Tower of London. His father was master of a merchant ship, and his uncle was a captain in the navy. "As to my mother's family; she was a master ropemaker's daughter, which had three rope-walks joining on the back of East Lane, and called Cantor's Rope-walks to this day."[2] The rope-walks can be seen alongside the adjoining timber yards on old maps of London. They were long, narrow sites where strands of hemp were twisted to form the lengths of rope used for the rigging and anchor cables of ships. Jack's father was captured by the French and died around 1706, leaving his mother a house in Deptford and about £14 a year. We hear nothing more about Jack's mother beyond the fact that her brother, who was a lieutenant in the Royal Navy, arranged for Jack to join the crew of his ship, HMS *Dover*, in 1708.

Another glimpse of a sailor's family of this period is provided by Ned Ward, a London publican and journalist, whose best-known and least reliable work is a satirical pamphlet about life in the Royal Navy entitled *The Wooden World Dissected*. He also published his observations on London life in a series of articles in *The London Spy*, which came out in book form in 1703. Unlike the navy, of which he had no firsthand experience, he had an intimate knowledge of London's streets, taverns, fairs, and customs. On one occasion around Christmastime, he and a friend took a stroll along the north bank of the Thames to Wapping, where they ventured into a public house to refresh themselves with a bowl of punch.

"The first figure that accosted us at our entrance was a female Wappineer, whose crimson countenance and double chin, contain'd within the borders of a white calico hood, and her fiery-face look, in my fancy, was like a red-hot iron glowing in a silver chafing dish."[3] The woman was the landlady of the pub and the mother of two sailors. One of her sons was sitting glumly in the corner smoking a short pipe of stinking tobacco. After she had served Ward and his friend, she subjected her son to a torrent of abuse for his idleness. She complained that she worked as hard as any woman in the parish but could not afford to support him, and urged him to get off his backside and sign on to one of several ships that were bound for the West Indies. He agreed to do so and had no sooner left the pub than in walked his sailor brother, Bartholomew, with a hat full of money clutched under his arm. He explained that he had been paid off when his ship reached the Downs and had made his way around to the Thames on a local vessel. He greeted his loud and corpulent mother with enthusiasm.

"Sure never any seafaring son of a whore had ever such a good mother upon shore as I have. 'Ounds, mother, let me have a bucket full of punch, that we may swim and toss in an ocean of good liquor, like a couple of little pinks in the Bay of Biscay."[4] The mother and her favorite son had been drinking for a while when the sailor's sister, Betty, entered the tavern, "and there was such a wonderful mess of slip-slop licked up between brother Bat and sister Bet that no two friends, met by accident in a foreign plantation, could have expressed more joy in their greeting."

The Wapping landlady was one of many sailors' women who earned a living in the taverns along the Thames, and in other British seaports. In the eighteenth century, as today, alehouses were often run by families.[5] In most cases the landlord was formally in charge, but it was the landlady and her daughters who did much of the work and who set the tone for the establishment. We see them in numerous engravings doling out drink for the sailors, and joining in their noisy celebrations as the men savored their precious few weeks ashore before returning to their ships. There were women licensees of alehouses, but they were a minority and were usually the widows of former land-lords. According to the 1796 directory for Liverpool, no less than 27 percent of licensed victuallers were female, but in most places the pro-portion was much lower.[6]

The sailors' women who were most in evidence in the East End of London were not landladies or sailors' mothers but the women de-scribed by Ward as strumpets or trulls. They were to be found plying their trade in the brothels that centered around the Ratcliffe Highway. This street lay to the north of the wharves on the riverfront at Wap-ping. It was described in 1600 by John Stow as "a continual street, or filthy straight passage, with alleys of small tenements or cottages builded, inhabited by sailors and victuallers."[7] Most sailors were young and unmarried, and every tide brought them flocking ashore from the hundreds of ships moored in serried ranks in the Pool of London. They were looking for women and drink, and the establishments along the Ratcliffe Highway provided for their needs. During the course of the seventeenth century, the neighborhood attracted prostitutes of several nationalities, including an influx of Flemish women who had a reputation for their sexual expertise and Venetian courtesans who were too expensive for ordinary seamen and were patronized by aristocrats and members of the court.

The most notorious of the local women in the 1650s and 1660s was Damaris Page, who was described by Samuel Pepys as "the great bawd of the seamen."[8] She was born in Stepney around 1620, became a pros-titute in her teens, and married a man named William Baker in 1640. During the course of the next fifteen years, she moved on from pros-titution to operating brothels. She had one on the Ratcliffe Highway that catered to ordinary seamen and dockworkers, and she also man-aged one on Rosemary Lane for naval officers and those who could af-ford the prices of the classier prostitutes. In 1653, she married a second husband, and two years later she was brought before the magistrates at Clerkenwell. The first charge of bigamy was dismissed on the grounds that her first marriage had not been sanctified, but the second charge was more serious. Accused of killing Eleanor Pooley while attempting to carry out an abortion with a two-pronged fork, she was charged with manslaughter and sentenced to be hanged. She was fortunate to be pregnant herself, however, and after being examined by a panel of matrons, she escaped the death sentence and spent three years in Newgate prison instead. On her release, she resumed her career as a madam and died a wealthy woman in her house on the Ratcliffe Highway in 1669.

The steady growth in London's maritime trade during the course of the eighteenth century brought more and more ships to the wharves and quays below London Bridge. A report published in 1800 estimated that there were 8,000 vessels and boats of all kinds in the port of London at any one time, and with the ships came the sailors.[9] Inevitably there was an increase in the supply of prostitutes to meet the demand. Some of these were girls who were forced into prostitution by sheer poverty. Others were young women who decided that they would rather sell their bodies than work sixteen hours a day as laundresses or seamstresses. According to the observations of Daniel Defoe in 1725, many prostitutes came from the huge army of young maidservants in London and took to prostitution to support themselves on the frequent occasions when they found themselves out of work: "This is the reason why our streets are swarming with strumpets. Thus many of them rove from place to place, from bawdy-house to service, and from service to bawdy-house again."[10]

While all too many prostitutes were downtrodden victims exposed to the dangers of disease and violence that were the hazards of their profession, it is evident that many women retained some measure of control over their lives. In the 1780s, Francis Place was apprenticed to a London leather breeches maker who had three daughters. The eldest daughter was a common prostitute, but the other daughters had more satisfactory arrangements. The youngest daughter, about age seventeen, had pleasant lodgings where she was visited by a gentleman, and the second daughter was kept by the captain of an East Indiaman "in whose absence she used to amuse herself as such women generally do."[11]

There was also a class of prostitutes who worked from home or could be approached in the theaters or pleasure gardens. These were the women who were sought out by the more discerning naval officers wishing for female entertainment. The names of these women, together with their addresses and details of their physical appearance and special skills, could be found in a variety of publications such as *The Covent Garden Magazine or Amorous Repository, The Man of Fashion's Companion*, and *The Rangers Magazine*. The first lists, produced in the 1740s, were handwritten and compiled by John Harris, who worked at the Shakespeare's Head, a Covent Garden tavern frequented by sea captains and directors of the East India Company. So popular were the lists that Harris went into print, as *Harris's List of Covent-Garden Ladies*, and some 8,000 copies of the 1758 edition were sold. Harris died in 1765 but his lists continued to be updated and issued on an annual basis up into the 1790s. The British Library has several editions and they make fascinating reading. Several of the women included in the slim volumes indicated a preference for sailors. Mrs. Crosby of 24 George Street, for instance, "being particularly attached to the sons of Neptune," had married an elderly sea captain. On his death, he left her a small annuity that was enough to keep her off the streets but not enough to live on, so she worked as a part-time prostitute. Readers of *Harris's List* were told that she could be contacted at home during the day or in one of the theaters in the evening, where she always sat in the side boxes. She was described as having dark hair flowing in ringlets down her back, languishing gray eyes, and a tolerable complexion. She charged one guinea for her services.[12]

Mrs. Grafton, who lived near Union Stairs in Wapping, let it be known that "her chief and best customers are sea officers, who she particularly likes, as they do not stay long at home, and always return fraught with love and presents."[13] She was described as a comely woman of forty who could give more pleasure than a dozen raw girls. She had acquired twenty years' experience working as a prostitute in Portsmouth before settling in London. Her price was 5 shillings, an attractive price for most naval officers, as a day's pay for the most senior captains in this period was 20 shillings.

Harris's List makes frequent use of nautical expressions in describing the physical accomplishments of some of the women. The most conspicuous example of this occurs in the description of Miss Devonshire of Queen Anne Street. After a description of her fair complexion, her cerulean eyes, her fine teeth, and her good figure, the reader is informed that "many a *man of war* hath been her willing prisoner, and paid a proper ransom; her port is said to be well guarded by a light brown *chevaux-de-freize*, and parted from *bumbay* by a very small pleasant isthmus. The entry is rather straight; but when once in there is very good *riding* . . . she is so brave, that she is ever ready for an engagement, cares not how soon she comes to *close quarters*, and loves to fight *yard arm* and *yard arm*, and be briskly *boarded*."[14]

By the 1840s and 1850s, the cheerful, noisy atmosphere of the East

End taverns and bawdy houses noted by Ward and pictured by Rowlandson had been replaced by a darker, more sinister area of slum dwellings, seedy dance halls, and down-at-the-heel brothels. The increase in the number of prostitutes and the dreadful conditions in which most of them worked led to a number of studies and investigations. In 1857, William Acton, a surgeon who specialized in female venereal diseases, published a book entitled *Prostitution, Considered in Its Moral, Social, and Sanitary Aspects in London and Other Large Cities*. This was based on information derived partly from his own observations and partly from figures supplied by the police. He reckoned that there were 2,825 brothels within the Metropolitan Police District and some 8,600 prostitutes. According to his figures, more than one-third of the brothels were situated in the East End of London, with the heaviest concentration in the area around the Ratcliffe Highway.

The cold statistics produced by Acton and other observers were brought to life by the descriptions of men like Bracebridge Hemyng, who interviewed the unhappy China Emma. Hemyng was aided in his investigations by a local police sergeant who knew his way around the brothels and drinking dens of the sailors' district. In one particularly sleazy and tumbledown hovel, they entered a room where a lascar was living with his woman. The East Indian sailor had been smoking opium and was lying on a straw mattress on the floor covered by two tattered blankets. He was stupefied by the opium and the room was filled with its sickly smell. The only piece of furniture was a table. The woman who crouched by his bedside looked like an animated bundle of rags. Her face was grimy and unwashed "and her hands so black and filthy that mustard-and-cress might have been sown successfully upon them."[15] Other lodging houses were more respectable, and Hemyng found the rooms to be larger than he expected. They were sometimes furnished with four-poster beds hung with faded chintz curtains. On the mantelpiece there would be some cheap crockery with a gilt or rosewood mirror hanging above. The sailors did not seem in the least concerned by the sudden appearance of the police sergeant and his companion and never showed any hostility.

The two men also visited a dance hall on the Ratcliffe Highway. This was on the upper floor of a public house and was a long room illuminated by gas lighting. There were benches along the walls and in the far corner a raised dais for the orchestra. Sitting behind a wooden ledge on which they placed their music sheets were four bearded and shaggy-looking musicians. Their instruments consisted of a trumpet, two flutes, and a fiddle, and with these they filled the room with a shrill, exhilarating sound that provoked the dancers to waltz around the room at great speed. Hemyng was astonished by the grace of the dancers, particularly the foreign sailors, who danced the waltzes and polkas with polished ease. The women were not such expert dancers but were self-possessed and decorous: "They did not look as if they had come here for pleasure exactly, they appeared too business-like for that; but they did seem as if they would like, and intended, to unite the two, business and pleasure, and enjoy themselves as much as the circumstances would allow."[16] He noted that the women did not change into their ball dresses in the dance hall but dressed at home and then walked through the streets in all their finery but without their bonnets.

John Binney, another contributor to Mayhew's *London Labour and the London Poor,* noted that within the category of sailors' women there were two classes. The lower class were little more than thieves. They would take a sailor into a coffeehouse or tavern, spike his drink with a drug such as laudanum, and then rob him. Or they would pick up a drunken sailor on the highway, lure him into a dark street with the promise of sex, and then steal his money and valuables. But there was also a better class of prostitute who did not resort to stealing and who did not work for male pimps.

> They dress tolerably well, in silk and merino gowns with crinolines, and bonnets gaily attired with flowers and ribbons. Many of them have velvet stripes across the breast and back of their gowns, and large brooches with the portrait of a sailor encased in them. They generally lay their hair back in front in the French style.[17]

Most of them lived in Albert Square, Palmer's Folly, Seven Star Alley, and the other streets around the Ratcliffe Highway. Binney reckoned the best-looking girls were Irish cockneys, but there were also a number of Dutch and German prostitutes, some of whom he thought were good-looking and others not. The foreign women spoke English pretty well, and one of the German women explained to an interviewer how she saw herself as a wife to visiting sailors. She was currently living with an English sailor whose ship was in the docks. She

had known him for a year and a half and he always lived with her when
he came ashore.

> He is a nice man and give me all his money when he land always.
> I take all his money while he with me, and not spend it quick as
> some of your English women do. If I not to care, he would spend
> all in one week. Sailor boy always spend money like rainwater;
> he throw it in the street and not care to pick it up again.[18]

She said that she was honest with him and he trusted her. If he had
£24 when he left his ship and he stayed six weeks with her, they would
spend £15 or £20 together and he would let her keep whatever was left
over when it was time for him to go. She knew that if he kept his money
himself he would fall into bad hands. He would order clothes at a slop-
seller who would overcharge him and ruin him. She was frank about
her relations with other sailors: "I know very many sailors—six, eight,
ten, oh! more than that. They are my husbands. I am not married, of
course not, but they think me their wife while they are on shore."
However, she admitted that she did not care much for any of them and
that she had a lover of her own who was a waiter in a coffeehouse. He
was German and came from Berlin, where she herself had been born.

It seems to have been a common practice for sailors to seek out the
same woman when they came ashore. Sergeant Prior of the Metropolitan Police told Hemyng that when sailors landed in the docks they
would draw their wages and go to live with the women they had been
with previously. They would give the women their money and considered themselves married to them for the time being. The women
usually treated them honorably, and when the money ran out, the men
went off to sea to earn some more.

IT IS INTERESTING TO COMPARE THE SAILORS' DISTRICT OF LONDON WITH
that of New York. Between 1800 and 1820, New York's population had
more than doubled, to around 123,000, and it had become the leading
port of North America. Sailing vessels of all sizes clustered along the
city's wharves, their masts forming a dense forest of weathered pine,
tarred rigging, and salt-stained sails stretching the length of South
Street. Today an elevated highway sweeps overhead toward the gleam-
ing skyscrapers of Wall Street, but in the early part of the nineteenth
century, the waterfront was a miscellaneous collection of warehouses,

sail lofts, timber yards, fish markets, taverns, ships' chandlers, and the houses of merchants and sea captains. Dozens of horses and carts threaded their way among the throngs of seamen and dockworkers. As with the waterfront alongside the Pool of London, the potent smells of fish and tar and horse manure mixed with the more pleasant aromas from cargoes of grain and tea and spices being unloaded from the ships.

Behind the buildings on the waterfront was an assortment of fine brick mansions, shops, seedy boardinghouses, bars, and dancing saloons. The area particularly frequented by sailors was centered around Water Street, and this is where the sailors' women were to be found. In 1853, there were reported to be thirty-eight houses of prostitution on Water Street alone and 138 young women working in them.[19] According to Matthew Hale Smith, the women there were the lowest and most debased of their class. They were flashy, untidy, and covered with tinsel and brass jewelry: "Their dresses are short, arms and necks bare, and their appearance as disgusting as can be conceived."[20] Equally notorious for vice and crime were Cherry Street, Fulton Street, and the waterfront adjoining Corlears Hook. The latter area is generally credited with giving rise to the term "hooker" and certainly had its fair share of rough characters, male and female. One observer thought the women there were bloated with rum, rotten with disease, drugged on opium, and victims of brutality and every kind of excess.

In some ways the dancing saloons, lodging houses, and brothels were similar to their equivalents in London's East End. The dancing saloons had three-piece bands that played noisy and energetic music on the violin, the banjo, and the tambourine. The bars were packed with weather-beaten sailors who were carefree and generous with their wages. "A sailor with cash in his pocket has a decided antipathy to drinking alone," wrote William Sanger, "and generally invites everyone in the room, male and female, to partake with him."[21] But there does seem to have been a difference between London and New York in the level of violence and in the way the prostitutes and their customers flaunted themselves on the streets. In Wapping and Stepney and Limehouse, most of the crime and vice went on behind closed doors or in dark alleys. In New York, it often took place in full view of respectable residents and shocked neighbors.

In 1839, a watchman arrested Edward Hogan and Catharine Riley for shamelessly copulating on the front steps of a house on Oliver Street. Ellen Robinson said it was impossible to live in her Water Street tenement because prostitutes were in the habit of sitting half-naked on the front stoop. In March 1847, the *National Police Gazette* reported the trial of George Beach on a charge of keeping a disorderly house.[22] Beach lived at 304 Water Street and faced an onslaught from hostile neighbors. John Robinson, who lived at number 309, complained that Beach's house was one of the worst in the city. It was a place of riot and drunkenness where men and women of the most infamous character gathered and used obscene and profane language. Robert Legget, who lived on Cherry Street, confirmed that it had been a riotous house for years and that he had seen thieves and prostitutes on the premises as late as one o'clock in the morning. But the most graphic account came from Charles Devlin, who was described as the principal complainant. He lived opposite, at number 318, with his wife and young daughters, and said that he had observed girls dancing naked in the house, and on Saturday nights "girls on Beach's steps take down men's pantaloons, which is a common practice." But his most damning charge was that Beach had girls as young as eleven years of age in the house and that he had cohabited with a girl of thirteen.

Child prostitution was rife in the city by the 1840s, and much of it went on in brothels run by women. In the same month that Beach was arrested, a woman named Jane White, alias Horn, alias Cook, was brought before the magistrates for conducting a system of juvenile prostitution from her house on Reade Street. A dozen young girls were sent out by their parents to sell fruit and candy in the local bars, offices, and stores. They would be befriended by unscrupulous men with perverted tastes and taken to White's house "to consummate their degradation by actual prostitution."[23] The girls received $2 or $3 a day from prostitution and were expected to give most of this to White. In May of the same year, Mary Ann Sterling was arrested for keeping a den of infamy at 27 Roosevelt Street. Six girls between the ages of twelve and sixteen were living in a miserable state of prostitution on her premises.[24] William Bell, a police officer, reported that a small fifteen-year-old girl who worked in a junk shop by the docks on Front Street was in the habit of going aboard coal boats in that vicinity and prostituting herself.[25]

Not all such girls were victims, and one of the surprising features of prostitution in New York is the number of women who retained control over their lives. Lucy Ann Brady, for instance, was a prostitute on an occasional basis. She was born in the city around 1820 and came from a poor family. As a teenager she used to attend the theater and began having sex with the men she met there. Her parents sent her to the House of Refuge, an institution for juvenile delinquents, but she ran away and for a year lived a life of casual promiscuity. She spent three nights with a steamboat captain. Another man paid her $5 for a night spent in a brothel on Orange Street. On another occasion she met a girlfriend in an oyster saloon, and they picked up two men and took them to another Orange Street brothel. Once she was arrested by the authorities and kept off the street for a while, but on being released she resumed her old life. Most of the time she worked as a servant but resorted to prostitution when she needed more money.[26]

As they grew older many New York prostitutes took to running their own establishments, and the newspapers frequently mentioned their arrest for keeping a disorderly house. Some of them were formidable characters. Mary or "Moll" Stephens, who was described as the keeper of a den of prostitution, was arrested on Christmas Day, 1846, for attempting to shoot a man named Briggs with a six-barreled pistol. Briggs had been noisy on her premises and refused to leave, so she discharged the pistol in his face. Fortunately for him, the barrel she fired was empty, although it was discovered that the other five barrels were loaded with powder and ball.[27]

Several New York prostitutes became wealthy property owners. Maria Williamson, who was reputed to run one of the greatest whorehouses in America, had saved enough money by 1819 to buy her brothel and adjoining real estate for $3,500. By 1820, she owned five brothels on Church Street, the total value of the houses being $10,000.[28] Fanny White bought a Mercer Street brothel in 1851 after working as a prostitute for some years. Two years later, she was assessed for $11,000 in real estate and $5,000 in personal property taxes. She then sailed for Europe with Dan Sickles, a married man who had been appointed secretary to James Buchanan, minister to Britain. She returned from Europe in 1854 and resumed the management of the brothel on Mercer Street. She accumulated several other houses, some of which were gifts from her numerous suitors, and married Edmond Blankman, a lawyer. On her death in 1860, she owned three fine city mansions as well as other property the total value of which was reckoned to be between $50,000 and $100,000.[29] This would make her a millionaire in today's terms.

Eliza Bowen Jumel was even more successful. She was born in Providence, Rhode Island, in 1775, the daughter of a prostitute. At an early age she became a prostitute herself, and when she was nineteen, she moved to New York, where she joined a theatrical troupe. She must have had considerable charms, because she was soon the talk of the town. In 1804, she married Stephen Jumel, a successful French wine merchant, who set her up in a fine mansion above Harlem. When her husband died, she took over his business and proved such a shrewd businesswoman that she is said to have become the wealthiest woman in America.[30]

The most famous New York prostitute in the 1840s was Julia Brown. She began in the 1830s by working in a brothel run by a notorious madam named Adeline Miller. After a while she set up on her own, and by 1842 she had a magnificent parlor house on Leonard Street. She attended the most fashionable balls and parties and became known as Princess Julia.[31]

These women were the tip of the iceberg. Recent studies of prostitution in New York have shown that dozens of other women made a good living from running brothels and boardinghouses. Marilynn Wood Hill has shown that at least twenty-four prostitutes had property valued at $5,000 or more in the years between 1840 and 1860, and both she and Timothy Gilfoyle have studied city records, newspapers, and the books of nineteenth-century reformers, which reveal that prostitution was not only a means to personal wealth for many women, but was sometimes an entrée into respectable society.

Things were rather different in San Francisco. This was the most notorious of all the ports in the Western world for its brothels, its nightlife, and the bizarre entertainments that were provided for the visiting sailors and the men who flocked into the city during and after the Gold Rush of 1849. Before then San Francisco was little more than a shantytown of wooden shacks, crudely constructed tents, and the mud huts of a few Mexican Indian families. The entire population of the place was reckoned to be no more than 459 people in June 1847, the majority of whom were men between the ages of twenty and forty.[32] Within a year of the finding of gold, some 50,000 men had arrived in the hope of making their fortune. The number of ships arriving in the booming town increased rapidly: 451 came in October 1851, and during the following year, a total of 1,147 entered the bay and dropped anchor offshore or tried to find a place alongside the one and only wharf.[33] Boardinghouses, bars, taverns, and gambling dens were hastily erected along the waterfront or in some cases were set up on board the ships lying on the beach. A doorway was cut in the side of the sailing ship *Niantic,* the interior was roughly converted into a doss-house, and the words "Rest for the Weary and Storage for Trunks" were painted on her sides. The brig *Euphemia* was turned into a jail.

The acute shortage of women was solved by shipping in prostitutes from New Orleans and the east coast of America. A batch of prostitutes was even brought over from France. Mexican women arrived in considerable numbers, and there was a brisk trade in women from China. The prettiest Chinese girls from the interior of the country were sold to the brothels that catered to the rapidly growing numbers of rich merchants and tradesmen, while the boat girls from Chinese seaports ended up in the inferior dens of prostitution frequented by sailors and gold miners. By the 1860s, San Francisco had developed into a flourishing frontier town with levels of crime, violence, and vice that matched those of long-established seaports.

An excerpt from a graphic article in the *San Francisco Herald* noted: "There are certain spots in our city, infested by the most abandoned men and women, that have acquired a reputation little better than the Five Points of New York or St. Giles of London. The upper part of Pacific Street, after dark, is crowded by thieves, gamblers, low women, drunken sailors and similar characters, who resort to the groggeries that line the street, and there spend the night in the most hideous orgies."

Pacific Street was the center of the area that became known as the Barbary Coast.[34] It stretched from the junction of Montgomery Street and Kearney Street down past Front Street to the water's edge. Every adventurous sailor looked forward to sampling its delights and being able to boast to his shipmates about his experiences there. The fact that many sailors were beaten up and robbed and infected with virulent forms of venereal disease on the Barbary Coast does not seem to have lessened its attraction. Apart from the inevitable gambling dens and bars, the Barbary Coast included an extraordinary variety of establishments catering to the sexual needs of visiting sailors. There were dance halls with small bands or orchestras in which the principal attractions were the women who were called "pretty waiter girls" whatever their age and looks. They wore gaudy and revealing costumes that usually consisted of black silk stockings, short skirts, and low-cut blouses. For the payment of the derisory fee of 50 cents, the patrons of some dance halls were allowed to strip the girls and view them naked. The enterprising manager of one of the Mexican dives somewhat preempted this custom by introducing a form of dress for his pretty waiter girls that he believed would give him an edge over his rivals. Instead of providing topless girls, as is the custom in similar establishments today, he provided bottomless girls. Their costume consisted of nothing more than short red jackets, black stockings, fancy garters, and red slippers. He was forced to abandon the experiment after a few weeks because the girls complained of the cold and it became impossible to control the hordes of men who crowded in to view the spectacle.

Then there were the "melodeons," so called because the music in them was originally provided by instruments called melodeons, which were small reed organs operated by foot treadles. These places provided liquor and staged theatrical performances ranging from the vulgar to the obscene; acts involving bestiality were not uncommon. The most famous of the melodeons was the Bella Union. The girls who performed on the stage were expected to sell drinks during intermissions, and if a customer wished to have sex with them, they retired to a room set aside with curtained booths or alcoves. The concert halls were similar to the melodeons and staged anything from lesbian acts to song-and-dance routines performed by women with stage names such as the Roaring Gimlet, the Little Lost Chicken, Lady Jane Grey, the Galloping Cow, and the Dancing Heifer. The latter two were sisters, enormous washerwomen who found it more profitable to perform on stage than to wash laundry. The Galloping Cow saved enough money to open her own saloon on Pacific Street in 1878. Any man who attempted to make advances to her was likely to have a bottle smashed over his head.

Whatever the entertainment provided in the dance halls, melodeons, and concert halls, it was usual for the women in them to work as prostitutes on the side. There were also brothels that made no attempt to provide music or dancing, and these fell into three main types: parlor houses, which usually housed the younger and prettier girls and charged anywhere from $2 to $10 for a brief visit and $20 for an all-night session; cribs, which were small, dirty, and dangerous; and cow yards, which were collections of cribs in one building housing as many as 300 prostitutes. Benjamin Estelle Lloyd, a local historian, summed up his impressions in a damning account in *Lights and Shades of San Francisco*, published in 1876: "The Barbary Coast is the haunt of the low and vile of every kind. The petty thief, the house-burglar, the tramp, the whoremonger, lewd women, cut-throats, murderers are all found here." He described the dance halls and concert saloons in which bleary-eyed men and faded women drank vile liquor, smoked offensive tobacco, and sang obscene songs. He concluded: "Licentiousness, debauchery, pollution, loathsome disease, insanity from dissipation, misery, poverty, wealth, profanity, blasphemy and death are there. And Hell, yawning to receive the putrid mass, is there also."

A few of the women who worked in the waterfront area of San Francisco managed to retain some measure of independence, but the vast majority of American, Mexican, Chinese, and European women working in the bars, dance halls, and brothels were degraded and exploited victims in an exceptionally rough, male-oriented world. This was not always the case with sailors' women elsewhere, as we have seen. However, it has to be said that the lives of most prostitutes in seaports were hard and dangerous and offered little hope for the future. Why, then, did so many women become prostitutes and who exactly were they?

Nineteenth-century observers were agreed on who the women were. They were young and they were working class. The most detailed survey of New York prostitutes was that carried out by Dr. William Sanger, published in 1858. Sanger was chief resident physician of Blackwell's Island Hospital in New York City and was appointed to investigate the extent of venereal disease among the poor in the city. He turned his original brief into an ambitious work, which he entitled *The History of Prostitution: Its Extent, Causes and Effects Throughout the World*. The basis of his study was the information obtained from 2,000 women, and this provides a remarkable insight into their lives. The limitations of the study are that it was dependent on information supplied by the police, who seem to have concentrated on women in brothels. Streetwalkers were largely ignored and child prostitutes were mysteriously omitted, although we know that large numbers of children under the age of fifteen were engaged in prostitution.

Sanger's study makes it clear that the great majority of adult prostitutes were between the ages of eighteen and twenty-three. Most of the rest were between twenty-four and thirty, after which the numbers drop sharply. Amazingly, his survey notes that there was a prostitute still working at the age of seventy-one and another at the age of seventy-seven. With regard to the occupations of the 2,000 women in his study, 933 had been servants before becoming prostitutes, 499 had lived with parents or friends, and most of the rest were dressmakers, tailoresses, or seamstresses. These figures are echoed in similar studies produced by the Reverend G. P. Merrick, chaplain of London's Millbank prison, who interviewed more than 100,000 women during the course of his work.[35] In an analysis of the trades and professions of 14,790 prostitutes, Merrick found that 8,001 were domestic servants, 2,667 were needlewomen, 1,617 were trade girls who worked in factories, 1,050 were barmaids, and the rest were street sellers, governesses, or dancers, or had no other job. Merrick also provided figures to show that the majority of the fathers of prostitutes were carpenters, laborers, shopkeepers, factory foremen, mechanics, soldiers, sailors, publicans, and farmers. Very few were professional men, officials in institutions, merchants, or shipowners, and only 13 were described as gentlemen. Merrick tested the reading and writing skills of the women and found that 3,237 were illiterate and 2,293 were of the lowest standard.

The traditional explanation for why women became prostitutes was that they were seduced by men and then abandoned. But of the 2,000 women studied by Sanger, only 258 gave this as a reason. The largest number, 525, gave destitution as the cause of their taking to the streets, and 515 gave "inclination." Sanger explains that "inclination" did not mean they wanted to become prostitutes but that they drifted into it for one reason or another: Some had been persuaded by other prostitutes; several had taken to drink as a result of problems in their lives and needed the money to satisfy their craving for liquor. Again Merrick's figures reflect similar findings. Out of a list of 16,022 women, 3,363 pleaded poverty and necessity resulting from lack of employment as the reason, 5,061 left their homes voluntarily for various reasons, 2,808 were led away by other girls, 3,154 were seduced and drifted onto the streets, and 1,636 fell into that category favored by the Victorian novelists: They were betrayed under a promise of marriage "and having lost their characters, and being abandoned by their seducers and relatives, felt that they had no alternative but to seek a home and livelihood amongst the 'fallen.' "[36] The reasons so many girls left their homes voluntarily would appear to be much the same as they are today: quarrels and tensions within the household; one or both parents taking to drink; violent or sexual abuse from the father or another male relation; or a wish to escape the confines and restrictions of family life. As one seventeen-year-old girl from Connecticut explained, "Mother is cross and home is an old, dull, dead place."[37]

Sanger provides several examples of young women driven to prostitution through poverty. One example in particular sums up the problems often faced by the wives of seamen. The woman, who is identified only by the initials C.H., told Sanger that her father and mother had died while she was a child. At the age of seventeen she married a sailor, and they had three children. The girl died but the two boys survived. She said that the family lived very comfortably until the youngest child was born, but then her husband began to drink. He stopped supporting the family and then went away, and she had not seen or heard from him for six months. Her older boy was five years old and her younger was eighteen months. She tried to keep going by washing and other work but could never manage to earn more than $2 or $3 a week. She came to New York with her two children "and I support them with what I earn by prostitution. It was only to keep them that I came here."[38]

Merrick and Sanger were agreed on the dreadful toll that prostitution took on the lives of those who practiced it. Sanger reckoned that the average duration of the life of a prostitute did not exceed four years from the commencement of her career. Merrick came up with a similar figure: "I find that the average number of years which they live after having taken to a 'life on the streets' is about three years and six weeks."[39] According to Merrick, the reasons for the high mortality of the women were the irregular hours, irregular meals, being out in all kinds of weather, short and broken sleep, and the constant drain on their natural strength.

While the lives of all too many prostitutes followed a tragic downward spiral, there were heartening examples of women who turned their earnings to good advantage. We have already noted examples of New York prostitutes who bought up properties and in some cases became wealthy women. Judith Walkowitz has shown in her studies of prostitution in the British ports of Plymouth and Southampton that women were not always the passive victims of male sexual abuse.[40] Many of them retained control of their lives. They negotiated their own prices. They established networks that enabled them to support each other in a male-dominated world. They often worked in pairs, both to protect themselves from violent customers and to enable them to overpower and rob drunken sailors. Many of them became lodging-house keepers, and while this made few women rich, it did give them a measure of independence.

2

The Sailors' Farewell

WHEN A WARSHIP WAS READY TO LEAVE HARBOR, THE BLUE PETER FLAG was hoisted at the masthead. This signal meant "All persons report on board—vessel is about to proceed to sea." Those sailors who had been allowed ashore swigged down their last drink, said farewell to their women, and made their way down to the waterfront with their sea chests. From there they had to find a boat to take them to their ship, which was anchored out in the fairway.

Sailors had no right to shore leave, and during times of war, many captains refused to allow their sailors ashore for fear that they would desert. In those cases it was the usual custom to permit wives to be ferried out to the ship. The wives were frequently outnumbered by local prostitutes, carried by enterprising boatmen who banked on the sailors' paying the women's fares.[1] To satisfy naval regulations, the women selected by the sailors to come aboard were signed on as their wives. The legal and illegal wives were allowed to live aboard the anchored ship for as long as she was in harbor. They shared the sailors' hammocks, and judging from contemporary reports and pictures, they danced and drank with them as merrily as the women in the sailors' taverns ashore. But when the blue peter flag was hoisted, it was time for the women to leave.

Whether it took place on the shore or aboard ship, the sailor's farewell to his woman was a theme that captured people's imaginations and was commemorated in numerous popular prints and poems, particularly in times of war. Although many of the prints and their accompanying verses were overtly sentimental and patriotic, they tell us a great deal about the mood of their times. Two engravings produced during Britain's war with France and Spain (1739 to 1748) are typical. The first, entitled *The Sailor's Farewell*, shows a seaman and his sweetheart standing on the shore with a ship anchored in the distance. The young woman clasps her lover around the neck and rests her head on his shoulder while the sailor points to the ship, which has pennants streaming from her mastheads and is raising her fore topsail as a signal for departure. The following verses are printed below the picture.

> See, see, you streamers! Lo, the wind sits fair,
>   And cruel calls the fondly parting pair.
> Oh, signal dire! the foresail too is bent;
>   And lo, they give their mutual anguish vent.
> The longboat waits, sly beck'ning are the crew;
>   They, death-like, struggle in a last adieu.

The second engraving, entitled *The Sailor's Parting*, shows a scene on the lower deck of a warship. A young sailor and his girl embrace beside a gunport, through which can be seen a billowing Union Jack. Another sailor sleeps in his hammock oblivious of the tender scene being enacted below. As in the previous engraving, the sailor's clothes and the dress of his woman are as carefully drawn as the accompanying detail. In this case, the poem underneath the picture reflects the thoughts of the young woman:

> Oh, there he goes, my dear is gone,
>   Gone is my heart's desire,
> Oh, may the bullets miss my John,
>   That's all that I require.

Such was the popularity of these engravings, and the similar prints that were produced during the Seven Years' War and the wars against Revolutionary France, that the pictures were frequently transferred as decorations onto ceramic tiles, jugs, bowls, plates, and mugs. Among the most charming of the objects that found their way into many homes were the earthenware figures usually designed as matching pairs: one depicting Jack-Tar bidding farewell to his weeping girl and the other showing their happy reunion on his return from the sea. The patriotic spirit that inspired the production and sale of such items is confirmed by the text beneath an illustration of *The Sailor's Adieu* on a creamware jug made in Liverpool around 1798: "What should tear me from the arms of my Dearest Polly but the undeniable calls of my country in whose cause I have engag'd my Honour and my Life."

Perhaps the most vivid depiction of the sailor's farewell is *Portsmouth Point,* an engraving by Thomas Rowlandson. This is a panoramic view of the waterfront at Portsmouth as the fleet prepares to set sail. A fresh offshore breeze is tugging at the washing hung out to dry, and everywhere there is bustle and confusion. Sailors are pushing barrows and carrying sea chests and sacks toward the water's edge, where two men are lifting a woman into one of the boats. A one-legged sailor scrapes away on a fiddle, and dogs are barking and yelping. In the doorway of the Ship tavern an officer says farewell to his family. With one hand he clasps his pretty wife and kisses her, with the other hand he waves to their baby who is clutched in the arms of a maidservant. Another child tugs at the wife's dress. Nearby a common seaman says a less decorous farewell to his girl. He has pushed her back against a barrel and has managed to get his leg across her. On the left of the picture, a drunken woman with her breasts exposed leers down at a laughing sailor sprawled on the ground at her feet.

Rowlandson views the scene with humorous detachment, but for the men who must return to the hard life at sea, and for the women who were left alone on the shore, the parting was fraught with emotions. Seafaring was a hazardous occupation at the best of times, but during wartime everyone was aware that the men might be killed or maimed in battle. Even if they survived the perils of the sea, it was more than likely that they would not see their families for months on end, sometimes not for years. Fanny Boscawen adored her husband, Admiral Boscawen, and wrote him the most wonderful letters, but she had to spend ten of the eighteen years of her marriage in a state of constant anxiety while he was away at sea. Captain Collingwood, Nelson's second in command at Trafalgar, was happily married to Sarah Blackett, and they had two young daughters. In the spring of 1803, Collingwood wrote to his father-in-law and told him that he had spent one year at home since 1793 and was a stranger to his own children.

One aspect of the sailor's farewell that was frequently highlighted by popular prints and ballads was the snatching of the sailor from his wife or sweetheart by the press gang. A savage cartoon by Gillray ironically entitled *The Liberty of the Subject* shows a group of thuggish sailors taking a terrified civilian in the street. The scissors in his pocket suggest that he is a tailor. A furious and powerful-looking woman has grabbed hold of the hair and one ear of the sailor who has taken her husband, and behind her another woman is laying into the press gang with a mop.

In a different mood is an engraving issued by the publisher Carington Bowles in 1785 that depicts a rural scene. An elegantly dressed young man is comforting a tearful woman who is distraught that her lover is about to be torn from her. A naval officer armed with a club has his hand on the young man's shoulder while two sailors smirk in the background. The accompanying verses explain what is happening:

> But, woe is me! the press-gang came,
>   And forc'd my love away
> Just when we named next morning fair
>   To be our wedding day.

The press gangs, which forcibly recruited men for the navy, frequently did drag young men from their wives and sweethearts, thereby acquiring a notorious reputation. They were hated by seamen and civilians alike. Few naval officers were in favor of impressment and reckoned that one volunteer was worth three men who had been press-ganged. And yet the system of forcible impressment, which went back to the beginnings of England's navy, continued in existence until well after the defeat of Napoleon and the end of the naval wars against France.[2] Why did the navy rely so heavily on impressment? How exactly did the system work and what was its effect on the men who were impressed and the women they left behind when their men were bundled off to sea?

The root cause of the press-gang system was the navy's need for thousands of men to man the ships in times of war and the lack of sufficient volunteers to fill that need. In 1793, at the commencement of the war against France, the navy's strength on paper was 45,000 men, made up of 36,000 seamen and 9,000 marines. By 1812, the number had risen to 145,000 men, which was 2.7 percent of Britain's male population.[3] This was not a large percentage (the army needed 6.7 percent), but the navy ideally wanted experienced seamen and not farm laborers or criminals. Britain had the advantage of a large merchant navy of some 120,000 men, which in theory she could draw on (and in practice frequently did), but merchant ships were even more important in wartime than they were in peacetime in order to maintain the nation's trade and thus help toward the cost of the army and navy.

Many young men did volunteer for the navy, partly for patriotic reasons, partly out of a sense of adventure, and partly for the generous bounty that was offered. In 1797, the bounty was £70, the equivalent of five and a half years' wages for an ordinary seaman. Nicholas Rodger quotes figures to show that in Plymouth during the period between 1770 and 1779 only 6 percent of the men on the ships' musters had been pressed into service.[4] However, by 1800 the navy was having to rely heavily on impressment to make up the necessary numbers.

Impressment was carried out in several different ways. The first was a land-based operation that was run by the Impress Service. By 1793, when it was formally recognized as a permanent body, the service was operating gangs in fifty-one ports in Britain and Ireland. The gangs were led by captains or commanders (usually called regulating captains) who were in charge of recruitment in a particular district. They had several lieutenants under them who took charge of the groups of men who went out and looked for recruits. In each district a rendezvous was established where volunteers could be enlisted, and where pressed men could be confined until they could be dispatched under armed guard to the fleet. In London there was a rendezvous on Tower Hill and another at St. Katharine's by the Tower, both of them conveniently placed for recruiting seamen from the hundreds of ships in the Pool of London.

The second and more productive method of recruiting was to intercept incoming merchant ships. Sometimes this was carried out by a warship coming alongside a merchant ship as she approached a port. Sometimes the operation was carried out by a naval party in a tender hired for the purpose. The tenders were usually brigs or sloops manned by a naval officer and a crew of armed seamen. The captains, mates, and boatswains of merchant vessels of fifty tons and upward were officially exempt from impressment; so were the crew of colliers, certain classes of fishermen, and all foreign nationals. However, the exemptions were frequently ignored, and captains of merchant ships went to considerable lengths to avoid putting in to a port where the press gang was known to be operating, sometimes using guns and small arms to prevent a naval party's boarding them at sea.

Although the press gangs operating in the streets of ports and harbors rarely encountered serious opposition, there were occasions when the families and friends of impressed seamen attempted to rescue them from the gangs. William Spavens was a former merchant seaman who had been pressed into the navy when his ship returned to Hull from a trading voyage to Russia. He was sent to join the crew of the 68-gun ship HMS *Buckingham,* and after a cruise to the West Indies, his ship returned to Britain with orders to procure men for the service. They put in to Liverpool, a port notorious for its opposition to the press gang, and sent a small group of sailors ashore. They picked up sixteen men, but only one proved to be a seaman, so they detained him and set the rest free. The next day, July 25, 1759, the captain sent a gang of eighty sailors ashore, including Spavens. They picked up several stragglers and then came across the crew of the ship *Lion* in the customhouse. The gang had no difficulty in taking seventeen of the seamen but then had to run the gauntlet of an infuriated mob as they led the impressed men along the streets back to the ship. Spavens describes how several hundred women, old men, and boys flocked after them and attacked them with stones and brickbats. The sailors from the *Buckingham* fired their pistols over the heads of the crowd and managed to reach the waterfront, "but the women proved very daring, and followed us down to the low water mark, being almost up to their knees in mud."[5]

On this occasion the crowd failed to rescue the impressed men, but in Bristol some women were more successful. Captain Brown was the regulating officer responsible for naval recruitment at Gloucester, a few miles up the River Severn from Bristol. In May 1759, he had to report a humiliating incident in which two women had been responsible for freeing fourteen men who had been taken by the press gang. On May 8, he had arranged that twenty men taken in the Gloucester area should be transported down the river to the Kingroad anchorage. Lieutenant McKinley was put in charge of the transport vessel, and he was accompanied by several members of the press gang who were fully armed. The remainder of the press gang under Lieutenant Hyde accompanied the transport vessel in a boat until she was clear of the town and on her way down the estuary.

On the morning of May 9, the vessel dropped anchor at Kingroad. Lieutenant McKinley, who had a drinking problem, decided to take the opportunity to go ashore with the master of the vessel. He carelessly left open the hatch over the area where the impressed men were confined, but since they were all handcuffed to one another he presumably thought there was no chance of their escaping. His mistake was to have allowed two of the impressed men's wives on board the vessel. While he was ashore the women produced an axe and a hatchet, which enabled the men to cut themselves free. Captain Brown later noted that the bolts securing the men required six or seven cuts with the axe before they parted.

Meanwhile, Lieutenant McKinley had gotten drunk, fallen down a bank, and broken his sword. When he eventually returned to the vessel, anchored out in the estuary, he found that fourteen of the twenty impressed men had taken a boat and all the guns on board, and had vanished. A few weeks later he went on a drunken rampage in Gloucester. He lurched down the street shouting and swearing obscenities, causing a riot among the inhabitants. When he fired a pistol at the chest of an onlooker, he was arrested by the constables and thrown into jail "without any other damage to his person than the insult of some thousands."[6]

Another recruiting officer in the Bristol area suffered a humiliating experience at the hands of some determined women. Lieutenant McKenzie was in charge of the hired vessel *United Brothers*, which lay in the anchorage at Kingroad. In October 1805, he was in the village of Pill on the outskirts of Bristol, searching for suitable men to impress into the navy. Entering an inn kept by Joseph Hook, he spotted a seaman and was attempting to take him when he was attacked by Mrs. Hook, her daughter, and a female servant. The three women rescued the seaman and enabled him to escape through a back door. Writing afterward to Captain Barker, his superior officer, McKenzie complained that the women had violently assaulted him and torn his uniform. He was particularly upset that Joseph Hook had looked on throughout and made no attempt to prevent his family from attacking him.[7]

It is little wonder that women should object to impressment. Their men were taken from them without warning, often leaving them with a house and children to support, and no income. Mary Creed was pregnant and living in lodgings at Mrs. James's on Griffin Lane, Bristol. A few days after Christmas 1806, she wrote the following letter to the secretary of the Admiralty:

> Sir, You will be pleased to lay before the Lords Commissioners of the Admiralty the deplorable situation I am in by having my husband, who is very sickly, and unfit for the service, taken from me by the Press Gang here. I am big with child, and have no other way of support but him, he likewise supporting his old father and mother, and if he was examined by any Doctor he would be found more fit for a hospital than a ship, having entirely lost the use of his right hand.[8]

Mary Creed's husband, John, had served as a steward on a West Indiaman, and although he was rated as a landman rather than a seaman, the regulating captain in charge of the impressment service at Bristol reckoned that he was "a very stout able man." His wife's plea was turned down, and John Creed was forced to join the Royal Navy.

Earlier the same year John Jacobs, the thirty-year-old boatswain of the merchant ship *Betsey*, was returning to Bristol in a convoy from the West Indies. His ship was intercepted by a vessel commanded by Lieutenant Lucas, and Jacobs found himself pressed into the navy. His wife, Mary Jacobs, immediately wrote to the Admiralty and begged their lordships to accept a substitute to serve in his place because "he is the sole support of me and four children."[9] The regulating captain noted that John Jacobs was Swedish, but because he had married in Bristol he was still liable for impressment. The scribbled note on the back of the letter suggests that Mary Jacobs also lost her husband to the navy.

In July 1806, Lucy Castle wrote to the Admiralty from Princes Street, Bristol, on behalf of her husband, William, who had been taken by the press gang and confined on board the naval brig *Enchantress* until such time as he could be dispatched to Plymouth to serve on a warship. Mrs. Castle explained that her husband was a native of America, but her plea was set aside because he had married an Englishwoman. From his confinement in the *Enchantress*, William Castle wrote a pathetic letter to the authorities in which he pointed out that his wife was pregnant, and that she and her other children were in great misery and had nobody to maintain them. The regulating captain noted that William Castle was twenty-two years of age, was formerly chief mate of a merchant ship, and "being an able seaman in every respect fit for the service cannot be discharged."[10]

What most upset the merchant seamen and their families was not so much the forcible impressment, though that was bad enough; it was the fact that the men were prevented from seeing their friends and loved ones. "It seems shocking to the feelings of humanity," wrote Spavens, "for a sailor, after he has been on a long voyage, endured innumerable hardships, and is just returning to his native land with the pleasing hope of shortly beholding a beloved wife and children, some kind relations, or respected friends, to be forced away to fight, perhaps to fall, and no more enjoy those dear connexions."[11] William Richardson, another merchant seaman who had been impressed, thought the navy's practice of intercepting homecoming merchant ships was as bad as Negro slavery and pointed out that if a man complained about being prevented from seeing his wife or friends and relations he was likely to be flogged "much more severe than the Negro driver's whip, and if he deserts he is flogged round the fleet nearly to death."[12] He reckoned that if men were allowed a few weeks' liberty after a long voyage, they would soon grow tired of shore life and return more contented to their ships.

The same message appears in many seamen's memoirs, and it is not surprising to find that this was one of the major grievances behind the Mutiny at the Nore in 1797. One of the nine articles of the document drawn up by Richard Parker and presented to the Lords Commissioners of the Admiralty expressed the seamen's demands in notably restrained language:

> That every Man upon a Ship's coming into Harbour, shall be at liberty (a certain number at a time, so as not to injure the Ship's duty) to go and see their friends and families; a convenient time to be allowed to each man.[13]

The more humane officers appreciated the men's situation, and when circumstances allowed they did give permission for shore leave. In June 1755, Admiral Hawke received a petition from seventeen men who had been on a two-year voyage to the East Indies. Their ship had been intercepted by a naval tender in the English Channel, and they had all volunteered for service. (The generous bounty persuaded many merchant seamen to volunteer for service in the Royal Navy.) In these circumstances volunteers tended to be treated exactly the same way as impressed men, and they were immediately dispatched to the fleet anchorage at Spithead and consigned to the *Prince George* under the command of Captain Rodney. The men got together and composed an eloquent letter to Hawke setting out their circumstances and explaining that "we have been so long out of land upon a very tedious voyage and several of us having wives and families who are in great distress by our long absence and others of us on private concerns we most humbly intreat your Honour that you would grant us leave of absence for three or four weeks. . . ."[14] Hawke secured permission from the Admiralty and directed Captain Rodney to allow the men three weeks' leave. This was by no means an isolated instance, but when the demands of war put captains and admirals under pressure to get their ships to sea, there was an obvious reluctance to allow men ashore and risk losing them through desertion.

WHILE MUCH HAS BEEN WRITTEN ABOUT THE HORRORS OF THE PRESS gang in Britain, it is often forgotten that the system was operated on a similar scale on the other side of the Atlantic. Indeed impressment was one of the causes of the War of 1812, which was fought by America for "Free Trade and Sailors' Rights." The war tends to be played down in British history books, partly because it was overshadowed by the events in Europe leading up to the defeat of Napoleon at Waterloo, and partly because the British suffered several humiliating defeats at sea during the course of the war in actions against formidable American ships such as the USS *Constitution*.

Throughout the eighteenth century, British warships sent press gangs into the ports along the east coast of America and forcibly recruited men for the Royal Navy. During a period of five months in 1745 and 1746, press gangs from the 14-gun HMS *Shirley* impressed 92 men from Boston. In 1771, HMS *Arethusa* took 31 men during a cruise along the coast of Virginia. One of the most draconian raids was a night raid on New York in 1757, when the navy sent in 3,000 seamen and impressed 800 men.[15] Nearly half of this number were subsequently found to be unsuitable and were released, but operations like this fueled the fury of all sections of the community. The merchants feared the effects on trade, the townspeople saw their communities devastated by the seizure of so many able-bodied men, the women lost husbands and sons, and the seamen themselves no longer felt safe in their own towns.

The American newspapers and the minutes of town meetings frequently recorded official protests, riots, and violent responses to the raids of the press gangs. There were three days of rioting in Boston in November 1747. An angry crowd that included Negroes, servants, and hundreds of seamen stormed the Town House where the General Court was sitting and demanded the seizure of the impressing officers and the release of the men they had taken. During the course of the riot, they besieged the governor's house, laid hold of a naval lieutenant, assaulted a sheriff, and put his deputy in the stocks.[16] In Newport, Rhode Island, in June 1765, around 500 seamen, boys, and Negroes went on a rampage in protest after suffering five weeks of impressment.

After the American Revolution of 1776, in which the British colonies achieved their independence, the Royal Navy could no longer impress American seamen. Any operations by British captains in American ports or aboard American ships were restricted in theory to searching for deserters from the navy, and the men who were seized were therefore not impressed but recovered. In practice, the navy did continue to impress American seamen. The British argued that a man who was born British remained a British subject and that applied to any man born in America before she achieved her independence. In an effort to safeguard their citizens, the American government issued their seamen with a document called a protection, a certificate headed by the seal of the United States and bearing a declaration signed by a public notary or customs officer that stated the bearer was an American citizen and was "to be respected at all times by sea and land." The name, age, and height of the bearer were included in order to identify him. In practice many American seamen found that a protection was no protection at all.

The experiences of an American sailor who was on the receiving end of the press gang are recounted in the memoirs of Captain William Nevens.[17] Born in Danville, Maine, in 1781, he was trained as a carpenter, but at the age of seventeen he joined the crew of a brig from Liverpool and sailed to Boston. After several voyages to the West Indies in different merchant ships, he sailed from Boston on the whaling ship *Essex* under the command of Captain Kilby and arrived in Barbados in February 1800. The ship was in such a poor state that the crew were paid off and Nevens planned to sail home in a schooner bound for Boston. He went ashore one evening with some of his shipmates, and as a precaution against the press gangs they armed themselves with clubs. After an evening of merrymaking, four of them wandered down to the beach to enjoy the cool sea breeze and work off the effects of the tamarind punch they had been drinking. They were taken by surprise when an officer and ten or twelve armed sailors surrounded them and hauled them into a boat. There they found ten other impressed seamen. The boat put off from the shore, and they were rowed among the anchored vessels until they came alongside a British warship, the 18-gun *Cyane*. The next morning, Nevens was interviewed by the ship's captain. When Nevens informed him that he was an American, the captain demanded to see his protection. Nevens produced the document from his pocket. The captain glanced at it and said, "You are an Irishman. What business have you with a protection? There are plenty of Nevenses in Ireland but there never was one born in America," and with that he tore up the protection and threw it overboard. Nevens managed to get a message to Captain Kilby, who came on board the warship, confirmed that Nevens was American, and demanded his release. The British captain swore that he knew Nevens's father in Ireland. He declared that Nevens was a damned Irish rebel and told Captain Kilby to get off his ship. Seeing his situation was hopeless, Nevens asked Kilby to take home his sea chest and bedding and if he did not return within a year to send them to his parents. "Having made these dispositions," writes Nevens, "I bade adieu to my liberty, and settled myself to the consoling prospect of serving Great Britain a few years for nothing." He noted that every vessel in the British Navy at this period had several Americans on board and though several escaped, the majority were compelled to serve under threat of flogging.

William Nevens was determined to escape, and his opportunity came when the *Cyane* sailed to St. Kitts. To prevent the crew deserting the captain anchored her three miles offshore, but Nevens saw that there was an American sloop of war anchored between the *Cyane* and the shore. He slipped overboard at night and swam toward the American sloop. Unfortunately, the tide swept him past her, and he was forced to continue swimming for nearly two hours before he came alongside another ship. This was a Scottish brig, *Sally* of Greenock, which was bound for New York. Her captain agreed to take him, and he eventually got back to Boston, where he married an English girl from Liverpool.

As with so much of maritime history, there are many accounts of men who were victims of the press gang but few accounts of what happened to the women whose husbands were taken from them. However, there were two women whose experiences were so unusual that they were recorded in some detail. They were Margaret Dickson, whose extraordinary story was published in the *Newgate Calendar,* and Ann Parker, who found herself at the center of one of the most notorious events in British maritime history—the Mutiny at the Nore.

3

Ann Parker
and the Mutiny at the Nore

SAILORS' WIVES HAD MORE THAN THEIR FAIR SHARE OF ANXIETY AND grief, but few had to endure the agony of Ann Parker. She arrived at Sheerness shortly before her husband was due to be executed. She was too late to be allowed on board HMS *Sandwich* to see him and exchange a few last words with him, but she was not too late to witness his body being hanged from the yardarm of the ship. Richard Parker went to his death not knowing that his wife was among the thousands of onlookers who had gathered to watch the final episode in a drama that had gripped the nation.[1]

Apart from the heroic determination that she showed in the days before and after the execution, nothing is known of Ann Parker beyond the fact that she was a farmer's daughter from Aberdeen. Her husband's early years are almost as obscure. Richard Parker was born in Exeter around 1764. He is believed to have come from a respectable family and to have obtained a good education, but at the age of nineteen he was taken by the press gang in Plymouth. He was imprisoned in a navy tender and transported to London, where he was forced to join the crew of the 74-gun ship HMS *Ganges*. Unusual for a pressed man, he was promoted to midshipman, which suggests that he may have had some seafaring experience in merchant ships. According to one source, he was discharged from the *Ganges* for immoral conduct and transferred to the sloop *Bulldog* as an ordinary seaman.[2] He served on the *Bulldog* until June 1784, when he was discharged sick to Haslar Hospital. He seems to have remained in the navy for a few more years and to have been promoted to petty officer or acting lieutenant.

At some point Parker came into an inheritance, left the navy, and settled in Scotland, where he met and married Ann. Like many others before him and others since, being unemployed and having money to spend led him into a life of gambling and dissipation. He soon spent his entire fortune, ran into debt, and ended up in an Edinburgh jail. At the outbreak of the war with Revolutionary France in 1793, he volunteered to rejoin the navy and was released from prison after paying his creditor with part of the bounty he received from the commissioning officer. From Edinburgh's port of Leith, he was transported south to the Nore with volunteers and pressed men, and was signed on to HMS *Sandwich* as a supernumerary.

Parker rejoined the navy at a critical time. After years of grumbling about their wretched conditions, the seamen of the channel fleet at Spithead had united in protest and on April 15, 1797, they submitted a petition to the Admiralty in which they demanded better food, shore leave on returning to port, pay for those injured, and above all, an increase in their wages, which had not changed since 1653. Senior officers were generally sympathetic to the men's requests, and with the country at war with France, they needed a fighting navy manned by loyal hands. Within eight days the Admiralty had agreed to all the demands, but when the fleet was ordered to sea on May 7, the men refused to obey their officers because they did not believe the promises that had been made. An Act of Parliament was hastily passed, and on May 14, Admiral Lord Howe arrived at Portsmouth with the news that all the men's demands would be met and that a pardon would be provided for the Spithead mutineers.

Meanwhile, unrest had spread among the ships anchored at the Nore, and Parker became a leading figure among the seamen's delegates. In addition to the concessions made to the men at Spithead, which had been extended to the whole navy by the act, the Nore seamen wanted a more equal distribution of prize money, the payment of arrears of wages before the ship went to sea, and the removal of the harshest of the Articles of War. The mutiny at the Nore began on May 12. At half past nine in the morning, the sailors climbed out on to the booms of the *Sandwich* and gave three cheers, which were at once answered by the crew of the nearest ship, the *Director*, commanded by William Bligh, who had already experienced a mutiny on his ship the *Bounty* eight years before. The men of the *Sandwich* trained the forecastle guns on the quarterdeck, and the officers had little option but to surrender the ship. Later that day the seamen unanimously chose Parker as their leader. There followed several days of confusion. Most of the other ships joined the mutiny. Parker held a number of meetings in the Chequers, a public house in Sheerness, and he and his committee of mutineers drew up a set of nine demands that they presented to the port admiral. Parker seems to have done his best to keep a check on the wilder actions of the rebellious seamen, but although there was no bloodshed, he could not prevent a certain amount of looting and other excesses. The seamen stole sheep from the Isle of Grain, robbed fishing boats of their catches, and so alarmed the local inhabitants that many respectable families sent their women away with their valuables for safety.

On June 4, the day when the fleet normally celebrated the King's birthday, some sailors took the opportunity to avenge themselves on their most unpopular officers. A mock trial was held on board HMS *Monmouth*, and four petty officers and a midshipman were subsequently flogged. Several officers were tarred and feathered and rowed in boats among the anchored ships. Effigies of William Pitt, the prime minister, were hoisted at the yardarms of some ships, and the seamen took potshots at them with guns and pistols, which inevitably led to rumors that real executions were taking place. The mutineers also began intercepting shipping on the Thames with the aim of blockading London. But soon the seamen began to have second thoughts. The Spithead mutineers had already won some major concessions, and it soon became clear that the authorities were not inclined to agree to the additional demands. The Admiralty brought up ships to surround the fleet at the Nore, and the mutiny began to collapse. Officers resumed command of their ships, and the crew of the *Sandwich* delivered up Parker as a prisoner. He was sent at once to Maidstone jail. On June 22, he found himself before a court-martial on board HMS *Neptune*, moored in the Thames off Greenhithe. There could be only one verdict for the ringleader of a mutiny, and he was duly sentenced to death. Parker, who had conducted his own defense, heard the verdict "with a degree of fortitude and undismayed composure which excited the astonishment and admiration of everyone."[3]

When Ann Parker learned that her husband had taken the bounty and rejoined the navy, she hurried to Leith, but when she arrived she discovered that the ship with the pressed men and volunteers aboard had already left the harbor and was sailing south to the Thames. She waited for further news, and when she heard of the mutiny at the Nore and Parker's imprisonment, she set off on the long journey from Scotland to London. By the time she arrived in the capital, her husband had been tried and convicted. The day before the execution was due to take place she made her way to St. James's Palace. There she handed a petition to the Earl of Morton for delivery to the Queen. Observers noted that she behaved in a manner appropriate to her unhappy situation. She waited until five o'clock in the afternoon, but with no response forthcoming from the palace, she abandoned all hope of a reprieve and set off to see her husband.

It was thirty-five miles from St. James's to the River Medway where the fleet was anchored. She managed to get a place on a coach that rattled east along the southern shores of the Thames through Dartford and Northfleet and Gravesend. It was eleven o'clock in the evening by the time she reached the ancient city of Rochester, huddled on the riverbank beneath its Norman castle and cathedral. She hurried down to the waterfront and found a boatman who had a cargo of garden produce for Sheerness. He agreed to take her with him early the next morning.

At four o'clock in the morning on the day set for the execution, the boatman helped Mrs. Parker aboard his boat and they set off downstream with the outgoing tide. As the winding river broadened out into the estuary of the Medway, the first light of dawn from an overcast sky revealed mile upon mile of marshes and mudflats on either side of them. There was a fresh easterly breeze, and even at that early hour, there was considerable activity on the river.[4] Local fishing boats headed out to the fishing grounds in the Thames estuary, and trading sloops and brigs set off for the ports of Kent, Suffolk, and farther afield.

By six o'clock, they could see the distant forest of masts marking the anchorage of the fleet at the Nore. This was the name given to the final stretch of the Medway before it joined the Thames. More than twenty warships were anchored there that morning, protected by the guns of Sheerness fort. It was nearly seven o'clock when they came alongside HMS *Sandwich*. The massive wooden hull of the 90-gun ship towered above them. Normally she was the flagship of the fleet, but the admiral had recently removed his flag to HMS *L'Espion*, leaving the *Sandwich* under the command of Captain Mosse. Mrs. Parker asked permission to speak to her husband, but the marine sentries on duty refused to allow her on board and ordered the boatman to pull clear, threatening to fire into his boat if he did not do so.

The boatman had no intention of endangering himself or his boat, and in spite of Mrs. Parker's desperate pleadings, he headed for the low fortress and the dockyard at Sheerness, which lay a few hundred yards away across the water. He assured her that no execution would take place that day because the yellow flag was not flying from any of the anchored ships. This flag was the signal to warn the fleet and onlookers that an execution was imminent.

As soon as they landed, Mrs. Parker spoke to another boatman on the garrison dock-stairs and persuaded him to take her back out to the *Sandwich*. At exactly eight o'clock, as she was being rowed up to Blackstakes, where the leading ships were anchored, a single gun was fired from the flagship *L'Espion*. Looking across she was horrified to see the fatal yellow flag hoisted to the masthead, and immediately afterward another yellow flag was hauled up on the foremast of HMS *Sandwich*. As they came alongside for the second time, she frantically renewed her entreaties to the sentries to let her come on board so she could speak to her husband. With the recent mutiny in everyone's minds, all officers present were aware that the execution of its ringleader might spark off more trouble. The sentries were under strict orders that no one should board or leave the ship, so once again they refused her permission. The boatman told her that he could not wait because he had promised to collect some people who had booked his services earlier.

The waterfront was now swarming with an expectant crowd of men, women, and children who were gathering to see the execution. Scaffolding had been erected on the shore of the Isle of Grain for spectators, and an increasing number of yachts, cutters, and rowboats were collecting in the vicinity of the *Sandwich*. Pushing through the curious onlookers on the shore, Ann Parker hired a third boatman and once again headed across the water toward the ships at anchor. But as she neared the *Sandwich* she saw a procession of men heading from the quarterdeck toward a platform that had been erected on the cathead, the heavy beam that supported the anchor near the bows of the ship. In the center of the procession she could clearly see the figure of her husband. Richard Parker was dressed in a black suit of mourning, and his hands were bound. Those present on deck observed that he looked a little paler than usual but that he carried himself with a remarkable composure and fortitude. As soon as she recognized his familiar figure and realized that he had only minutes to live, Ann Parker shrieked, "Oh, my dear husband!" and fainted. After a few minutes she recovered, and looking across toward the flagship, she saw the chaplain in his robes turn away from her husband.

While she lay unconscious in the bottom of the boat, Richard Parker had spoken briefly to the assembled ship's company. He had knelt and prayed, and had then stood up and said, "I am ready." The provost marshal had placed the greased halter around his neck but had done it so clumsily that Parker spoke to the boatswain's mate who was standing nearby and said, "Do you do it, for he seems to know nothing about it." The boatswain's mate expertly made fast the halter to the reeve-rope and indicated that all was ready. Parker turned around and looked for the last time at his shipmates gathered on the forecastle. He nodded his head toward them and with an affectionate smile said, "Goodbye to you." He then turned to Captain Mosse and asked him whether the gun was primed. He was told that it was.

"Is the match alight?"

"All is ready."

Parker asked whether any gentleman would lend him a white handkerchief so that he could give the signal, and after a pause a gentleman stepped forward and handed him one. Parker bowed and thanked him and ascended the platform. A cap was drawn over his face, and he stepped firmly to the edge of the platform. He dropped the handkerchief and quickly placed his hands in his coat pockets. As the reeve-rope swung him in the air, the gun at the bows of the ship fired with a shattering boom that echoed across the water. The explosion was followed by a rising cloud of gunpowder smoke, but the eyes of the hundreds of seamen on the anchored ships and the waiting crowds on the shore were fixed on the black figure suspended from the yardarm on the flagship's foremast. It was noted that Parker's body appeared extremely convulsed for a few seconds and then hung lifeless.

In all, some 3,000 people watched the last moments of Richard Parker, but his wife was not one of them. She lay senseless in the boat among the dozens of other small craft gathered around the warship. She said later that she "saw nothing but the sea, which appeared covered with blood."

For the third time she was rowed back to the shore. Almost overcome with shock and grief but still determined to be with her husband, she hired a fourth boat, and as she was once again rowed back to the flagship, she saw his body being lowered to the deck. By the time she came alongside, she was told that the corpse had been taken into a boat for burial ashore at Sheerness.

This might seem to be the end of the story, but Ann Parker continued to demonstrate that desperate and heroic determination which enables some people to fight on when all seems lost. With some difficulty she managed to secure an audience with Vice Admiral Skeffington Lutwidge, who had recently been appointed commander in chief of the fleet at Sheerness. She told him she wanted to remove her husband's body from the burial ground in the garrison. Lutwidge asked her why she wanted to take her husband's body. She replied, "To have him interred like a gentleman, as he had been bred."

Ann Parker knew her husband was no criminal, and she wanted him to have a decent burial and the blessing of the church. Vice Admiral Lutwidge had no sympathy for the wife of the notorious leader of the recent mutiny and categorically refused her request. Having failed to get her way by official means, Mrs. Parker resorted to desperate measures. The place where her husband was buried was alongside the walls of the garrison and was enclosed by a new stockade fence that was nearly ten feet high. She tried to find out who kept the key to the gate of the stockade, but failing to do so, she waited until nightfall and returned to the burial place. At about ten o'clock, she came across three women and persuaded them to help her recover the body of her husband. The women were probably sailors' wives or prostitutes; the commissioner of the dockyard at Sheerness frequently complained that the area was "a common resort of Whores and Rogues by day and night."[5] When the coast was clear, the four women climbed over the gate and into the stockaded area.

Although Richard Parker's coffin was buried in a shallow grave, the women had no tools and had to dig away the earth with their bare hands. They lifted the coffin from the ground, carried it across to the fence, and managed with some difficulty to heave it over the gate. They laid it on the ground outside, and in order to conceal it from the sentries manning the Barrier Gate nearby, they sat on the coffin for the remainder of the night. At four o'clock in the morning, the draw-bridge of the fort was lowered and a fish cart rumbled through the gateway onto the road outside. Mrs. Parker accosted the driver and, finding that he was heading for Rochester, persuaded him to add the coffin to his load for the price of a guinea. Having arrived in the town she found the driver of a wagon who, for six guineas, agreed to take the coffin to London and to deliver it to the Hoop and Horseshoe, on Queen Street, Little Tower Hill. Mrs. Parker had hired a room there where she arranged for the coffin to be deposited.

The mutiny of the seamen at the Nore and the subsequent court-martial of Richard Parker had been widely reported and had caused considerable interest not only among seafarers and their families, but among people from all classes, particularly in London. When the word got out that Parker's corpse had been brought to the East End by his widow, a crowd began to gather outside the Hoop and Horseshoe. Some of the more unscrupulous women appear to have been charging people to see Parker's body. By Monday, the crowds of the curious had grown so big that the local magistrates were forced to intervene. Ann Parker was called to the police office on Lambert Street, where she was asked why she had removed her husband's body from its burial place at Sheerness. She said that she wished to take him to his family in Ex-eter or to her family in Scotland so that she could bury him like a Christian. She was asked whether the rumors were true that she had been charging people money to view the corpse. At this she burst into floods of tears and replied, "Do I appear like a monster so unnatural?" Subsequent inquiries confirmed that there was no truth in the accusa-tion. The magistrates were concerned that elements in the population would use the occasion of the funeral to cause a riot, and they there-fore decided that the coffin should be moved immediately to the work-house on Nightingale Lane and then buried in the churchyard of Aldgate Church the next morning. However, the crowds continued to gather in the Minories all that evening, and fearing a tumultuous as-sembly the next day, they arranged for the body to be moved at one o'clock in the morning from the workhouse to the burying vault of the church of St. Mary at Whitechapel.

In the afternoon of Tuesday, July 4, Ann Parker was permitted to attend the funeral service for her husband, which was officiated by Mr. Wright, the rector of St. Mary, Whitechapel. At her particular request, the coffin lid was taken off and she was allowed to look at her husband for the last time. After the ceremony was over she signed a certificate to confirm that the burial service had been duly performed.[6] No doubt to cover themselves in the event of any inquiry into the proceedings, the minister and officers of the parish asked her to state that she was perfectly satisfied with the mode of his interment and with the treatment that she had received. This she agreed to. The following inscription can still be found in the church register under the heading of burials: "4 July, 1797, Richard Parker, Sheerness, Kent, age 33. Cause of death, execution."[7]

THE STORY OF ANN PARKER IS OBVIOUSLY UNUSUAL AND CANNOT BE regarded as typical of the experiences of sailors' women. Of the hundreds of thousands of sailors who served at sea in the eighteenth century, relatively few were hanged for mutiny, and it would be hard to find another sailor's wife who went to such extreme lengths to rescue her husband's corpse and give him a Christian burial. But the story does encapsulate, in an unusually dramatic form, the tragedy that was the lot of so many wives and families of seamen. We are allowed a glimpse of a few days in the life of Ann Parker because of the notoriety of her husband, and because the mutiny at the Nore aroused strong passions and was widely reported at the time. But what of the other seamen who were present that day and what of their families?

On the morning of Parker's execution, there were fourteen warships lying at anchor in the River Medway. Most of these ships had between 500 and 600 seamen on board, and we can therefore assume that around 8,000 seamen and marines were assembled on the decks of their ships to watch Parker die. The majority of these men were not allowed ashore and were confined to their ships for as long as they remained in the harbor. Only the officers and the more long-serving and reliable hands would be given permission to spend time ashore. The remainder must endure an existence that was hard but bearable for the younger and more adaptable, but for older men and for landsmen unaccustomed to the confined life on board, it was nothing less than a floating hell.

Richard Hall was at the Nore in June 1800, when he wrote to his wife from HMS *Zealand*. He told her that it was worse than a prison: "If I had known it was so bad I would not have entered. I would give all I had if it was a hundred guineas if I could get on shore." He said that they flogged men every day and that many other men would give all the world if they could get onshore. He concluded, "Dear wife, do the best you can for the children and God prosper them till I come back, which there is no fear of and send an answer as soon as possible."[8]

The captains were very aware that many of the sailors had been impressed into the navy and had good reason to believe that they would run away if allowed ashore. Between 1795 and 1805, more men were court-martialed for desertion than for drunkenness, theft, or any other offense. The punishment for desertion was brutal: floggings of 200 or 300 lashes were common, and in some cases men were hanged.

Richard Parker paid the ultimate price for leading a protest against some of the worst aspects of naval life, and his wife was left a widow. There was another wife of an impressed seaman whose story was equally dramatic but had a happier ending. Margaret Dickson was born around 1700 in Musselburgh, a tiny fishing village on the Firth of Forth, a few miles from Edinburgh.[9] Her parents were poor but ensured that she had a good religious education and was versed in the household duties that might be expected of her. She duly married a local fisherman and bore him several children. At some time around 1726 or 1727, her husband was taken by the press gang during one of the navy's periodic recruitment sweeps of the Firth of Forth.

Left on her own, Margaret Dickson had a brief affair with another Musselburgh man and became pregnant. She was so frightened of causing a scandal (it was a local custom that adulterous women should be publicly rebuked in church) that she attempted to hide her pregnant state until the last moment. She was alone when she went into labor. Unable to get assistance from her neighbors, she fell unconscious and had no recollection whether she gave birth to a baby that was alive or stillborn. When a dead baby was found near her house, she was accused of murder, arrested, and sent to the jail in Edinburgh. At her trial, a surgeon gave damning evidence. He had put the baby's lungs in water and found that they floated, which according to him meant the child had been born alive because it had breathed air into the lungs. Margaret Dickson was found guilty of murder and condemned to death.

During the subsequent days in prison she confessed that she was guilty of adultery but constantly denied that she had murdered her child "or even formed an idea of so horrid a crime." She was hanged at Edinburgh in 1728, and afterward her body was delivered to her friends, who placed it in a coffin and sent it on a cart for burial in Musselburgh. The weather was sultry, and the people in charge of the cart decided to stop for a drink at the village of Pepper-Mill outside Edinburgh. While they were drinking, one of them saw the lid of the coffin move. They went to remove it and were startled when the hanged woman sat up. Most of the spectators ran off in terror, but someone had the presence of mind to take her indoors, bleed her, and put her to bed. The following morning she woke up and had recovered sufficiently to be able to walk back to her home in Musselburgh.

Under Scottish law, a person could not be punished twice for the same offense, and since she had already suffered the due punishment, she was now a free person. Her sailor husband had meanwhile returned to Musselburgh, and since the marriage of an executed person was automatically dissolved, they were married for a second time a few days later. According to the account in the *Newgate Calendar,* she continued to deny that she had murdered her child, and we learn that "she was living as late as the year 1753."

Margaret Dickson's recovery may seem miraculous, but in fact there are several accounts of people who survived hanging in Britain during the eighteenth century. Presumably, if the drop was not sufficient to break the neck, one simply suffered temporary asphyxiation, became unconscious for a while, and when the pressure of the rope was released, was able to make a complete recovery.

4

Female Sailors: Fact and Fiction

IN AUGUST 1815, A BOOK WAS PUBLISHED IN BOSTON ENTITLED *THE Adventures of Louisa Baker*. The heroine of the book was a young woman from Massachusetts, and the story was told in her own words.[1] She described how she had been seduced and abandoned by the son of a local trader, and had run away from home to spare her respectable parents the shame. In bitterly cold weather she walked to Boston, where a kindly woman took pity on her and gave her a bed for the night. The woman told her to avoid the area of town that was inhabited by prostitutes and warned her against the pimps who were continually in search of new victims.

With a heavy heart, Louisa set forth to look for a job as a chambermaid with a respectable family. She described herself as "a young and slender female thinly clad, and in a tedious snowstorm, with a handkerchief in one hand containing a few articles of clothing."[2] Faint with cold and hunger, she eventually came to a house on the heights of west Boston where she was welcomed by a matronly woman and a number of girls whom she took to be her daughters. Interviewed by the matron, she revealed why she had left her home. She was allowed to stay until she had given birth to her baby (who did not survive) and recovered her health. But when she then expressed a wish to leave the house and return to her friends, the woman turned nasty. She told Louisa she must pay for the days she had spent with her and threatened to expose the secret of her seduction. Louisa was persuaded that she had no alternative but to entertain gentlemen in the manner practiced by the other girls—prostitutes, she now realized—of the household.

The house was in the notorious red-light area known as Negro Hill, and several pages of the book are devoted to an account of the area and its inhabitants. The author described the dancing halls where the girls endeavored to please the patrons with their obscene gestures. She also described the different grades of harlots. These ranged from the strumpets of distinction who lived in some style down to the women she called "arch hags," whose chief qualifications were swearing, drinking, and obscenity: "Their companions are principally composed of sailors of the lowest grade and straggling mulattoes and blacks."[3]

In 1812, after three years in which she learned to attract the attention of men and to "practice vices perhaps before unthought of," she met the first lieutenant of a privateer. During an evening's conversation, he explained what he would do if he were a female and wanted to see the world: He said he would dress as a man and was confident that it would be possible for a female to travel abroad by land and sea without her sex being exposed.

Louisa at once determined to leave the brothel. She dressed herself in a sailor's suit, sneaked out of the house, and made her way through town. On Fish Street she entered a house where men were being enlisted to join the crew of one of the U.S. frigates that were in the harbor. She entered as a marine, which enabled her to avoid the strip search that new recruits joining as sailors had to undergo. The next day she went on board the ship: "I had taken the precaution to provide myself with a tight pair of under draws, which I had never shifted but with the greatest precaution, which, together with a close waistcoat or bandage about my breasts, effectually concealed my sex from all on board."[4]

In August 1812, they sailed out of Boston toward the Gulf of St. Lawrence. They captured two merchant vessels, and learning that a British squadron was on the Grand Banks, they headed south. On August 19, they sighted a British frigate and gave chase. Louisa was stationed in the tops, and far from feeling daunted by the prospect of battle, she found that she was entirely composed and keen to distinguish herself. As they came within range, the British ship fired her broadside, which fell short. At 6:00 P.M., the two ships came alongside each other and the battle commenced in earnest. From her position in the tops, Louisa aimed her musket at the enemy sailors on the deck of the ship below. When a ball of grapeshot struck and splintered the butt of her musket, one of her comrades saw what had happened and said, "Never mind, George, you have already won laurels sufficient to recommend you to the pretty girls when you return to port!"

Half an hour after the action had begun, the mainmast and foremast of the British ship crashed to the deck, and her captain surrendered. Her crew members were taken prisoner, the ship was set on fire, and at quarter past three, she blew up and sank. The British had lost 15 men killed and 63 wounded. The Americans had 7 killed and 13 wounded.

The victorious frigate returned to Boston to undergo repairs, and Louisa went ashore to enjoy herself with her shipmates. On more than one occasion she was in the company of girls from the brothel where she had worked, but her disguise was so effective that they failed to recognize her. As soon as the ship was ready they sailed, and in December they were cruising along the coast of South America, where they encountered another British warship. A fierce action took place, and after nearly four hours of bombarding each other with round- and grapeshot, the British ship surrendered with heavy casualties. During the course of the action, Louisa discharged her musket nineteen times, and with some effect since she had now learned to take pretty exact aim. Shortly after the battle she was climbing down the shrouds when she missed her hold and fell overboard. A boat was lowered to rescue her, and as soon as they had pulled her back on deck, her shipmates were ordered to strip off her wet clothes and replace them with dry ones. They had nearly undressed her when she recovered sufficiently to prevent them from going too far. She was able to get dressed without her sex being discovered.

For three years Louisa served as a marine. She took part in three battles, never deserted her post, and although she mixed freely with the crew both at sea and ashore, at no time did anyone suspect that she was a woman. She had now been away from home for nearly six years, and after receiving her wages and prize money she decided it was time to abandon her male disguise. She went shopping in Boston and bought a suitable outfit so that she was able to resume her former character as a respectable young woman. When she returned to her family home, her parents did not recognize her at first, but when she reminded them of events in her past, they saw she was their long-lost daughter. They welcomed her back and listened to the story of her adventures with tears running down their cheeks. In the final paragraph of the book, Louisa explained how she had been unwilling to make public the worst aspects of her recent experiences but had been persuaded by a friend that her story would provide an example and a warning to other young people "never to listen to the voice of love, unless sanctioned by paternal approbation." She further explained that she had withheld any details that would enable readers to discover her real name, or the names of her parents.

Although her identity remained a mystery, the people of Boston had no difficulty in identifying the U.S. frigate on which she served as the USS *Constitution*. This magnificent 44-gun ship had returned to Boston harbor in 1815 after a succession of spectacular victories over ships of the Royal Navy. In August 1812, she had encountered the 38-gun HMS *Guerriere*, dismasted her, and forced her surrender in a manner similar to the action described in Louisa's narrative. And later the same year, she had engaged in a ferocious action off the coast of Brazil against HMS *Java*, which was reduced to a complete wreck. The British commander, Captain Lambert, was killed by a musket ball fired by a marine sharpshooter in the maintop of the *Constitution*, which must have led readers of Louisa's story to think she might have played an extremely significant part in the action. The *Constitution* had then gone on to capture the *Cyane*, a 22-gun frigate, and the sloop *Levant* as news was received of the conclusion of the naval war.

Not surprisingly, *The Adventures of Louisa Baker* sold extremely well. It cashed in on the patriotic mood of the day but also provided what appeared to be a firsthand account of life among the prostitutes on Negro Hill, or what is today Beacon Hill. Within a few months, a sequel was published entitled *The Adventures of Lucy Brewer, alias Louisa Baker*. The author explained that she had published the first book with extreme reluctance, but "contrary to all expectation, so great has been its circulation, and so great the avidity with which it has been sought after and perused, that I have, contrary to my determination, even again consented to become my own biographer."[5] She now admitted that her real name was Lucy Brewer and that she had been born in the small town of Plymouth, Massachusetts. She summarized her early adventures and the three awful years she had spent among "the detestable harlots who inhabit those vile brothel-houses which the Hill contains." She briefly recounted her experiences as a marine and confirmed that the ship she served on was the frigate *Constitution*.

After her return from sea, she spent a while on her parents' farm, but her previous adventures had made her restless and she decided to continue her travels. She once again assumed male clothes and took the stagecoach to Newport. Traveling with her were a midshipman, a sea captain, a venerable old gentleman, and a seventeen-year-old girl. They stopped to dine at an inn where the captain and the midshipman got drunk. They insulted the girl with rude jokes and obscene language until Lucy rebuked them. The midshipman was enraged. He had a dirk dangling at his side and hinted that with this little weapon he had withstood and overcome formidable foes upon the ocean. Lucy challenged him to a duel, but the midshipman's courage deserted him when faced with the sight of a cocked pistol. He was forced to apologize to the girl, and when they arrived at Newport, he beat a hasty retreat. Lucy traveled on to New York, where she met the young lady she had defended. Her name was Miss West and she was accompanied by her brother. They were from a wealthy New York family, and Lucy spent some time with them before traveling back to Boston. Dressed as a military officer, she revisited her old haunts on Negro Hill and even called on the madam who ran the brothel where she had been taught her first lessons in vice. The old woman was completely fooled by her disguise. Satisfied with her recent adventures, Lucy returned once again to the peaceful home of her fond parents.

In May 1816, the third part of Lucy's story appeared under the title *The Awful Beacon, to the Rising Generation of Both Sexes.* This time the author was given on the title page as "Mrs. Lucy West (Late Miss Lucy Brewer)." This volume described how Charles West, the handsome brother of Miss West, had read Lucy Brewer's autobiography and discovered the identity of the young man who had defended his sister's honor. He wrote to Lucy from New York to say he would like to see her again, and some time later he arrived at her parents' farm in a carriage. After some further adventures, they were married, and Lucy concluded her book with some moralizing stories and reflections.

This was not the end of the saga, however, because in the summer of 1816, Mrs. Rachel Sperry, the madam of the brothel where Lucy had worked for three years, published her side of the story. In a pamphlet entitled *A Brief Reply to the Late Writings of Louisa Baker (alias Lucy Brewer)*, she revealed that the real name of the author of the three publications was Eliza Bowen. She pointed out that, far from being a reluctant innocent who had been corrupted by an old bawd, Miss Bowen had made such rapid strides in the arts of harlotry that she had decoyed countless youths with her feminine wiles, and had been an enthusiastic participant in the midnight revels at the dancing halls. Mrs. Sperry justified her own career by recounting how her husband had drowned in a boating accident near Boston lighthouse in the spring of 1806, leaving her to support three small children. The starving condition of her family had prompted her to open a lodging house on the Hill. She had made sure that her female boarders were quiet and well behaved when they had company in the evenings, and was grateful for their assistance with her sewing work in the daytime. She provided examples of Miss Bowen's disgraceful behavior and refused to believe that she had sincerely repented of her past life. She concluded her pamphlet with the words "I therefore now furnish the public with a true statement of the whole affair—let the candid examine and judge for themselves."

We do not know for certain what the public made of Lucy Brewer's adventures, but we do know that her story proved so popular that the various parts were combined in a single volume entitled *The Female Marine* and that nine editions of this were published between 1816 and 1818. (This was in addition to the six editions of *The Adventures of Louisa Baker* and the three editions of *The Adventures of Lucy Brewer*.) Many of the readers seem to have been young women who were fascinated by the heroine's racy life. Inside the cover of one surviving copy, a woman wrote that *The Female Marine* was "a very interesting Book indeed," underlining the words for emphasis. Several accounts had already appeared of women dressing as soldiers and fighting in the U.S. Army,[6] and it therefore seems likely that contemporary readers assumed this was a true account of a woman who had had similar experiences in the U.S. Navy.

We now know that the stories are entirely fictitious and that they were written by a man. Research by the American historian Alexander Medlicott, Jr., in the 1960s showed that there was no evidence to prove the existence of Louisa Baker, Lucy Brewer, Lucy West, or Eliza Bowen in any of the towns of Plymouth County, nor could any marine with the first or last name of George be found on the muster rolls of the USS *Constitution*. Further research by Professor Daniel A. Cohen has made it abundantly clear that the mastermind behind the pamphlets was an enterprising Boston publisher named Nathaniel Coverly, Jr. It was he who arranged for their publication and subsequent promotion, but he was not their author. He employed a writer who produced prose and verse for him to order. This was Nathaniel Hill Wright, a poet and printer in his late twenties who turned his hand to a variety of tasks to support himself and his family. It was said that Wright "could do the grave or the gay, as necessity demanded, and with equal facility." He evidently had considerable gifts as a writer because his account of Lucy Brewer's adventures is remarkably convincing. In the tradition of Daniel Defoe, he concealed his own identity and cunningly combined real events and real places with entirely imaginary characters.

Encouraged by the success of *The Female Marine*, Coverly published another story about a female sailor in September 1816. This was entitled *The Surprising Adventures of Almira Paul*. Like Coverly's earlier publications, this has often been regarded as a true account although the story is harder to believe than the story of Lucy Brewer. It was also written in the form of an autobiography and described how Almira Paul was born in Halifax, Nova Scotia, in 1790. At the age of fifteen, she married William Paul, a sailor, by whom she had two children. When her husband was killed in a sea battle in 1811, she decided to go to sea herself. Leaving her children with her mother, she dressed as a man and joined the British cutter *Dolphin* as the cook's mate. She took the name of Jack Brown and subsequently saw action on a variety of British and American ships.

During the course of the next three years, she survived some difficult times. She was bullied by the ship's cook and took her revenge by kicking him overboard. For this offense she was ordered to be flogged, and she avoided revealing her sex by wearing a shirt during the flogging. She fell from the main yard onto the deck and fractured her skull but recovered. She was captured by Algerian pirates in the Mediterranean and was released in Algiers by the British consul. She made her way to Portsmouth, where she married a woman who had lost her sailor husband at the Battle of Trafalgar. Before the widow had time to discover that she had married a woman, Almira Paul was on a ship bound for Jamaica. She went down with fever in Demerara but recovered with the aid of a black nurse. She then sailed to Liverpool, where she went ashore and was wooed by the local girls who attempted "by their expressions of love and regard for me, to decoy me into their favorite ports; where they might be the better enabled to induce me to part with a few guineas." She returned to the Mediterranean and joined the crew of the *Macedonian*, which she deserted in Baltimore; to avoid being arrested as a deserter she resumed female clothes. However, after three years associating with sailors, she was reluctant to leave their company and therefore became a prostitute in the red-light district of the port. After six weeks of this, she traveled to New York and then on to Boston, where she joined the prostitutes on West Boston Hill. The story ends with her imprisonment in a Boston jail for failing to pay her landlord.

While the adventures of Almira Paul might seem to stretch our credulity to the limit, the story of Lucy Brewer is by no means far-fetched. A real-life parallel can be found for most of the incidents in Brewer's life: a number of female sailors left home because they had been seduced and become pregnant; many sailors' wives resorted to prostitution in order to support themselves and their families; there is at least one account of a female sailor binding her breasts to conceal her sex; many women disguised as men took part in sea battles; and at least three female sailors subsequently had accounts of their lives published.[7] It is possible that the publisher or the author of the stories in *The Female Marine* had read or heard of some of these accounts and made use of them in much the same way as Daniel Defoe drew on the life of the shipwrecked mariner Alexander Selkirk as his inspiration for the character of Robinson Crusoe.

The most famous of the women who served in the Royal Navy were Hannah Snell and Mary Anne Talbot, whose lives will be examined in the next chapter, but there are a number of other women whose lives are equally fascinating. The American writer Suzanne Stark has investigated the stories of twenty of the women who are believed to

have served in the Royal Navy between 1650 and 1815, and by check-
ing with captains' logs, ships' musters, and contemporary newspaper
articles, she has been able to sort out fact from fiction.[8] The most impressive naval career of all the female sailors is that of William Brown,
a black woman who spent at least twelve years on British warships,
much of this time in the extremely demanding role of captain of the
foretop. A good description of her appeared in London's *Annual Register* in September 1815: "She is a smart, well-formed figure, about five
feet four inches in height, possessed of considerable strength and great
activity; her features are rather handsome for a black, and she appears
to be about twenty-six years of age." The article also noted that "in
her manner she exhibits all the traits of a British tar and takes her grog
with her late messmates with the greatest gaiety."[9]

Brown was a married woman and had joined the navy around 1804
following a quarrel with her husband. For several years she served on
the *Queen Charlotte*, a three-decker with 104 guns and one of the
largest ships in the Royal Navy. The *Queen Charlotte* had a crew of 850
men and usually served as the flagship of the fleet. Brown must have
had nerve, strength, and unusual ability to have been made captain of
the foretop on such a ship. The topmen were responsible for going
aloft in all weathers and furling or setting the highest sails (the topsails
and topgallants). The captain of the foretop had to lead a team of seamen up the shrouds of the foremast, and then up the shrouds of the
fore-topmast and out along the yards a hundred feet or more above the
deck. With their feet on a swaying foot-rope, the men had to heave up
or let go of the heavy canvas sails, difficult enough in fine weather but
a hard and dangerous job in driving rain and rough seas.

At some point in 1815, it was discovered that Brown was a woman
and her story was published in the papers, but this does not seem to
have affected her naval career. She had by this stage earned a large sum
of prize money, and she visited the pay office on Somerset Place to collect this. Her husband attempted to cheat her out of the money, though
whether he was successful in this is not known. What is certain is that
Brown returned to the *Queen Charlotte* and rejoined the crew. The
entry in the ship's muster book for the period December 31, 1815, to
February 1, 1816, reads, "William Brown, AB, entered 31 December,
1815, 1st Warrt., place of origin, Edinburgh, age 32."[10] This indicates
that she was rated as able seaman and confirms her age as thirty-two,

not twenty-six as recorded in the newspapers. In January 1816, she was made captain of the forecastle, which was a more senior role but did not usually entail going aloft. In the summer of 1816, she and several other seamen were transferred from the *Queen Charlotte* to the *Bombay*, a 74-gun ship; according to the *Bombay*'s muster book, William Brown joined the ship on June 29. The muster books for the succeeding years are missing, so we do not know what happened to her after that date.

William Prothero, like the fictional Lucy Brewer, was a marine; that is to say, she served on board ship as a soldier rather than as a sailor. The details about her are tantalizingly brief. The muster books of HMS *Amazon* tell us that Private William Prothero entered the ship on December 1, 1760, and was discharged on April 30, 1761. The *Amazon* was a Sixth Rate ship of 22 guns under the command of Captain Basil Keith. On April 20, 1761, the ship was at Yarmouth and the captain noted in his log, "One of the marines going by the name of Wm. Protherow was discovered to be a woman. She had done her duty on board nine months." A further snippet of information is provided in the journal of J. C. Atkinson, who was a surgeon's mate on the *Amazon*. He noted that she was "an eighteen-year-old Welsh girl who had followed her sweetheart to sea."

The extraordinary life of Mary Lacy is recorded in almost as much detail as that of Lucy Brewer and Almira Paul but with the vital difference that at several points it checks out with surviving documents.[11] Her story was first published in London in 1773, under the title *The History of the Female Shipwright . . . Written by Herself*, and an American edition was published in New York with a similar title in 1807. Mary Lacy was born of poor parents on January 12, 1740, at Wickham in Kent. She was the eldest of three children and received a good education in a charity school. When she was about twelve, she went into domestic service in the town of Ash and worked in various households for the next seven years. An unrequited love affair so unsettled her that she decided to leave Ash. Carrying an old frock coat and pair of breeches, a pair of stockings and pumps, and a hat, she left the town at six o'clock on the morning of May 1, 1759. As soon as she was out in the countryside, she changed into the men's clothes and left her own under a hedge. She traveled via Canterbury to Chatham, home of one of the royal dockyards. There she learned that the 90-gun ship *Sandwich* had recently been launched and was still short of her full complement of crew. She went on board and introduced herself to the gunner, telling him her name was William Chandler. He gave her some biscuits and cheese and suggested that she apply to Richard Baker, the carpenter, who promptly took her on as his servant. Her duties included making his bed, fetching him beer, boiling him beefsteak, and cleaning his shoes. Unfortunately, Baker had a quick temper and would suddenly fly into a rage and beat her. When not working aboard the ship, Baker lived with his wife in a house in Chatham; Mrs. Baker proved kinder than her husband to Mary Lacy. She provided the young carpenter's mate with "a clean shirt, a pair of stockings, a pair of shoes, a coat and a waistcoat, a checked handkerchief, and a red nightcap for me to wear at sea."

On May 20, 1759, the *Sandwich* was moved downstream to take her guns aboard. Three weeks later she was at the Nore to take on the rest of her crew, and on June 21 she set sail down the Thames estuary and headed across the English Channel to join Admiral Hawke's squadron off Brest. In July, Rear Admiral Francis Geary came aboard and raised his flag at the mizzenmast. His flag captain, and the commander of the 750 men on the ship, was Captain Richard Norbury.

At this stage in the Seven Years' War between Britain and France, the Royal Navy was engaged in a holding operation that involved a constant blockade of the ports where the French ships were gathered. From the summer of 1759 to the autumn of 1760, HMS *Sandwich* joined the extended line of British warships patrolling the seas off Ushant. The Bay of Biscay has always been notorious for its storms— so bad were the conditions that every two months or so the ship was forced to head back to England and put in to Plymouth in order to carry out repairs, take fresh provisions on board, and allow sick and exhausted crews to recover. Mary Lacy learned to survive the gales, but at one point she was so badly affected with rheumatoid arthritis that she could not walk and had to be confined to the sick bay for several weeks. She had another severe bout of arthritis when the *Sandwich* was in Portsmouth in the autumn of 1760 and was confined to the naval hospital. By the time she recovered, the ship had sailed.

She now joined the *Royal Sovereign* as a supernumerary. This 100-gun ship was the guardship for the port and was permanently stationed offshore at Spithead. Although the crew were in sheltered waters and in sight of land, they were seldom allowed ashore. Mary was confined to the ship for a year and nine months. Fortunately she made a number of friends, notably a young woman who was living on board with a sailor named John Grant. She writes, "The young woman and I were very intimate, and as she was exceeding fond of me, we used to play together like young children." Grant did not see their friendship in such an innocent light and became so resentful that he took his jealousy out on the young woman by beating her and threatening to send her ashore.

Although Mary's autobiography provides a vivid picture of life on board a British warship, she makes surprisingly few references to any problems she might have experienced in disguising her sex. One of the few occasions when she might have been discovered took place on the *Royal Sovereign*. While working on deck, she tripped and fell down an open hatch. She cut her head badly and was taken to the doctor.

> When I came to myself I was very apprehensive lest the doctor in searching for bruises about my body should have discovered that I was a woman, but it fortunately happened that he being a middle-aged gentleman, he was not very inquisitive, and my messmates being advanced in years, and not so active as young people, did not tumble me about or undress me.

Mary now decided to become a shipwright's apprentice, and thanks to recommendations from her former shipmates and her own determination, she succeeded in her aim. In March 1763, she was signed on as apprentice to Alexander McLean, the acting carpenter of the *Royal William*, an 84-gun ship that was out of commission and based at Portsmouth Dockyard. McLean was currently living on board the ship together with his mistress and several other warrant officers and their wives, but he later rented a house ashore.

For the next three or four years, Mary put in twelve-hour days in the dockyard and in the evenings joined their drunken revels. She must have had stamina as well as considerable ability as a craftsman, because she not only survived the long hours and physical demands of the job, but she also earned the men's respect. She records that they would say she was "the best boy on board." She also continued to attract the women. McLean's mistress was obviously fond of her and on one occasion "came and placed herself in my lap, stroking me down the face, telling the watermen what she would do for me, so that the people present could not forbear laughing to see her sit in such a young boy's lap as she thought I was." She became particularly friendly with a very handsome girl named Sarah How, who became "very free and intimate with me." She also carried on a flirtation with a prostitute named Betsey, and then became such close friends with Sarah Chase, a servant girl, that her fellow workers thought they would soon get married. Mary tells us that they were very intimate together and that they agreed that neither of them would go out with any other person without the consent of the other.

During her time on the *Sandwich*, she had written to her parents and explained her situation. In 1767, she went to see them for the first time since she had left home at the age of nineteen. She told them all about her adventures, but unfortunately when she returned to Portsmouth, a friend of the family came to live in the town and let it be known that the shipwright's apprentice known as William Chandler was really a woman. The rumor rapidly spread around the dockyard, and some of the other apprentices wanted to examine her to discover the truth. She was saved by two of the shipwrights she had worked for. They took her aside, questioned her very seriously, and said that it would be better if she told them the truth rather than expose herself to the rudeness of the dockyard boys. Mary burst into tears and admitted that she was indeed a woman. They were astonished but swore to keep her secret. They assured the dockyard people that William was a man and pointed out that if he were a girl he would not have gone after so many women.

Mary qualified as a shipwright in the spring of 1770 and was duly awarded the certificate to confirm that she had completed her apprenticeship. Unhappily, after surviving six years at sea and seven years as an apprentice, she suffered another bout of rheumatoid arthritis that was so crippling she could scarcely walk. She recovered sufficiently to be able to return to work, but while helping to dismantle a 40-gun ship, she seriously strained herself and found that she could no longer cope with the physical demands of the job. She had no option but to leave the dockyard and apply to the Admiralty for a disability pension. Her case was examined, and on January 28, 1772, the Lords of the Admiralty agreed to her request. The following report must be one of the most unusual entries ever to appear in the volumes of Admiralty minutes:

A Petition was read from Mary Lacey [*sic*] setting forth that in the Year 1759 she disguised herself in Men's Cloaths and enter'd on board His Maj^{ts} Fleet, where having served til the end of the

War, she bound herself apprentice to the Carpenter of the *Royal
William* and having served Seven Years, then enter'd as a Shipwright in Portsmouth Yard where she has continued ever since;
but that finding her health and constitution impaired by so laborious an Employment, she is obliged to give it up for the future,
and therefore, praying some Allowance for her Support during
the remainder of her life:

   Resolved, in consideration of the particular Circumstances
attending this Woman's case, the truth of which has been attested
by the Commissioner of the Yard at Portsmouth, that she be allowed a Pension equal to that granted to Superannuated Shipwrights.[12]

This marked the end of Mary Lacy's life as William Chandler. Her
autobiography ends abruptly with her meeting a Mr. Slade at Deptford
who proposed marriage.

She had always planned to remain single but at length decided to
accept his offer, convinced that the hand of Providence had brought
them together. Her husband was sober and industrious, and the book
concludes with Mary looking forward to enjoying the utmost happiness the married state affords. While the essential facts of Mary Lacy's
story check out with contemporary documents, it seems likely that the
tidy ending was provided by her publisher, who was happy to allow
readers to be titillated by her lesbian flirtations but felt that the book
must have a more traditional conclusion.

The adventures of William Brown, William Prothero, and Mary
Lacy bring up a number of interesting questions. How many other
women cross-dressed as men and went to sea in the great age of sail?
How was it possible for them to fool their shipmates for so long when
they were living in such close proximity? Why on earth would a
woman want to run away from her home and family and put herself
through the notorious hardships and dangers of life at sea? And why
has the whole subject of cross-dressing women so fascinated people
that fictional accounts of female sailors became best-sellers, sea
chanties and ballads were written about them, and they even appeared
in plays and melodramas on the London stage?

We will never know how many women went to sea as men because
the only cases we have any evidence of are those in which the
woman's sex was revealed and publicized in some way, or those cases

where a woman left the sea and had her story published. There must have been many women who sailed as men whose sex was never discovered and who lived and died as anonymously as their sisters who never went to sea. Stark's research has revealed twenty cases of female sailors in the Royal Navy in the seventeenth and eighteenth centuries that appear to be genuine and two accounts that are largely fictitious. Another fifteen cases of female sailors on board merchant vessels and fishing boats are recorded in newspaper articles, reports in the *Naval Chronicle*, and other sources, though the accuracy of these cannot be guaranteed. As there were up to 145,000 men in the Royal Navy in 1810, and some 120,000 men in the merchant navy at the same period, it is evident that female sailors were very rare indeed, and it is little wonder that when they were discovered their stories found their way into the newspapers.

What is striking about the genuine cases of female sailors is how they were able to fool the men on board for weeks, months, and in some cases, several years. On the face of it the women had an almost impossible task. Anyone who has been belowdecks on HMS *Victory* or the USS *Constitution* will recall the lack of headroom and the cramped conditions. The *Victory* and the *Constitution* were among the largest ships of their day, so that life on a more typical warship of, say, 74 guns was even more confined. The officers had the benefit of living in small cabins constructed of wood or canvas screens, but the ordinary seamen lived literally on top of each other in a low, cavernous space dominated by the rows of guns. The off-duty watch slept in hammocks suspended below the deck beams. A female sailor could find herself in a hammock with no more than a few inches separating her from the seamen snoring in the hammocks on either side of her. Below the hammocks, the seamen sat on their sea chests or lay on the deck with their backs against the gun carriages. For meals they gathered around temporary tables slung between the guns, usually six to a table or a mess. One of their number would fetch the food for the mess from the galley, and broth or salt beef would be shared among them and eaten out of wooden bowls.

A 74-gun ship had a crew of around 550 to 650 men, most of whom were crammed into the area in front of the quarterdeck, about half its 176-foot length. The stern of the ship was largely taken up by the captain's cabin, appropriately called the great cabin, and by the quarters and stores of the officers and warrant officers. Much of the remaining space that was not occupied by the guns was filled with anchor cable, spare sails, and pens containing an assortment of animals. Cows, goats, pigs, and chickens predominated but many sailors kept pets, and so the barking of dogs and the screeching of parrots and monkeys were added to the clucking of chickens and the lowing of cattle. Most ships also had several cats, whose job it was to keep down the population of rats that lurked in dark corners and ate their way through any food not firmly contained in barrels.

While life belowdecks was damp, dark, and reeking of tar, bilge water, and unwashed bodies, life on deck was equally forbidding in an entirely different way. There the female sailor was at the mercy of the boatswain's lash and the physical demands of sailing in all weathers. Even in light breezes, she must constantly haul on coarse ropes and climb aloft to handle the sails, but in heavy weather she must make her way across a heaving, slippery deck in driving rain and stinging clouds of salt spray. If called on to do so, she must clamber up the shrouds and out onto the yardarms that would be swinging in a slow, giddy arc backward and forward above the ocean. A missed foothold or handhold could mean a fall resulting in death or a crippling injury.

So how did a young woman cope with this? Most working-class women in the seventeenth and eighteenth centuries were accustomed to a hard life that involved long hours and a great deal of physical labor so that, provided the female sailor was reasonably strong and fit, she would not have found most of the demands of the sailors' work beyond her. She obviously had to develop a head for heights, and this proved the undoing of at least one woman. Captain Malony was short of hands when his ship *Daedalus* put in to the port of St. Johns, New Brunswick, in 1835. He went to the local jail, and the governor supplied him with an apparently robust and able-bodied seaman who went by the name Thomas Hanford. The *Daedalus* had been at sea for some time when a gale blew up and all hands were sent aloft to reef the topsails. Thomas reluctantly climbed toward the mizzentop but there his courage failed him. He came down and confessed to the mate that he was a woman whose real name was Sarah Busker. The captain agreed that for the rest of the voyage to London she should work in the cabin as a servant. She had already made a previous voyage to Labrador on a fishing boat but now decided to give up further thoughts of the sea.[13]

The sex of a female sailor named Rebecca Young was revealed in a tragic accident that came about because she was too confident of her ability to go aloft. She had spent two years sailing out of the Thames estuary on a hatch-boat. She went by the name Billy Bridle and dressed herself in a sailor's trousers, shirt, jacket, and neckerchief. One afternoon in June 1833, she challenged a man to climb the masthead with her, and after some hesitation he joined her at the maintop. She urged him to go higher, and they both climbed to the topmast crosstrees. After sitting there for a few minutes the man was called down. Five minutes later Rebecca followed, but in attempting to slide down the topgallant halyards, she burnt her hands so badly that she was forced to let go and fell twenty feet to the deck. She died on the spot, and an inquest held at the town hall in Gravesend a few days later returned a verdict of accidental death.[14]

Most of the women who went to sea were able to cope with working aloft, and several excelled at it. We have already seen that William Brown was promoted to captain of the foretop, and Mary Ann Arnold, who served as a cabin boy on a number of merchant ships, was commended by her captain in 1839: "I have seen Miss Arnold among the first aloft to reef the mizen-top-gallant sail during a heavy gale in the Bay of Biscay."[15] But however active and courageous these women may have been, they still had to look like men. Or did they?

The chief reason why women were so successful in fooling their shipmates was that they looked like adolescent boys. Every ship, whether naval or merchant, had several boys in the crew. Some were as young as nine or ten, and many were in their teens. The navy welcomed boys because they were quick and agile aloft, and they could be trained from a young age in the complexities of navigation and seamanship. Those training to be officers were often fully equipped to command a ship before the age of twenty, and an able seaman in his early twenties who had been at sea since he was a boy was a priceless asset on any ship. The clothes worn by sailors were ideal for disguising a woman's shape. They consisted of a loose shirt and a waistcoat or jacket, baggy trousers or petticoat-breeches, which were like culottes, and a handkerchief tied around the neck. Hair was often worn long and tied in a pigtail or a ponytail. All that was needed was to bind the breasts sufficiently for them to be hidden beneath the shirt, in the manner described by Mary Lacy and the fictitious Lucy Brewer. In

1849, the *Carlisle Journal* carried a report about a sailor named Ann Johnson, the daughter of George Johnson, a shoemaker who lived at 22 Oak Street in New York. While at sea she had gone aloft in the heaviest weather, and the report concluded, "Her appearance is said to be that of a good-looking boy of 16 or 17 years."[16]

The trickiest problem facing the female sailor every day was using the toilet facilities, which in most ships were extremely primitive. The seamen usually climbed over the sides onto the leeward channels and urinated into the sea, or they went forward to the heads. This was the name given to the platform at the bows that was built over the beakhead and behind the figurehead. There the seaman crouched over a hole to defecate or sat on a crude box with a hole in the top, called a "seat of easement." Presumably most women would have gone to the heads rather than attempting to urinate over the sides, although there is evidence to show that some women who cross-dressed made use of a small funnel of horn or metal to assist them.[17]

The subject of menstruation is not mentioned in any of the accounts of female sailors, but women historians have suggested that this might not have been such a problem. One theory is that the young women on board ship lived such ferociously active lives that, like modern athletes in training today, they may have ceased to have periods. In the case of prepubescent girls, the hard life and poor diet could have delayed the onset of puberty for several years. Another theory is that so many seamen suffered from a range of diseases and ailments including piles and gonorrhea that they were not likely to comment on one of their number having bloodstained clothing on occasion.

Which brings us to the question of why a woman would want to go to sea dressed as a man. The traditional reason, and the one made popular in numerous ballads, was that women went to sea to join their sailor lovers. We have already seen it suggested that the young woman known as William Prothero followed her lover to sea. So did the seventeen-year-old Margaret Thompson, who left her uncle's home in London in 1781 and joined the navy under the name George Thompson. She revealed that she was a woman when she was blamed for a theft and condemned to be flogged. When asked by the captain why she had taken the extraordinary step of going to sea disguised as a man she said it was "to see her sweetheart, who quitted England three years since, and is now resident at Bombay."[18] Hannah Snell is said to have married a Dutch sailor and followed him to sea. And according to the *History of the Pirates* by Captain Charles Johnson, the pirate Anne Bonny left her father's house in the Carolinas and ran away to sea with a feckless sailor. Perhaps these and others were prompted to go to sea because of love affairs, but the evidence suggests that most of the women who went to sea disguised as men did so for hard economic reasons or because they wished to escape from something in their past.

Anne McLean is a typical example of one who went to sea for economic reasons. She was born of poor parents in Ireland around 1829. When they died she found it difficult to obtain a livelihood, and "being stout and hardy, thought she might pass for a boy."[19] She had a brother who was a seaman in the service of the East India Company, and this prompted her to go to Cork to sign on as a sailor. She made two voyages to the West Indies, but on her return in November 1846, she left the sea and spent three weeks in a factory in Glasgow. She did not like the confinement of the work there, so she found employment as a coal porter and then did some field labor at Pollokshaws on the outskirts of the city. She decided to go to sea again and applied to the recruiting sergeant of the East India Company in Glasgow. He was delighted to sign on a fit and experienced young seaman, but a sharp-eyed onlooker saw through her disguise and she had to confess that she was a woman. A newspaper report described her appearance in detail. She was eighteen years old and was exactly five feet, five and three-quarter inches in height. She had a manly look, "and was dressed in corduroy jacket, moleskin trousers, blue bonnet, striped shirt, and hob-nailed shoes." She had a rather shrill voice but attempted to overcome this drawback by adopting such male habits as smoking and swigging back glasses of whiskey or porter. When she left the recruiting rendezvous after her gender had been revealed, she said she would try to get work on the railways as a navvy.

Forces of circumstance led to eighteen-year-old Betty Wilson's going to sea. She was staying at a lodging house in the English town of Whitehaven when she was robbed of her clothes. We read that "in her extremity she was induced to rig herself in the clothes of a sailor who was asleep at the time in the same house."[20] She had no friends or relations to help her, so she resolved to find employment as a seaman and embarked on the merchant ship *Charlotte* of Dundalk. She made two voyages to Ireland disguised as a man and would have made more but on going ashore in Belfast in September 1832, she got so drunk that she passed out in the street. She was picked up and taken in a handcart to the police station. It was while they were trying to resuscitate her that it was discovered she was a woman. She said that she had assumed the name James Wilson and was apparently deeply ashamed of the awkward situation she found herself in. A collection was taken to enable her to buy some women's clothes.

The Morning Chronicle of May 22, 1813, carried a story of another woman who took to the sea when she lost her clothes. She was traveling on a coastal voyage as servant to a family when the vessel was wrecked and everyone else on board was drowned. She was cast naked on the shore, and finding the dead body of a seaman lying near her, she dressed herself in his clothes and begged her way to the nearest port. She managed to find work as a landsman on a ship and then transferred to the American schooner *Revenge*. She spent three years as a member of that crew, but when the *Revenge* was captured by the British frigate *Belle Poule,* she became a prisoner of war. Rather than be sent to a British prison, she revealed her sex and told her captors that she would like to be sent home to America. She said she was owed about $200 in wages and prize money. There was no mention of the woman's name in the newspaper article, but there was a brief description: "She has a comely face, sun-burnt, as well as her hands; and appeared, while in men's clothes, a decent, well-looking young man."

A few women evidently went to sea to escape problems at home. It will be recalled that the fictitious Lucy Brewer left home to save her parents from shame when she realized she was pregnant. There are several real-life accounts of young women pursuing the same course. In 1813, Captain Embleton, master of the British collier *Edmund and Mary,* was sailing from Blyth to Ipswich when he discovered that one of the boy apprentices on his ship was female. His wife, who was traveling on board with him, interviewed the girl and learned that she was the daughter of a Northumberland widow. She had become pregnant and after she had given birth decided to leave home and never to return. She got hold of some men's clothes, made one coastal voyage, and then applied to the owners of the *Edmund and Mary,* who agreed to take her on as an apprentice mariner. The discovery of her gender was made on the vessel's second voyage. It seems that the girl had behaved well "and was considered a very active lad."[21]

Many of the women who went to sea disguised as men or boys attracted no more than a brief mention in the newspapers of the day and were quickly forgotten. But there were four female sailors whose stories circulated more widely. Their biographies were frequently reprinted, their lives inspired plays and ballads, and their names continue to crop up in books and discussions relating to the theme of the female warrior. Their names are Hannah Snell, Mary Anne Talbot, and the pirates Mary Read and Anne Bonny.

5

Hannah Snell, Mary Anne Talbot, and the Female Pirates

THE NEW WELLS THEATER WAS IN GOODMAN'S FIELDS, A FEW HUNDRED yards north of the Tower of London. In the 1750s, it lay on the edge of the City. To the west was a jumble of rooftops and church spires dominated by the dome of St. Paul's, and to the east were green fields and the scattered houses forming the village of Stepney. The theater was managed by William Hallam, who presented nightly performances of shows called harlequinades. These consisted of a series of acts that included anything from tightrope walking and acrobatics to song-and-dance routines. The performances usually began at five o'clock in the afternoon and sometimes lasted four or five hours. On June 29, 1750, an unusually large crowd assembled to see a twenty-seven-year-old woman named Hannah Snell sing two songs. The *Whitehall and General Evening Post* noted that "She appeared in her Marine Habit, and met with universal applause, as she behaved with great decency and good manners."

Hannah Snell had spent four and a half years dressed as a man.[1] She had joined the marines, sailed to India, and taken part in the siege of Pondicherry, where she had been badly wounded. After nine months recovering in the hospital at Cuddalore, she sailed back to England on

HMS *Eltham* and served as a seaman during the voyage. On her return she revealed her identity. She was discharged from the navy, and when the press got hold of her story, she became a celebrity. Her portrait was painted by several artists, a London publisher issued a vivid account of her life story, and everyone was curious to see the young woman who had bravely fought for her country disguised as a man.

It was a shrewd idea to cash in on her popularity by appearing on the London stage. Exactly how much she was paid for her appearances is not recorded, but her biographer noted that she persuaded the manager of the theater to pay her a weekly salary for the season, "which is such a stipend that not one woman in ten thousand of her low extraction and want of literature could, by any act of industry (how laborious soever) with any possibility procure."[2] So between June 29 and September 6, Hannah performed every night except Sundays at the New Wells. For the first three weeks she restricted herself to singing two specially written songs. A typical verse gives an idea of the rousing, patriotic nature of the material:

> In the midst of blood and slaughter, bravely fighting for my king,
>   Facing death from every quarter, fame and conquest home to
>   bring,
> Sure you'll own 'tis more than common, and the world proclaim it,
>   too,
> Never yet did any woman more for love and glory do.[3]

On July 19, it was decided to extend her repertoire by having her demonstrate the military exercises normally carried out by the marines on parade. Dressed in a red coat with brass buttons, white breeches, and a tricorn hat, she marched onto the stage to the sound of tabor and drum and accompanied by female attendants. It was reported that she performed the military exercises with such precision that even veteran soldiers who came out of curiosity were full of admiration.

There are articles in the London papers, and brief details appear in ships' muster books and the records of Chelsea Hospital, but the prime source for the life of Hannah Snell is the biography that was written and published by Robert Walker. The first edition came out in July 1750 under the title *The Female Soldier; Or, The Surprising Life and Adventures of Hannah Snell*. A second and somewhat extended edition was published a few months later. Most of the basic facts recorded by Walker appear to be true and are confirmed by other sources, but he could not resist embellishing the story with sensational incidents, several of which are probably fictitious.

Hannah Snell was born in Worcester on April 23, 1723. Her father was a hosier and cloth-dyer.[4] Her parents died when she was twenty, and she moved to London to stay with her sister, Susannah, and her sister's husband, James Gray, who was a house carpenter. They had a house on Ship Street in Wapping, not far from the waterfront.[5] Hannah spent two or three years with them, and during that time she met a Dutch sailor named James Summs. According to Walker, she married Summs on January 6, 1744, at the Fleet. There is no record of the marriage, but this is not surprising: The area near today's Fleet Street was notorious in the eighteenth century for "Fleet Marriages." These were originally carried out in the chapel of the Fleet prison by clergymen confined for debt but later took place in taverns and rooms in the neighborhood. No licenses or other formalities were involved, and therefore they were much favored by runaway couples and by sailors in a hurry to marry before rejoining their ships.

Walker tells us that Summs proved to be a bad choice for a husband. He not only kept company with criminals but took up with other women and sold off Hannah's possessions in order to support his dissolute way of life. After a while he deserted her, but not before he had gotten her pregnant. She gave birth to a daughter, whom she named Susannah after her sister. The infant's baptism is recorded in the registers of the church of St. George-in-the-East, Middlesex, in September 1746. The child lived for only six or seven months, and soon after her death Hannah decided to disguise herself as a man and set off to join the army. She dressed in her brother-in-law's clothes and adopted his name. As James Gray, she traveled to Coventry, where she joined Colonel Guise's 6th Regiment of Foot. According to her biographer, she intended to track down her husband to seek her revenge. This may or may not be the case, but it is curious that instead of looking for James Summs on a ship she headed inland to Coventry.

The regiment was sent to Carlisle, and there an incident reportedly took place that must surely be fictitious. Her sergeant wanted Hannah to act as an intermediary so he could have his way with a young woman. Hannah warned the woman of his intentions, and when the sergeant found out what she had done, he took his revenge on Hannah by accusing her of neglect of duty. She was sentenced to receive 600 lashes, and according to Walker's account, she was tied to the city gates and received 500 lashes before some of the officers intervened. Since 200 or 300 lashes often amounted to a death sentence for hardened soldiers and seamen, it seems unlikely that she not only lived through this ordeal but managed to maintain her male disguise: It was standard practice for the flogging to be administered on a man's bare back. Walker explained, "At that time her breasts were but very small; and her arms being extended and fix'd to the city gates, her breasts were towards the wall, so that then there was little or no danger of her comrades finding out the important secret, which she took such uncommon pains to conceal."[6]

She served as a soldier for between four months and two years and then deserted. Still using the name James Gray, she went to Portsmouth and in 1747 enlisted in Colonel Fraser's regiment of marines. On October 24, 1747, she joined the sloop *Swallow* as a marine, and shortly afterward she sailed aboard her to India, where the vessel met up with the fleet commanded by Admiral Boscawen.[7] In August 1748, Boscawen's fleet arrived at Cuddalore on the southeastern coast of India, and Hannah was dispatched with the other marines to take part in the siege of Pondicherry. Standing knee-deep in water, she reportedly fired thirty-seven rounds of shot before she was hit herself. She received six shot in her right leg, five shot in her left, and another shot in the groin. She lay wounded in the camp for a day and a night before she was carried to the hospital at Cuddalore. She allowed the surgeons to treat the gunshot wounds in her legs, but in spite of the dreadful pain, she did not let them see the wound in her groin because she did not wish to be revealed as a woman. The biography contains a graphic description of how she probed the wound and managed to extract the musket ball with her thumb and finger. She persuaded an Indian nurse to bring her lint and healing ointment to dress the wound, and as a result she recovered sufficiently from her injuries to be able to get up and about.

She was released from the hospital on August 2, 1749, and was temporarily assigned as a seaman to the frigate *Tartar*. On October 13, she was transferred to HMS *Eltham*, 44 guns, which set sail for England.[8] Among the various incidents on the voyage home two would appear to be entirely fanciful. In Lisbon she supposedly met an English sailor who told her that her husband was in prison for murdering a Genoese. While there is no reason why she should not have had news of her husband at some point, the picturesque details of James Summs's life since abandoning her do not ring true. Even less convincing is her biographer's description of a flogging she was subjected to while on board the *Eltham*. On this occasion, Hannah was accused of stealing a shirt from one of her shipmates. She was ordered to be clapped in irons for five days, flogged with twelve lashes, and then sent up to the foretop for four hours. Again Walker has to use some ingenuity to explain why she was not revealed to be a woman: "When her hands were lashed to the gang-way, she was in much greater danger of being discovered; but she stood as upright as possible, and tied a large silk handkerchief round her neck, the ends whereof entirely covered her breasts, insomuch that she went through the martial discipline with great resolution, without being the least suspected." Walker concludes, "At this time, 'tis true, the boatswain of the ship taking notice of her breasts, seemed surprised, and said, they were the most like a woman's he ever saw; but as no person on board ever had the least suspicion of her sex, the whole dropped without any farther notice being taken."[9]

The *Eltham* arrived at Spithead on May 25, 1750.[10] The crew went ashore, and Hannah and some of her shipmates took lodging at the sign of the Jolly Marine and Sailor in Portsmouth. While she was staying there, Hannah met a young woman named Catharine, who was the sister-in-law of the man who ran the lodging house. Within a few hours they became very intimate, and Hannah found that "her amorous caresses were so engaging to Mrs. Catharine, that she fell victim to the young God of Love."[11] Catharine would have liked to marry her, but Hannah told her that first she must go to London to collect her pay. She set off in the company of her shipmates, and when she reached the capital she went to see her sister and brother-in-law in Wapping. In spite of her marine uniform, her sister recognized her at once, flung her arms around her neck, and stifled her with kisses. After Hannah had told them about her adventures, they went to Downing Street. There Hannah met up with the other marines, and they called at the house of John Winter, who was agent to their regiment. He very readily paid them what they were due. Hannah was owed two and a half years' pay and received £15 plus two civilian suits, which she later sold for 15 shillings.

In a jovial mood, they repaired to the Two Fighting Cocks, a tavern next door to Mr. Winter's house on Downing Street. After they had drunk the health of the King, Hannah decided to tell them who she really was. Turning to a marine she had sometimes shared a bed with she said, "Had you known, Master Moody, who you had between a pair of sheets with you, you would have come to closer quarters. In a word, gentlemen, I am as much a woman as my mother ever was and my name is Hannah Snell."

Her companions were at first shocked and unbelieving, but her sister and brother-in-law assured them it was the truth and said that they would swear it upon oath if necessary. When they had gotten over their initial surprise, her companions suggested that she should submit a petition to the Duke of Cumberland, captain general of the British army, for financial recompense for her injuries. On June 16, Hannah, dressed in a man's suit, went to St. James's Park to see whether she could meet him. She spotted him in an open carriage accompanied by Colonel Napier. Fortunately, the carriage was standing still while a servant was sent on some errand, so she had no difficulty in handing over her petition. The duke read it through in a leisurely manner and then handed it to Colonel Napier, asking him to look into the merits of Hannah's case.

On June 27, the *Penny London Post* reported that the duke had put her on the King's List, which in theory meant that she would receive a pension of £30 per annum for the rest of her life, but there is some doubt as to whether she ever received any money from this source. Later in the year, however, she was admitted as an out-pensioner to the Royal Hospital, Chelsea. There is a brief entry in the admission book for November 21, 1750, which notes that Hannah Snell, age twenty-seven, served in Fraser's regiment of the 2nd Marines and in Guise's regiment for four and a half years, and was "Wounded at Pondicherry in the thigh of both legs, born at Worcester, her father a Dyer."[12] The Royal Hospital had been founded by King Charles II in 1682 as a retreat for veteran soldiers, and Hannah Snell was one of only two women to be granted a pension by the institution. The other was Christian Davies, who had fought in Marlborough's campaigns as a foot soldier in the 2nd Dragoons.[13] She had enlisted under the name Christopher Welsh, but her identity was revealed by army surgeons when she was wounded at the Battle of Ramilles in 1705.

Meanwhile, Hannah had become famous, partly through the reports in the newspapers and partly through Robert Walker's biography. As we have seen, she took advantage of the publicity to get onto the London stage, and she enjoyed three months of public adulation. When London audiences eventually tired of her act, she looked elsewhere for a living because the pension from Chelsea Hospital of 5 pence a day was not enough to support her. According to Walker's biography, she opened a pub in Wapping called the Woman in Masquerade, but no evidence can be found of a pub by that name or of any licensee named Hannah Snell or James Gray. What seems to have happened is that she moved out of London to the country. Advertisements in the newspapers indicate that she took her stage act on tour in the provinces for a while. She performed at the Merchant's Hall in Bristol in January 1751, and she was at the New Theatre in Bath on February 25.[14] We then lose sight of her for eight years.

In November 1759, the following item appeared in *The Universal Chronicle:*

> Marriages. At Newbury, in the county of Berks, the famous Hannah Snell, who served as a marine in the last war, and was wounded at the Siege of Pondicherry, to a carpenter of that place.[15]

The carpenter's name was Richard Eyles, and we know from the marriage registers of Newbury that the marriage took place on November 3. They had two sons, George and Thomas. George grew up to become a lawyer in London: It seems that a wealthy lady who admired Hannah's heroism became his godmother and contributed to his education. In 1781, he was married at St. Paul's, Covent Garden, and he lived to the age of eighty-five.[16] It is not known what happened to Thomas.

There is no record of the death of Hannah's husband, Richard Eyles, but on November 16, 1772, she married Richard Habgood at Wickham Chapel at Welford in Berkshire. Nothing whatsoever is known about him, and by 1778 he had apparently disappeared from her life, because in that year we get a fascinating glimpse of Hannah in the pages of the Reverend James Woodforde's diary. Woodforde was rector of Weston Longeville in Norfolk, and when he learned that Hannah was in the neighborhood he went to see her. The entry in his diary for May 21, 1778, is worth quoting at length:

I walked up to the White Hart with Mr Lewis and Bill to see a famous Woman in Men's Cloaths, by name Hannah Snell, who was 21 years as a common soldier in the Army, and not discovered by any as a woman. Cousin Lewis has mounted guard with her abroad. She went in the Army by the name of John Gray. She has a Pension from the Crown now of £18, 5 shillings per annum and the liberty of wearing Men's Cloaths and also a Cockade in her Hat, which she still wears. She had laid in a room with 70 Soldiers and not discovered by any of them. The forefinger of her right hand was cut off by a Sword at the taking of Pondicherry. She is now about 60 yrs of age and talks very sensible and well, and travels the country with a Basket at her back, selling Buttons, Garters, laces etc. I took 4 Pr of 4d Buttons and gave her 2 shillings, 6 pence.[17]

It is curious that of all the wounds that Hannah was reported to have received during the siege of Pondicherry, no mention was made of her losing a finger, the only injury that would normally have been visible. Perhaps this was the result of a later accident that she decided to claim as a war wound while she wandered the countryside as a peddler selling buttons. By 1785, Hannah was living with her son George in Stoke Newington, and both of them had hit hard times. George was later admitted to Ratcliffe Workhouse in London, but Hannah suffered an even more ignominious ending to her days. On August 6, 1791, she was admitted to Bethlem Royal Hospital, the notorious lunatic asylum more familiarly known as Bedlam. One newspaper recorded that she was admitted because she was "a victim of the most deplorable infirmity that can afflict human nature."[18]

It is impossible to be certain what this infirmity was, but it is unlikely to have been Alzheimer's disease or Parkinson's disease because these do not produce the sort of violent behavior that would have compelled her son George to commit her to a place like Bedlam. The most likely explanation is that she picked up syphilis from her first husband, the dissolute sailor James Summs, and that in 1791 she fell victim to tertiary syphilis, or what was called "general paralysis of the insane." In the days before antibiotics, syphilis was widespread among the population and in its later stages was one of the most feared of all diseases. It could be picked up from a single sexual encounter and lie dormant for twenty or thirty years. When it reached the third stage, it attacked the brain and nervous system, resulting in wild and uncontrollable behavior. Whatever struck down Hannah rapidly took its toll, because she died on February 8, 1792, six months after being admitted to Bedlam.[19] She was sixty-eight years old.

THE ONLY OTHER FEMALE SAILOR FROM BRITAIN TO RECEIVE SIMILAR publicity was Mary Anne Talbot. The story of her action-packed years in the army and the Royal Navy was published in 1804 by Robert Kirby, a London publisher who had taken her on as a domestic servant. The book sold so well that he produced a second, enlarged edition in 1809. The biography brought her temporary fame but did not prevent her from falling into debt and spending time in Newgate prison. She died on February 4, 1808, at the age of thirty. Her story was republished in 1893 alongside the stories of Hannah Snell, Madame Velasquez, and Mrs. Christian Davies in a book entitled *Women Adventurers.*[20] This gave an added credibility to her adventures and has resulted in her receiving a mention in most subsequent books dealing with female sailors and soldiers. However, recent research has cast doubts on her story, and it seems that much of it may have been fabricated either by her or by her publisher.

Robert Kirby's extended edition of the story was entitled *The Life and Surprising Adventures of Mary Anne Talbot in the Name of John Taylor, a Natural Daughter of the Late Earl Talbot . . . Related by Herself.* It tells how she was born in London on February 2, 1778, and was the illegitimate daughter of Lord William Talbot. After being educated at a boarding school in Chester, she fell into the hands of Captain Essex Bowen of the 82nd Regiment of Foot: "Intimidated by his manners, and knowing I had no friend near me, I became everything he could desire." When Captain Bowen's regiment was posted to Santo Domingo, he took her with him as his footboy. After various adventures in the West Indies, the regiment was ordered to Europe, and Mary became a drummer boy. She took part in several skirmishes and was present at the siege of Valenciennes, during which Captain Bowen was killed. She decided to desert from the army and made her way through the countryside to the coast, where she embarked on a French privateer.

Soon afterward the privateer ran into the British fleet under the command of Admiral Howe. The crew of the privateer were captured, and Mary was interrogated by the admiral on board his flagship, the *Queen Charlotte.* Howe dispatched her to the 74-gun ship *Brunswick,* where she was appointed cabin boy to Captain John Hervey. Within a few months she found herself taking part in the Battle of the Glorious First of June 1794. The *Brunswick* engaged the French ship *Vengeur,* and an epic duel ensued, lasting three hours and ending with the sinking of the French ship. During the course of the action, Mary received two serious wounds: A musket ball went right through her left thigh, and a grapeshot lodged in the same leg near her ankle. The ship's surgeon was unable to extract the grapeshot, so when the *Brunswick* returned to Portsmouth, Mary was sent to Haslar Hospital, where she spent four months as an outpatient.

When she was discharged from the hospital, Mary joined the crew of the bomb ketch *Vesuvius,* commanded by Captain Tomlinson. The *Vesuvius* was dispatched with a British squadron to cruise down the French coast. Separated from the squadron by a gale, the vessel was intercepted and captured by two French privateers. Mary and the rest of the crew were sent ashore and confined in the prison at Dunkirk. After spending eighteen months as a prisoner of war, she was released during an exchange of prisoners. She became a steward on the merchant ship *Ariel* and sailed to America and back to London. When she went ashore at St. Katharine's Dock, she and a fellow crew member fell into the hands of the press gang.

> I accosted the inspecting officers and told them I was unfit to serve His Majesty in the way of my fellow-sufferers, being a female. On this assertion they both appeared greatly surprised, and at first thought I had fabricated a story to be discharged, and sent me to the surgeon whom I soon convinced of the truth of my assertion.[21]

She was duly discharged, marking the end of her life at sea. She was only nineteen years old and spent the remaining years of her life in London. She made several applications to the navy pay office in Somerset House and apparently received most of the pay due to her for her service aboard the *Brunswick* and the *Vesuvius.* She seems to have drifted from job to job but found difficulty in making ends meet. She joined the Thespian Society in Tottenham Court Road and performed onstage in several women's parts. Sometimes she dressed in male clothes and frequented sailors' taverns. Eventually her debts mounted up, and she was consigned to Newgate prison. Her time there was made more bearable by the devoted attention of a woman friend she had been living with before her arrest. The woman joined her in the prison and helped to support her with her needlework: "She has continued with me ever since and remains a constant friend in every change I have since experienced."

The wounds in her leg constantly gave her trouble, and at various times she was treated in St. Bartholomew's Hospital, St. George's Hospital, and the Middlesex Hospital. While a patient at Middlesex, she was interviewed by a reporter from *The Times* of London. He described her as "a young and delicate female" and published his interview with her in the issue of November 4, 1799. The account that she gave him of her adventures differed in several respects from the story she later told the publisher Robert Kirby. She maintained that she was related to some families of distinction but said that at an early age she had been villainously deprived of a sum of money bequeathed to her by a deceased relation of high rank. She had fallen in love with a young naval officer and followed him to sea, where she had impersonated a common sailor before the mast. During a cruise on the North Sea, she had quarreled with her lover, left the ship, and gone into the army. However, her passion for the sea caused her to rejoin the navy. Instead of describing her experiences with Howe's fleet at the Battle of the Glorious First of June, she told the reporter that she "received a severe wound, on board Earl St. Vincent's ship, on the glorious 14th of February [the Battle of Cape St. Vincent, February 14, 1797], and again bled in the cause of her country in the engagement off Camperdown [October 11, 1797]." She told the reporter that her knee was shattered in the battle, which was not what she subsequently told Kirby.

The name that Mary went by when she was masquerading as a boy in the army and the navy was John Taylor. The research of Stark has shown that there was a John Taylor who was a fourteen-year-old captain's servant on board the *Brunswick*.[22] According to the ship's muster book, he had joined the ship at Portsmouth on December 18, 1793 (and not been taken from a French privateer) and was discharged by request together with his brother Isaac on July 4, 1794. There is no mention of his being wounded at the battle on June 1, 1794, nor does his name appear in the muster books of Haslar Hospital for June and July 1794.

Mary Talbot told Kirby that the bomb ketch *Vesuvius* was captured by the French in the English Channel, but the *Vesuvius* was in the West Indies at this time and was never captured by the French. There are also discrepancies in her description of her life in the army. There was no officer named Captain Bowen in the army lists of 1791 to 1796, and the 82nd Regiment of Foot was not in existence in 1792 nor was it sent to the West Indies until 1795, by which time Mary Talbot, according to her story, was in the navy. Her description of herself as "a natural [i.e., illegitimate] daughter of the late Earl Talbot" is equally suspect. Lord William Talbot never became an earl, and the late earl in 1804 was the fourteenth, George, who died in 1787.

Perhaps we should not dismiss Mary Talbot's story completely. It seems possible that she did dress as a man and spend time in the army and at sea. She certainly suffered from a wound of some sort in her leg, but whether this was received at the Battle of Camperdown, the Glorious First of June, or a shipboard accident is in doubt. It may be that when she fell on hard times she decided to embroider the experiences she had been through in the hope that she might make some money from her subsequent celebrity. Or it may be that Robert Kirby invented the entire story in the same way that the American publisher Nathaniel Coverly, Jr., and his hack writer invented the stories of Louisa Baker and Almira Paul.

OF ALL THE WOMEN WHO WENT TO SEA DRESSED AS MEN, THE MOST fascinating must surely be the two pirates Mary Read and Anne Bonny. As their biographer said, "The odd incidents of their rambling story are such, that some may be tempted to think the whole story no better than a novel or romance," but he went on to point out that their story was witnessed by the people of Jamaica who were present at their trial in 1720. The transcript of that trial has been preserved, as have several other contemporary documents, so there is enough evidence to confirm the events that they experienced at sea.[23] However, a considerable stretch of the imagination is required to picture the life they must have led while members of a pirate crew. There is a wealth of information available about life on board naval and merchant ships in the eighteenth century but relatively few documentary sources for the pirates. Apart from occasional reports from colonial governors, the records of pirate trials, and some accounts by men who survived pirate attacks, the primary source for the lives of female pirates, and most of the other pirates of the so-called Golden Age of Piracy, is a book entitled *A General History of . . . the Most Notorious Pyrates,* first published in London in 1724. It was so popular that four editions followed within two years and it was rapidly translated into French, Dutch, and German. The author was Captain Charles Johnson, of whom virtually nothing is known.[24] At one stage it was suggested that this was a nom de plume for Daniel Defoe but this attractive theory has since been discredited. What is certain is that Captain Johnson must have attended several pirate trials in London and that he interviewed pirates and seamen who had voyaged with them. He assured his readers that "there is not a fact or circumstance in the whole book but he is able to prove by credible witnesses."

If we assume that Johnson's description of the pirates is accurate, it is astonishing that Mary Read and Anne Bonny could have survived in such an alien world.[25] It was a world in which murder, torture, and casual violence were commonplace and where foulmouthed men indulged in drunken orgies that lasted for days on end. When pirates attacked a ship, they did not simply rob the passengers and crew of their money and valuables. They ransacked the ship, hurled unwanted goods and gear overboard, killed or mutilated anyone who offered opposition, and frequently finished the operation by setting fire to the vessel and marooning any survivors on some deserted, mosquito-infested island. In today's terms, they were the maritime equivalent of the paramilitary gangs who have been responsible for massacres, rapes, and burnings in war-torn parts of Africa, the Balkans, and elsewhere. They were beyond the law and the normal decencies of human behavior, and among their number were men who took an active pleasure in killing.

As far as the pirates were concerned, women were for recreation and pleasure and were not welcome on board their ships. Among the written articles that many pirates agreed to before a voyage was a rule that made the position clear: The crew of Bartholomew Roberts, one of the most formidable pirates, agreed: "No boy or woman to be allowed amongst them. If any man were to be found seducing any of the latter sex, and carried her to sea, disguised, he was to suffer death." This makes the adventures of Mary Read and Anne Bonny all the more remarkable.

According to Captain Johnson's account, Mary Read was born in England. Her mother had married a sailor and had a son, but the sailor disappeared, leaving her on her own. She was young and careless and found herself pregnant again. To conceal her shame, she left her husband's relations and went to stay with friends in the country, where she gave birth to Mary Read. Soon after this, the son died and Mary decided to pass her daughter off as her son and to ask her wealthy mother-in-law for financial assistance. Mary was dressed as a boy, and the mother-in-law agreed to provide a crown a week toward the child's maintenance. When the old woman died, Mary was thirteen and was sent out to work as a footboy for a French lady. However, Mary tired of this menial life and "growing bold and strong, and having also a roving mind" she went to Flanders and joined a foot regiment as a cadet. She fought in several engagements and then fell in love with a handsome young Flemish soldier in her regiment. They were sharing a tent, and in due course "she found a way of letting him discover her sex." He was surprised and delighted at this revelation, but she refused to allow him to take further liberties unless he agreed to marry her. When the campaign was over they were duly married, obtained their discharge from the army, and set themselves up as proprietors of an eating house near Breda under the sign of the Three Horse Shoes.

Unhappily, her husband soon died, and Mary decided to assume men's clothing again and seek her fortune elsewhere. After a brief spell in another foot regiment, she boarded a ship and sailed to the West Indies. Her ship was captured by English pirates, and she was persuaded to join their crew. She later said that "the life of the pirate was what she always abhorred, and went into it only upon compulsion," but evidence given by witnesses at her trial suggested she was as fierce and resolute as any of her fellow pirates. In September 1717, a proclamation was issued in the name of King George I declaring that any pirates who surrendered themselves by a certain date "should have his most gracious pardon."[26] This was part of a concerted move by the British authorities to put an end to piracy in the West Indies. The crew of Mary Read's ship decided to take advantage of the pardon and made their way to Nassau in the Bahamas. It was from this notorious pirate haven that Mary Read was to set out on her last voyage in the company of Anne Bonny.

Anne Bonny was born near Cork, Ireland, and was the illegitimate daughter of a lawyer and his maidservant. As a result of a complex saga involving the theft of some silver spoons, the lawyer sleeping with his wife when he thought he was sleeping with the maid, and the maid being sent to prison, the lawyer and his wife had a quarrel and separated. The lawyer became so fond of his illegitimate daughter that he arranged for her to come to live with him. To prevent his wife and the townsfolk from suspecting anything, he dressed her in breeches as a boy and pretended that he was training her to be his clerk. His wife eventually found out, and the resulting scandal so affected the lawyer's practice that he decided to go abroad. Taking Anne and the maid with him, he sailed to Carolina, where he became a successful merchant and purchased a plantation.

Anne grew up to be a bold and headstrong young woman, and in 1718 she married a penniless sailor named James Bonny. This so upset her father that he threw her out of the house. Anne and her sailor husband made their way to the island of New Providence in the Bahamas, where they hoped to find employment. There Anne was courted by the pirate John Rackam, a somewhat reckless character whose colorful clothes had earned him the nickname of Calico Jack. Rackam, like the crew of Mary Read's ship, had arrived in the Bahamas in 1719 in order to take advantage of the royal pardon extended to pirates. He persuaded Anne to leave her husband and go to sea with him. When she became pregnant, he took her to some friends in Cuba where she had their child. As soon as she had recovered, he sent for her and she rejoined his crew, dressed as usual in men's clothes.

It was around this time that the two women met on Rackam's ship. They were both dressed as men, and Anne Bonny took such a liking to the handsome Mary Read that she let her know she was a woman. According to Johnson she was greatly disappointed when Mary let her know that she was a woman also. It has been suggested—and is perhaps true—that the two women subsequently enjoyed a lesbian affair. But the most surprising aspect of the matter was that their paths could have crossed at all. It is generally reckoned that there were between 2,000 and 3,000 pirates operating in the western Atlantic and among the hundreds of Caribbean islands around 1720. Mary Read and Anne Bonny are the only women who are known to have entered this male world disguised as men, and yet they both ended up on a small pirate ship with a crew of less than a dozen. We might be tempted to think that Captain Johnson was using some artistic license in his story, but his description of their time with Rackam is borne out by other contemporary documents. On September 5, 1720, for instance, Captain Woodes Rogers, the governor of the Bahamas, issued the following proclamation, which subsequently appeared in the *Boston Gazette* and elsewhere:

> Whereas John Rackum, George Featherstone, John Davis, Andrew Gibson, John Howell, Noah Patrick &c, and two Women, by name Ann Fulford alias Bonny, & Mary Read, did on the 22nd of August last combine together to enter on board, take, steal and run away with out of this Road of Providence, a Certain Sloop call'd the William, Burthen about 12 tons, mounted with 4 great Guns and 2 swivel ones, also Ammunition, Sails, Rigging, Anchor, Cables, and a Canoe owned and belonging to Capt. John Ham, and with the said Sloop did proceed to commit Robbery and Piracy . . . the said John Rackum and his said Company are hereby proclaimed Pirates and Enemies to the Crown of Great Britain, and are to be so treated and Deem'd by all his Majesty's Subjects.[27]

In October 1720, *The Boston Gazette* reported that several pirates were operating on the coast of the Bahamas, including Rackam, who had with him twelve men and two women. The paper went on to say that the governor of the Bahamas had sent a sloop with a crew of forty-five men after them. The sloop failed to find Rackam and his crew, but thanks to details that came to light during the subsequent trial of the pirates, we are able to follow their movements in some detail from the time they stole the sloop *William* on August 22. On that day they sailed out of the sheltered anchorage at Nassau and headed northwest until they came to the snaking length of the low-lying island of Eleuthera. They failed to find any suitable victims along its sandy shores, but on September 1 they sighted the tiny settlement of wooden houses on Harbour Island. There they plundered seven local fishing boats of their fish and gear before heading south to escape any search parties sent out by Governor Woodes Rogers. They threaded their way through the dozens of islands and cays of the Bahamas toward the great island of Hispaniola. It took them a month of sailing with the tropical sun beating down on the hot deck of their sloop before they sighted its thickly wooded mountains. On October 1 they came across two British ships a mile or so offshore. The pirates fired their guns, and the two small merchant vessels heaved to and surrendered. We learn that the crew of the ships were put in fear of their lives and that the pirates proceeded to "steal, take, and carry away the two said merchant sloops, and the apparel and tackle of the same sloops to the value of one thousand pounds of current money of Jamaica."[28]

From Hispaniola the pirates sailed through the Windward Passage and on to the north coast of Jamaica. There, on October 19, they came across a schooner lying in the beautiful bay of Port Maria. Thomas Spenlow, the owner of the vessel, and two other seamen later swore that they saw the two female pirates wearing men's clothes and handing gunpowder to the men at the guns as they attacked his vessel. The pirates plundered the ship of fifty rolls of tobacco and nine bags of pimiento, kept Spenlow a prisoner for forty-eight hours, and then released him and his vessel. They then proceeded westward along the Jamaican coast until they came to Dry Harbor, where the sloop *Mary and Sarah* was lying at anchor. Rackam fired a gun at her, which prompted her captain, Thomas Dillon, and his men to pile into the ship's boat and head for shore to get help. One of Rackam's crew shouted that they were English pirates and they had nothing to fear from them, whereupon Dillon and his men decided to return to their ship. Dillon noted that Anne Bonny had a gun in her hand and later recalled that the women "were both very profligate, cursing and swearing much, and very ready and willing to do anything on board."[29] Once again the pirates ransacked the ship and moved on.

The last recorded attack made by Rackam and his crew was on a large, provision-loaded dugout canoe, in which there was a local woman named Dorothy Spenlow. She later said that Mary Read and Anne Bonny were wearing men's jackets and long trousers and had handkerchiefs tied around their heads. Each of them had a pistol and a cutlass in her hands and swore at the men that they must murder her. She said that she knew they were women because of the size of their breasts. Rackam's men did not kill the woman but took all her provisions and sailed away.

At Negril Bay, on the extreme western end of the island, the pirates' raiding expedition came to an end. Word of their attacks had reached the governor, who dispatched two armed merchant sloops

under the command of Captain Jonathan Barnet and Captain Bon-
nevie. Barnet was a tough, experienced seaman with a commission
from the governor of Jamaica to capture pirates.[30] The two vessels
reached Negril Point late in the afternoon and saw a heavily built sloop
lying at anchor in a small cove ahead of them. Barnet suspected that
this was the pirate ship they were looking for, as there was no good reason for a vessel to be anchored off this part of the island. The coast beyond the four-mile stretch of sandy beach was mostly swamp and a
breeding ground for mosquitoes.

The light was fading fast, but Barnet decided to investigate. As he
changed course and headed inshore, the sloop weighed anchor and set
sail. Barnet maintained a steady course and slowly closed the gap between them, but it was ten o'clock at night before he was close enough
to hail the sloop. Across the water came the reply, "John Rackam from
Cuba."

Barnet ordered him to strike immediately to the flag of the King
of England. Rackam shouted back that he would strike no strikes and
ordered his crew to fire a swivel gun at the approaching merchant ship.
Barnet promptly gave the order to his men to fire a broadside from the
carriage guns on his deck and followed this up with a volley of musket shot. The broadside carried away the boom of the pirate vessel and
effectively disabled her. Several of the pirates called for quarter, indi-
cating that they wanted to surrender. Barnet swung his vessel alongside and boarded the sloop. Mary Read and Anne Bonny were the only
two members of the pirate crew to remain on deck and put up any resistance.

The next day Barnet put in to a cove farther along the coast and delivered the pirates into the charge of Major Richard James, a local mili-
tia officer. The pirates were taken to Spanish Town jail to await trial.
On November 17, 1720, an Admiralty Court, presided over by Sir
Nicholas Lawes, the governor of Jamaica, condemned Calico Jack and
the ten men in his crew to death. Anne Bonny was permitted to see
Rackam on the day of his execution and is reputed to have told him that
if he had fought like a man he would not have been hanged like a dog.
The day after the death sentence had been passed, the men were hanged
at Gallows Point, a windswept promontory on the narrow spit of land
that leads out to Port Royal. The body of Calico Jack was bound in
chains and suspended from a wooden gibbet on a small island at the en-

trance of Kingston Harbor as a warning to seafarers who might be tempted to take up piracy. Today the island is called Rackam Cay.

The trial of the two women pirates took place on November 28. Exactly why they should have been tried separately is not made clear, because the charges they faced were exactly the same as the men's. They were accused of piratically and feloniously attacking and plundering seven fishing boats at Harbor Island, of shooting at and taking two merchant ships off Hispaniola, and of attacking the sloops of Thomas Spenlow and Thomas Dillon and assaulting their crews. When the charges had been read, the women were asked whether they were guilty of the piracies, robberies, and felonies, and they both pleaded not guilty. Some of the people whose vessels had been attacked by Rackam and his crew were then called as prosecution witnesses, and they all swore that Mary Read and Anne Bonny had been active and willing participants in the piracies. The women could produce no witnesses in their defense, nor did they have any questions to ask, and so the verdict was inevitable. Sir Nicholas consulted the twelve commissioners who were sitting in judgment with him and then informed the women that the court had unanimously found them both guilty. He asked them whether there was any reason why the sentence of death should not be passed upon them, but neither of the women had anything to say. He therefore declared that they would be taken to the place of execution and hanged by the neck until they were dead.

It was not until after this dreadful sentence had been passed that the women spoke up. The transcript of the trial notes that "the prisoners informed the court that they were both quick with child, and prayed that execution of sentence might be stayed. Whereupon the Court ordered that execution of the said sentence should be respited, and that an inspection should be made."[31] When an examination was carried out, they were both found to be pregnant and therefore escaped the death penalty. Captain Johnson records that Mary Read contracted a violent fever soon after her trial and died in prison, and this is confirmed by the parish registers for the Jamaican district of St. Catharine, which indicate that she was buried on April 28, 1721.[32] There has been much speculation about the fate of Anne Bonny. There is some evidence to suggest that her father, William Cormac, persuaded the Jamaican authorities to release her from jail and took her back to Charleston, South Carolina, where she married a respectable local man named James Burleigh and had eight children by him. The same source indicates that her father also managed to locate the son she had by Rackam in Cuba. The boy was brought back to Charleston, adopted by Anne, and named John in memory of his pirate father. Anne is believed to have died in 1782 at the age of eighty-four.[33]

What is certain is that the authorities, who were engaged in a vigorous campaign against piracy in the West Indies, were able to report that one more pirate ship and her crew had been eliminated. Sir Nicholas Lawes wrote to London and reported the fate of Rackam and his men. He added that "the women, spinsters of Providence Island, were proved to have taken an active part in piracies, wearing men's clothes, and armed, etc."[34] On January 31, 1721, a ship arrived in New York with the news of Rackam's capture and trial. A brief report appeared in *The Boston Gazette* a week or so later, which noted that he and ten of his men had been executed for piracy and hung up in chains, and that two women who were with them were likewise condemned but "pleaded their bellies."[35]

It was not until Captain Johnson's *General History of . . . the Pyrates* was published three years later that the full story came out. Evidently aware that female pirates were likely to interest the reading public, the publisher drew particular attention to their remarkable actions and adventures on the title page, and the only illustrations in the first edition were of Blackbeard, Bartholomew Roberts, and a fold-out picture of Anne Bonny and Mary Read. The two women are shown dressed in baggy sailors' clothes, brandishing weapons and standing together on a tropical shore.

6

Wives in Warships

IN OCTOBER 1811, *THE BOSTON GAZETTE* REPORTED THAT A FIVE-MONTH-old girl had been sent anonymously to the Royal Naval Hospital at Greenwich with £50 in banknotes sewed up in her clothes.[1] Inquiries revealed that the child's father was a seaman in a British man-of-war. He had been allowed to take his wife to sea with him, but sadly he had been killed in action. The day after his death, his wife gave birth to a baby girl between two guns and then died herself. The shipmates of the dead seaman took care of the baby. They fed her with crackers and water and took turns acting as nurses, moving her from hammock to hammock whenever they were called on deck. When the ship eventually returned to England, the sailors collected £50 from the ship's company and arranged for the child and the money to be delivered to Greenwich. The child was reported to be remarkably healthy. She had been baptized Sally Trunnion, in reference to her place of birth—trunnions being the term for the two lugs that support a gun barrel on a gun carriage.

Another birth on a warship was reported by a young seaman with an American squadron in the Mediterranean in 1803.[2] Henry Wadsworth was a seventeen-year-old sailor in the American 38-gun frigate *Chesapeake*. He was so fond of writing that he had persuaded the ship's carpenter to build him a writing desk, and he kept a journal of life on board the ship during her cruise. On February 21, 1803, the ship left Algiers, and from Wadsworth's journal we learn that the following day Mrs. Low, the wife of James Low, captain of the forecastle, bore a son in the boatswain's storeroom. A few days later the baby was baptized in the midshipmen's mess. The christening was organized by a midshipman named Melancthon Taylor Woolsey, who became godfather to the child and provided refreshments of wine and fruit to celebrate the occasion. As Mrs. Low was feeling unwell, Mrs. Hays, the gunner's wife, officiated. The divine service was led by the ship's chaplain, the Reverend Alexander McFarlan. Wadsworth tells us that all was conducted with due decorum and decency and that this must have given great satisfaction to the parents. However, it failed to give any satisfaction to those ladies of the lower deck who were not invited to celebrate the christening of Melancthon Woolsey Low. We learn from Wadsworth that Mrs. Watson, the boatswain's wife, Mrs. Myres, the carpenter's lady, and Mrs. Crosby, the corporal's wife, got drunk in their own quarters out of pure spite.

These were not the only women on board the *Chesapeake*. The commander of the ship, Commodore Morris, had obtained permission from the secretary of the navy to bring his wife along with him, as well as their young son, Gerard, and the boy's nurse. Wadsworth described Mrs. Morris in a letter to his girlfriend at home and said that she had all the virtues of the female sex. Her knowledge of geography and history was extensive, and she had a passion for reading. He noted, however, that "her person is not beautiful, or even handsome, but she looks very well in a veil." Mrs. Morris did not number diplomacy among her accomplishments, and she became extremely unpopular among the officers in the squadron, who believed she had an undue influence over her husband. She was blamed for the fact that Morris allowed the squadron to spend far too much time in the fashionable ports of the Mediterranean so that she could pursue her social life. In due course, Morris was recalled to Washington, and in November 1803 he had to face a court of inquiry in which he was censured for the inactive and dilatory conduct of his squadron.

Another American warship in the Mediterranean at this time is known to have had women on board. John Cannon, the boatswain of the 36-gun frigate *New York*, had his wife with him, and so did John

Staines, a quarter-gunner in the same ship. During the course of the cruise, Staines's nineteen-year-old wife, Nancy, had a miscarriage and developed a serious infection. In spite of all the efforts of the ship's surgeon, who prescribed warm baths, elixir vitriol, and an antiemetic, she succumbed to a high fever and died within twelve days.[3]

Ten years later, during the War of 1812, we find Commodore Stephen Decatur, one of America's naval heroes, arranging for two women to be taken onto the *United States* as supernumeraries.[4] The women were wives of seamen on the ship, and it was Decatur's intention that they should act as nurses. They were signed on to the ship's books on May 10, 1813, and two weeks later the *United States* sailed from New York, evaded a British squadron that was blockading the coast, and sailed north to New London, Connecticut. On October 28, John Allen, the husband of one of the women, fell overboard and drowned. His wife, Mary, received Decatur's permission to leave the ship and return to New York. It is not known what happened to Mary Marshall, the other woman. She may have stayed on board until her husband was transferred to the *President* in May 1814.

The examples quoted above suggest that the American navy, which only came into existence in the years following the Revolution of 1776, was remarkably relaxed in its attitude toward women on board warships. But the case of little Sally Trunnion, which was by no means an isolated one, indicates that the British also allowed wives of seamen on board their ships. Indeed, it was not unusual in the Royal Navy for warships to have several wives living on board when the ship was at sea. Sometimes the women were the wives of officers or colonial governors who were taking passage on a ship to overseas postings. Sometimes naval captains were given permission by their commanding officers to have their wives living on board, but this was only in peacetime and usually when the ship was stationed for a length of time in harbor. Usually the women who went to sea were the wives of those warrant officers known as standing officers—the gunner, the boatswain, and the carpenter.

The reason that the standing officers were often allowed to take their wives to sea can be explained by the special position they held on a warship. Although they were inferior in rank to the commissioned officers (the captain and the lieutenants), they were key members of the ship's company. They received their warrants from the Navy

Board and in theory were attached to the same ship from the moment she was built to the day she was broken up. By contrast, the commissioned officers received their commissions from the Admiralty and were appointed to a particular ship for a particular commission, which could be a matter of only a few months. When the commission was completed, they were unemployed. The more permanent position of the standing officers was reflected in the fact that when a ship was laid up for repairs they stayed with her. They continued to live in the ship, and their wives and children often joined them on board.

The warrant officers fell into two unofficial categories. Those of wardroom rank, who lived and ate with the commissioned officers in the stern of the ship, included the master, the purser, the surgeon, and the chaplain. The other warrant officers, who included the gunner, the boatswain, the carpenter, and the cook, usually had cabins in the forward part of the ship, conveniently near the boatswain's and carpenter's stores and the galley. Their wives were thus able to live with them relatively unnoticed by most of the crew and well out of the way of the officers on the quarterdeck. This may be why many captains were prepared to overlook their presence on board. There was also the fact that the warrant officers were generally regarded as reliable, steady men. They were older than the young men who formed the bulk of a warship's crew, and their wives seem to have been equally steady and responsible. If they had been young and flighty they would have been a disruptive influence and unlikely to have been tolerated on board by the captain. Sometimes the warrant officers' wives came to the fore during battle, but mostly they seem to have melted into the background and to have played a motherly role.

These women of the lower deck were not recorded in the ship's muster book, so they did not officially exist. They had to make their own arrangements with the purser for victualing or share their husband's food ration. (It was common practice for standing officers to provide their own food and drink rather than eat the ship's food.) Since there was no official record of their existence, they rarely appear in captains' letters or logbooks and we only learn of them by chance through other means, such as the journals of naval surgeons or chaplains, the transcripts of courts-martial, or the memoirs of seamen. Occasionally, there are passing references to them in official records. Many captains produced their own sets of orders for the conduct of the officers and men on their ships, and in some of these we catch a glimpse of the women carried on board. In the orders that Edward Riou, captain of HMS *Amazon,* issued in 1799, the following instruction appeared: "Screens are never to be admitted except where women sleep and then only during the night and to be taken down (not rolled up) during the day."[5]

The official attitude of the Royal Navy to taking women to sea was set out in a series of instructions that went back to the seventeenth century and even earlier. In 1731, the British Admiralty issued a set of printed instructions entitled *Regulations and Instructions Relating to His Majesty's Service at Sea.* These were based on instructions issued by James, Duke of York, in 1663, which had been amended and reissued several times during the next seventy years. Part Two of the 1731 regulations sets out precise details for the captains and commanders of His Majesty's ships, and Article 38 made the navy's attitude toward women abundantly clear: "He is not to carry any woman to sea, nor to entertain any foreigners to serve in the ship who are officers or gentlemen, without orders from the Admiralty."[6]

In 1756, the Admiralty issued *Additional Regulations Relating to His Majesty's Service at Sea.* The position of women on ships was further clarified in Article 11, which dealt with cleanliness on ships. In addition to the captain's making sure that his men constantly kept themselves clean, that the ship be aired between decks, and that precautions were taken to prevent people relieving themselves in the hold "or throwing anything there that may occasion nastiness," there was the following instruction: "That no women be ever permitted to be on board but such as are really the wives of the men they come to, and the ship not to be too much pestered even with them. But this indulgence is only tolerated while the ship is in port and not under sailing orders."[7]

In 1806, a revised and much enlarged set of regulations was issued at the instigation of Lord Barham, the First Lord of the Admiralty. Article 14 of these regulations was much the same as Article 28 of the earlier ones, instructing the captain as follows: "He is not to allow of any woman being carried to sea in the ship, nor of any foreigners who are officers and gentlemen being received on board ship either as passengers or as part of the crew without orders from his superior officer, or the Lords Commissioners of the Admiralty."[8]

It is interesting to compare these instructions concerning women

with those issued by the British army during the same period. Unlike
the navy, which frequently took women to sea but acted as if they did
not exist, the army was accustomed to having women accompanying
regiments. Loose women and prostitutes were discouraged, but the
wives of officers often accompanied their husbands overseas, and a
limited number of soldiers' wives were allowed to travel with the regiments on campaigns. The soldiers' wives were expected to make
themselves useful by washing the soldiers' linen, searching for victuals,
cooking, and acting as nurses. When the regiment was on the march,
they accompanied the baggage wagons at the rear of the column, but
when they arrived in camp or barracks, they were permitted to share a
tent with their husbands or join them in a corner of the barracks.

In the early part of the eighteenth century, the number of soldiers'
wives allowed to accompany a regiment varied from three to ten for
each company, but the situation was regularized in 1800 when the
Duke of York issued an order setting out that "His Royal Highness
permits women, being the lawful wives of soldiers, to embark in the
proportion of 6 to 100 men (Non-commissioned Officers included)."[9]
This number is confirmed by orders issued for individual regiments.
In 1801, for instance, the Corps of Riflemen published "Rules for the
Soldiers' Wives," which began, "The number of women allowed by
Government to embark on service are six for every hundred men, in-
clusive of all Non-commissioned Officers' wives. This number is
ample and indeed more than sufficient for a light corps. . . ."[10] In 1807,
a General Order for troops destined for service on the Continent further specified that the wives should be carefully selected "as being of
good character and having the inclination to render themselves useful;
it is very desirable that those who have children should be left at
home."[11]

There were about 4,500 wives with the army in Spain in December 1813, and memoirs of army officers who served under the Duke of
Wellington in the Peninsular campaign suggest that the women had a
hard time.[12] They were subject to army discipline and punishment, suffered from exposure and hunger, and gained a reputation for plundering on and off the battlefield. Like their husbands, they were exposed
to enemy attack. However, as they were in such short supply, the
women were never likely to remain widows for long if their husbands
were killed. Lieutenant William Gratton noted that "when a married

man was shot, and his wife was a capable and desirable person, she
would receive half a dozen proposals before her husband was 48 hours
in the grave."[13]

Much less is known about wives at sea than is known about army
wives, and the evidence we have is fragmentary. In the Public Record
Office in London are twelve private journals by a young Irish physician named Leonard Gillespie, which provide a vivid insight into life
on a small warship. Gillespie was appointed surgeon of the 16-gun
sloop *Racehorse* in August 1787, and he spent the next three and a half
years on the ship as she patrolled up and down the east coast of Britain,
impressing seamen and chasing smugglers. Women mostly feature in
his journal when the *Racehorse* is in port. In December 1787, for instance, the sloop was anchored at the Nore, and he recorded the presence of four prostitutes on board. They had infected several members
of the crew with venereal disease, "yet these women are seemingly
well in health, are in good spirits and having been turned over from
their first paramours are entertained by others who seem to remain un-
affected by any syphilitic complaints."[14]

Gillespie's journal reveals that in January 1789, a member of the
crew had his wife on board while they were at sea. Gillespie noted that
on January 11, when the *Racehorse* was en route from North Shields to
Sheerness, McKenzie's child, who was twelve months old, was suffering from a cough, a fever, and respiratory difficulties following a bout
of measles. Three days later the child was vomiting and seriously ill.
At six o'clock on the morning of January 16, the child died. Three
weeks later, as they were sailing off Whitby, he recorded that "McKenzie's wife menstruated but has not been well since from affliction for
the loss of the child. . . ."[15] The next day she was still ill but was taking some nourishment and getting some sleep. By the time they
reached Sheerness, Mrs. McKenzie was up and looking healthy. From
the muster book of the *Racehorse*, we learn that her husband was a
twenty-four-year-old Scotsman from Sutherland named Charles
McKenzie.[16] He was listed as an able seaman, which makes his case unusual. As we have seen, it was common practice to allow warrant officers to take their wives to sea, but although McKenzie was rated an able
seaman (which meant that he had some two years' experience at sea),
he would not normally have been allowed any special privileges. Mrs.
McKenzie does not, of course, appear anywhere in the muster book.

Dr. Gillespie did not enjoy his time on board the *Racehorse,* and in November 1790, he left the ship and headed for Paris, where he spent some time furthering his medical studies. There is a gap in his journals, and they resume when he took up the appointment of senior surgeon at the naval hospital in Martinique. The British had taken the West Indian island from the French, and it was used as a naval base before being given back to the French under the terms of the Peace of Amiens. Gillespie spent seven years at the naval hospital, which was located by the harbor at Fort Royal, the island's capital. Much of his time there was taken up with the thankless and usually hopeless task of looking after victims of the deadly tropical fevers that decimated the crews of ships in West Indian ports. One of these victims was the wife of William Richardson, the gunner on HMS *Tromp,* who later published a book entitled *A Mariner of England: An Account of the Career of William Richardson from Cabin Boy in the Merchant Service to Warrant Officer in the Royal Navy As Told By Himself.* Like Gillespie's private journals, Richardson's memoirs provide a graphic picture of daily life in the navy, and most of his text is concerned with his fellow seamen, his disapproving comments on the press-gang system, and his observations on the foreign ports he visited during his extensive travels. But he also provides some useful information about sailors' women.

Richardson was born in the port of South Shields, County Durham, in 1768, and was the son of a merchant sea captain. He went to sea as a boy and spent several years on colliers and merchant ships in the North Sea and the Baltic. He then joined a slave ship and sailed to the Guinea coast and across to the West Indies. On his return, he was press-ganged into the navy while his ship was anchored in the Thames. He served in several large warships and became a warrant officer. In 1797, his ship was ordered into Portsmouth Dockyard for repairs, and while he was on leave that summer he married Sarah Thompson, a local girl from Portsea. Her father was a master stonemason, and Richardson tells us that he had met her before his last sailing to the West Indies "and she had promised to wait for my return, which she did. I have every reason to be satisfied with my choice, and her kind care and affection for my welfare."[17] In March 1800, Richardson was appointed gunner on HMS *Tromp,* an elderly 54-gun ship lying at Chatham. This meant moving all his chests, bedding, cabin furniture, and cooking utensils from his former ship, loading them on

to a passage boat, and sailing with his wife around the coast to the
Medway. When they arrived, they found the cabins in the *Tromp* were
being painted, so they took up residence ashore at the Red Lion pub.

On July 10, 1800, the ship sailed from Chatham to Portsmouth,
where she was to join two other warships so she could escort a convoy
of nineteen merchant ships across to Martinique. Richardson was
ashore at Portsmouth when he saw the signal for sailing flying from the
masthead of the *Tromp*. He hurried to Portsea to say good-bye to his
wife and found that she had decided to sail with him. Knowing from
firsthand experience of the dangers of tropical diseases in the West Indies, he was reluctant for her to go, but eventually he agreed. He then
found that nearly a dozen other women were also intending to sail on
the *Tromp,* including the wives of the captain, the master, the purser,
the boatswain, and the sergeant of marines. Richardson's comment
was that "a person would have thought they were all insane wishing to
go to such a sickly country!"[18] There were emotional scenes as Mrs.
Richardson bade farewell to her parents, and so quick had been her decision that they had to retrieve their clothing all wet from the washer-
woman.

On August 1, the convoy sighted Madeira. At half past one in the
early hours of the next morning, the captain's wife gave birth to a fine
boy, and at ten o'clock they came to anchor in Funchal Roads,
Madeira. Richardson and his wife went ashore, drank some of the
worst Madeira wine they had ever come across, and did some sight-
seeing. Having stocked up with water and fresh beef, fruit, and vegetables, the convoy weighed anchor and set sail across the Atlantic.
After an easy passage, they arrived at Barbados on September 2, where
they left the merchant ships and then headed north-northwest to Martinique. Two days later, they dropped anchor in nineteen fathoms in
Fort Royal Bay.

Within days of their arrival, Richardson's worst fears were realized as the *Tromp*'s crew began to go down with fever (almost certainly
malignant yellow fever, the prime killer of new arrivals in the
Caribbean). The death toll was appalling. The first lieutenant and the
clerk were the first to die; then the master and his wife, the marine officer, the boatswain, the surgeon's mate, and most of the midshipmen;
"then the master-at-arms, the armourer, gunner's mate (a fine stout
fellow), the captain's steward, cook and tailor, then the captain's lady
maid, and many brave men."[19] When Richardson's wife showed signs

that she too had the fever, he took her ashore and put her under the care of Madame Janet, a French black woman who was reputed to be an excellent nurse, and a French doctor named Dash. They put her to bed in an airy room, gave her herbal tea to drink, and would not allow her to eat anything. The starvation diet produced results, and after a few days she began to recover.

Around this time Richardson recorded that Dr. Gillespie came on board the *Tromp* to see what could be done about the fever-stricken ship, but as the men had already sprinkled the decks with vinegar, smoked out the ship below deck, and pumped clean water in and out of the hold, the only additional advice that he could give them was to wear flannel next to the skin. Gillespie received another mention in Richardson's memoirs when the gunner asked his permission to bury the mangled body of a marine in the graveyard of the hospital. The man had fallen overboard while drunk, and a shark had bitten off his head, one arm, and one leg. At first Dr. Gillespie refused Richardson's request on the grounds that only people who died in the hospital could be buried there, but on viewing the body, he changed his mind and allowed him to be buried in the hospital grounds.

Richardson and his wife had hoped the ship would soon be ordered home again, but Admiral Duckworth decided that the *Tromp* should be turned into a prison ship, and they had to spend two years in Martinique before they could return home. It was not until September 1802 that they sailed back to Portsmouth.

Other mentions of women on warships appear in the transcripts of courts-martial. In 1755, for instance, Mr. Mackenzie, the purser of HMS *Guarland*, made a number of complaints against his commander, Captain Arbuthnot, resulting in the captain's having to face a court-martial on board HMS *Syren* in Hampton Roads, Virginia.[20] During the course of the proceedings, it was revealed that the captain had allowed the boatswain's wife and the master's wife and child to go to sea on his ship. Most of the purser's complaints were about the ship's stores, the stowing of ballast, and the use of water, and the court's conclusion was that these charges were malicious, frivolous, and groundless. However, Captain Arbuthnot was blamed for carrying women to sea and giving them passage from England to Virginia, "contrary to the 38th Article of his General Instructions," and for this he was sentenced to be reprimanded.

Complaints of ill-treatment made by John Piper, another purser, led to the court-martial of Captain Vaughan and Lieutenant Pike of HM sloop *Baltimore* at Chatham in October 1750.[21] Among the purser's many complaints was the fact that Lieutenant Pike had a woman on board. Captain Vaughan told the court that the woman, who was named Nancy, was in the sloop when he took command of her and as the ship was only going from port to port and not going abroad he did not at first take any notice of it. However, when the purser complained that Miss Nancy was causing "some uneasiness," he ordered the lieutenant to put her ashore when they got to Cork. George Banbury, the captain's clerk, was given the task of taking Nancy ashore, but she managed to persuade him to take her back on board without the knowledge of the captain or the lieutenant. George agreed to do so, and she hid below until the ship was well on her way to Plymouth. When they anchored in Plymouth Sound, Nancy was again rowed ashore. She was obviously a determined woman, because the captain had to admit to the court that when the *Baltimore* arrived at the Nore, he found that Miss Nancy had managed to get on board again. In the summation of the case, no mention was made of the woman, and the court acquitted Captain Vaughan and dismissed the purser's complaints as vexatious and groundless.

One of the most bizarre cases of a woman being present on a warship at sea was revealed in a court-martial that took place on July 10, 1763.[22] A dead woman's body had been found sewn up in a hammock in the bread room of HMS *Defiance*. When the ship's commander, Captain Mackenzie, was questioned about the body, he said:

> I inquired how that woman could have got in the Bread Room, and who kept the keys of that room, on which it was found that Rumbold habitually kept those keys. He then acknowledged that he had concealed her and that when she came on board she was in good health. The reason for their not making any report of the death they said was, the fear of my punishing them.

Further questioning of Adam Rumbold, the purser's steward, and Christopher Gutteno, the surgeon's mate, revealed that the woman had been smuggled on board the *Defiance* from another ship. She had complained of a stomach ailment, and the surgeon's mate had bled her and given her a vomit and a grain of opium. She also complained of a violent headache. They had sat up two nights with her, but she had died at five o'clock in the morning. She had apparently stowed away in the *Defiance* while the ship was stationed in the West Indies, and the seaman who had smuggled her aboard had since been discharged. The verdict of the court was that the woman had died a natural death, and the seamen who attended her were acquitted.

The presence of a woman on board a naval ship was revealed in another court-martial, which took place on March 15, 1799.[23] On trial were five members of the crew of HMS *Hermione*. They were charged with murder, mutiny, and delivering up the ship to the enemy. The mutiny was as notorious in its day as the mutiny on the *Bounty*, which took place ten years before. There was no equivalent to the epic confrontation between Captain Bligh and Fletcher Christian, but the mutiny itself was much more savage. Its cause was the excessive cruelty of Captain Hugh Pigot. The son of an admiral, he had joined the navy in 1782 at the age of twelve, gained his first command at twenty-four, and was appointed post captain in 1794. While in command of HMS *Success*, he had ordered eighty-five floggings in the span of nine months, and so severe were some of these punishments that two men had died from the number of lashes inflicted on them.[24]

In February 1797, Pigot was appointed to the command of the 32-gun frigate *Hermione*, on the Jamaica station, which was lying at Cape Nicholas Mole at the western end of Haiti. After a disastrous cruise in which a second ship under his command was wrecked, Captain Pigot returned to Haiti. In June, William Martin joined the *Hermione* as her boatswain, and he was accompanied by his wife, Frances. Some later reports suggested that there were several other women on the ship, but it is clear from the evidence of the court-martial that Mrs. Martin was the only woman on board.

On August 16, Captain Pigot sailed from Haiti in command of a squadron of three ships. He continued to flog his men mercilessly; on September 20 he provoked some of them beyond endurance. At six o'clock in the evening, as the ship was heading northward through the Mona Passage, she was hit by a squall and the men were ordered aloft to reef the topsails. Pigot swore at them for not working fast enough, and as they battled to tie the reef points, with the wind whipping at the flogging sails, he bellowed through his speaking trumpet, "I'll flog the last man down." In their desperate scramble to complete the job, three of the young sailors lost their hold and fell to the deck. They were

killed instantly. Pigot brutally barked, "Throw the lubbers overboard," and ordered the boatswain's mates to go aloft and lash the remaining topmen into completing the job. Midshipman Casey, who had
been publicly humiliated and flogged by Pigot the week before, observed that the deaths of the sailors "greatly increased the previous
dislike of the Captain and no doubt hastened, if not entirely decided,
the mutiny."

At eleven o'clock the following night, a group of seamen armed
with cutlasses and boarding axes gathered outside the captain's cabin.
Private McNeill, the marine sentry guarding the door of the cabin, was
knocked down with a single blow with the flat side of a cutlass, and the
men broke their way into Pigot's quarters. After a frenzied fight in
which the captain was slashed, stabbed, and run through with a bayo-
net, the men smashed one of the stern windows and threw his blood-
soaked body into the sea. During the next few hours of darkness, the
mutineers roamed the ship seeking out additional victims. All three
lieutenants were attacked and thrown overboard, and after the men
had broken into the spirit room and helped themselves to rum, they became increasingly aggressive and began to pay off old scores. The
purser and the surgeon were dragged up on deck and shoved out
through the gunports, as was the captain's clerk. They even hauled the
marine lieutenant from his sickbed where he was dying of yellow fever
and threw him over the side. By morning the next day, they had murdered ten men. Among them was William Martin, the boatswain, who
had become the target of Richard Redman, the quartermaster's mate.

While groups of men were roaming the ship, Redman went to
Jones, the steward, with a sword in his hand and demanded to be let
into the captain's wine store. "I gave him a bottle of Madeira," Jones
said later. "He knocked off the head of it with his sword and drunk
half a pint or more. . . ." Stoked up with liquor and carrying two additional bottles, Redman made his way to the boatswain's cabin and
was heard to say, "By the Holy Ghost, the Boatswain shall go with the
rest!" He dragged the wretched man out of his cabin to the maindeck
and pushed him out through one of the gunports. Martin was heard
crying out when he hit the water. Redman then returned to the cabin,
and according to Jones, he "remained in the cabin with the Boatswain's
wife, and I saw him no more that night." When Redman emerged the
next morning, he was observed to be wearing a ruffed shirt and white

waistcoat. None of the witnesses at the court-martial reported any screams or cries for help from Mrs. Martin, and while there seems to have been a suggestion that she therefore submitted to Redman's embraces willingly, it seems far more likely that she was raped. She must have been terrified by the hideous sounds of murder and mayhem on the darkened ship, and when confronted by the drunken man who had just drowned her husband, she must have felt that resistance was useless if she was to save her life.

By daybreak the mutineers had elected one of their number to take command of the ship, and they headed for the Spanish port of La Guaira on the coast of Venezuela, 500 miles away. On Sunday, September 27, the *Hermione* dropped anchor in the roadstead under the guns of the fort. Several of the mutineers went ashore under a white flag and reported to the Spanish governor. The Spanish agreed to take over the ship and renamed her the *Santa Cecilia.* (The ship was recaptured a month later in a daring night attack by seamen from HMS *Surprise:* They crept into the Spanish harbor in boats, overcame the crew, cut the anchor cables, and towed the ship out to sea.) In due course, many of the mutineers were caught or gave themselves up, and twenty-four of them were hanged. Mrs. Martin made her way to America and vanished.

However, a document in the Public Record Office reveals that in August 1803, she appeared before the Court of the Commissioners in London, which managed the charity that granted relief to the poor widows of naval officers. In the transactions of the court it is noted that "Frances, Widow of Wm. Martin, who was murdered while acting as Boatswain of the Hermione" was detained as a prisoner in the Spanish port and did not return to England until April 1802.[25] The court agreed that she should be granted a pension from the day on which her husband was murdered.

A number of seamen's wives were present at battles. John Nicol was a seaman on board HMS *Goliath* during the Battle of the Nile in 1798 and later wrote an account of his experiences that mentioned the part played by women that day.[26] The *Goliath* was a 74-gun ship, and under the command of Captain Foley, she led Nelson's fleet into the battle. The French fleet was lying at anchor in Aboukir Bay, between Alexandria and the mouth of the Nile. The French had a strong defensive position, and when they sighted the British fleet on the horizon

on the afternoon of August 1, they assumed that the enemy would wait
until the next morning before attacking. Nelson decided to take them
by surprise. With the sun low in the sky and many of the French sailors
still ashore, the British ships swept into the bay on a fresh northwesterly wind. Much of the battle took place in the dark.

Nicol would have preferred to be on the deck of the *Goliath* so that
he could see what was happening, but his station was down below in
the powder magazine with the gunner. He noted, "Any information we
got was from the boys and women who carried the powder." As they
drew near the enemy, the British seamen stripped to their waists,
opened the gunports, and gave three cheers every time they fired a
broadside. The two fleets were evenly matched until the huge French
flagship *L'Orient* of 120 guns was seen to be on fire. Admiral Brueys
had had both legs shot off but was continuing to direct the action until
around ten o'clock that night when the ship's magazine caught fire and
the ship blew up. The explosion could be heard in Alexandria, fifteen
miles away. The *Goliath* was so shaken by the blast that Nicol and his
shipmates thought the after part of their ship had been blown off until
some of the boys told them what had happened. There was a nasty moment when a shot came bursting through the hull into the magazine,
but no serious harm was done and the carpenters plugged the hole to
stop the water that was pouring in. It was hot work manning the guns,
and Nicol later recalled:

> I was much indebted to the gunner's wife, who gave her husband
> and me a drink of wine every now and then which lessened our
> fatigue much. There were some of the women wounded and one
> woman belonging to Leith died of her wounds, and was buried
> on a small island in the bay. One woman bore a son in the heat of
> the action; she belonged to Edinburgh.[27]

One after the other, the French ships struck their colors and surrendered, and at dawn the next day, Nicol went on deck to view the aftermath of the battle. "The whole bay was covered with dead bodies,
mangled, wounded and scorched, not a bit of clothes on them except
their trousers," he recalled. "Thus terminated the glorious first of August, the busiest night of my life."

Nicol's references to women are confirmed by two other sources.
Most unusually, the names of four women were recorded in the muster

book of HMS *Goliath*. They were Sarah Bates, Ann Taylor, Elizabeth Moore, and Mary French, and it was noted they were "victualled at ⅔ allowance per Captain's order in consideration of their assistance in dressing and attending on the wounded, being widows of men slain in fight with the enemy on 1ˢᵗ August 1798."[28] Two other women who were present at the battle, Ann Hopping and Mary Ann Riley, put in a claim for the Naval General Service Medal many years later but were not awarded it because it was decreed that it could be given only to males.[29]

The records of the Naval General Service Medal provide evidence of another birth on a warship. The medal was established in 1847, and it was intended that it be awarded to all who could prove that they had been present at specified naval actions between 1793 and 1840. Among the claims was one from Daniel Tremendous McKenzie, who had been born on HMS *Tremendous* shortly before the Battle of the Glorious First of June, 1794. His rating on the medal roll is given as "Baby." His mother's name does not appear on the ship's muster book, but his father is there, listed as Daniel McKenzie, age twenty-seven, an able seaman.[30] There was an obvious injustice in issuing a medal to a baby boy but not allowing it to be awarded to the women who took part in battles, many of whom had done heroic work as nurses or had carried powder to the guns.

Queen Victoria seems to have played a key part in the decision to exclude women from the medal. Jane Townshend was present at the Battle of Trafalgar on board HMS *Defiance*, and when she put in a claim for the medal, Admiral Sir Thomas Byam Martin, who was a member of the committee that vetted the claims, wrote, "The Queen in the *Gazette* of the first of June [1847] directs all who were *present* in this action shall have medals, without any reservation as to sex, and as this woman produces from the captain of the *Defiance* strong and highly satisfactory certificates of her useful services during the action, she is fully entitled to the medal."[31] However, Admiral Byam Martin subsequently noted in the committee's minutes, "Upon further consideration this cannot be allowed. There were many women in the fleet equally useful, and it will leave the Army exposed to innumerable applications of the same nature." This provided the committee with an excuse for the decision, but it seems likely that the Queen was responsible for the change of heart: She was no supporter of women's rights and believed that a woman's place was in the home.

Evidence that the French also had women on their warships was provided in the aftermath of the Battle of Trafalgar. In the closing stages of the battle, the French ship *Achille* caught fire. Shooting from the musket men stationed in the tops caused her mizzentop to catch alight. This was a deadly threat to the ship, and the French seamen immediately began to hack down the mast, hoping that the flaming spars would fall overboard into the water. Their efforts were in vain, because two devastating broadsides from the British ship *Prince* brought down all three masts. The burning mizzentop fell on the boats amidships and red-hot wreckage dropped through to the deck below. The fire rapidly spread, and the French had no option but to abandon ship before her magazine caught fire and she exploded. The *Achille* had been bravely fought, and though she did not strike her colors and surrender, the British ships in the vicinity held their fire and went to her aid. The *Prince* launched her boats and began to pick up some of the hundreds of French seamen who had jumped into the water. Boats from the *Belleisle* and the *Euryalus* were sent to help, and the schooner *Pickle* and a cutter joined in the rescue. The *Achille* exploded at 6:10 P.M., and the surrounding boats closed in to pick up the last survivors from the wreckage. Among them was a naked woman who was found clinging to a spar and was taken aboard the *Pickle*. She was given a jacket and trousers and transferred with fifty French survivors to the *Revenge*.[32]

The woman's name was Jeanette. Her husband was a member of the *Achille*'s crew, and she had dressed in men's clothes and stowed away in the ship. When the fire broke out, she had tried to find her husband but, failing to do so, had attempted to escape by climbing out of a port in the gunroom and sitting on the rudder chains. The heat melted the lead of the rudder stock, which dripped on her, and she decided to take off her clothes and jump into the sea. She managed to grab hold of a floating spar, but one of the men clinging to the spar bit and kicked her, forcing her to swim to another. The British seamen in the *Pickle* were considerably more gallant than the shipwrecked Frenchmen. An officer gave her some sprigged blue muslin that had been taken from a Spanish ship, and the captain ordered that two shirts from the purser's stores be made into a petticoat for her. A few days later she rejoined her husband, who had survived the fire and was found among the survivors.

More examples of women on warships can be found in the years following the Napoleonic Wars. Charles M'Pherson, a sailor on board HMS *Genoa* during the Battle of Navarino in 1827, recalled that nine of the petty officers on his ship had their wives on board. During the action, the wives helped the surgeon by dressing the injured men's wounds and bringing them drinking water when they needed it: "Two of their number, I think it but justice to mention, acted with the greatest calmness and self possession. One of them was a Mrs. Buckley, and the other a Mrs. Clark, the latter a Marine's wife."[33] On another ship a few years later, a naval captain was informed by his surgeon that a woman on board had been in labor for twelve hours, and if he would permit the firing of a broadside to leeward "nature would be assisted by the shock."[34] The captain agreed to fire the ship's guns and the woman delivered a fine baby boy. Like other boys born belowdecks on warships, he would inevitably be known as "a son of a gun" because it was usual for such births to take place alongside the guns.

If the wives of warrant officers (and even ordinary seamen on occasion) were unofficially allowed to go to sea with their husbands, what about the wives and mistresses of captains? The great majority of captains undoubtedly felt that a warship at sea was no place for a woman, particularly a gentlewoman. This was not simply because of the discomforts of life at sea and the obvious dangers involved when going into action—it was also because the Royal Navy, like the merchant service and the fishing fleet, was a predominantly male society with masculine values and traditions. Admirals and captains were happy to entertain ladies in harbor with elegant dinners and concerts, but however much they might like women and however much they might miss their wives when they were away, they felt that a woman's place was at home.

There were occasions when a captain would take a woman to sea, but it was not a usual practice. In 1787, the twenty-eight-year-old Captain Horatio Nelson married Fanny Nisbet on the island of Nevis in the West Indies. It is notable that he did not take her back to England with him in his ship HMS *Boreas*. The 28-gun frigate was considered too cramped for passengers, and so while Nelson returned home in the *Boreas,* Fanny, her son, Josiah, and her uncle crossed the Atlantic in the *Roehampton,* a large and comfortable West Indiaman. However, eleven years later, following his victory at the Battle of the Nile, Nelson invited Sir William and Lady Hamilton on board his flagship, the *Foudroyant*, and they spent an idyllic six weeks cruising from Palermo to Syracuse and Malta. It was during this cruise that Horatia, the daughter of Nelson and Lady Hamilton, was conceived.

A conspicuous example of a naval wife accompanying her husband on a warship was that of Lady Cochrane, the wife of Admiral Lord Cochrane, who was one of the most dashing and colorful of the generation of naval officers that followed Nelson. Thomas Cochrane was born in 1775, the son of the Earl of Dundonald. After a spell in the army, he joined the navy as a midshipman at the unusually advanced age of seventeen. By 1798, he was commander of the *Speedy*, a naval brig, and he captured several prizes off the French and Spanish coasts. In 1801, he was captured by a French squadron but was released during an exchange of prisoners. He combined a successful naval career with duties as a member of Parliament until 1814, when he was falsely accused of connivance in a stock exchange fraud. He was expelled from the navy and from Parliament. In 1817, he was offered and accepted the command of the navy of Chile, which was then engaged in the struggle for independence from Spain.

In 1812, Cochrane had met Katharine Barnes, a spirited woman whom he described as "the orphan daughter of a family of honourable standing in the Midland Counties."[35] His uncle, who wanted him to marry the rich daughter of an admiralty official, refused to give his permission for the marriage, so the couple traveled to Annan in Scotland, where they were married in secret. By the time Cochrane was appointed vice admiral of Chile they had two young sons. At the end of August 1817, the family set sail for South America in the *Rose*, an old merchantman of 300 tons. Upon their arrival in Valparaiso, Cochrane took charge of the Chilean fleet. While Cochrane engaged in a series of actions against Spanish ships, his wife traveled on horseback into the mountainous interior of Chile in the hope that a change of air would improve the health of their younger son, who was seriously ill. News of the approach of a royalist army forced her to return to the coast by a circuitous and dangerous route that involved crossing a vast gorge on a frail, swaying rope bridge with her little boy clutched in her arms.

Safely back in Callao Bay, Lady Cochrane joined her husband on his flagship, a captured Spanish frigate of 50 guns. She was no sooner aboard than Cochrane learned that a warship laden with treasure had escaped from the harbor. He at once set off in pursuit, overtook the ship, and opened fire. In his autobiography, Cochrane later described his wife's role in the action:

> Lady Cochrane remained on deck during the conflict. Seeing a gunner hesitate to fire his gun, close to which she was standing, and imagining his hesitation from her proximity might, if observed, expose him to punishment, she seized the man's arm and, directing the match, fired the gun. The effort was, however, too much for her, as she immediately fainted, and was carried below.[36]

Concerned about the safety of her children, Lady Cochrane returned to England soon after this, traveling in the British frigate *Andromache*. Cochrane's naval actions were so successful that he was instrumental in securing the independence of Chile and Peru. When he returned to Britain, he was reinstated in the Royal Navy and promoted to rear admiral in 1832 and full admiral in 1851.

Lady Cochrane's experience was not typical, but the novels of Jane Austen suggest that it was not wholly unusual for a naval wife to spend time at sea. Several of the principal characters in her last novel, *Persuasion,* are naval officers and their wives. One of the most formidable of these is Mrs. Croft, the wife of an admiral. She is described as having a reddened and weather-beaten complexion as a result of having been much at sea. She informed the well-meaning but unworldly Mrs. Musgrove that during her fifteen years of marriage to the admiral, she had crossed the Atlantic four times, been once to the East Indies and back again, and visited Cork, Lisbon, and Gibraltar.

> "And I do assure you, ma'am," she told Mrs. Musgrove, "that nothing can exceed the accommodations of a man of war; I speak, you know, of the higher rates. When you come to a frigate, of course, you are more confined—though any reasonable woman may be perfectly happy in one of them; and I can safely say, that the happiest part of my life has been spent on board a ship."

Jane Austen knew about such things because two of her four brothers were captains in the Royal Navy at the time she was writing

Persuasion. Frances Austen (the family called him Frank) served under
Nelson, spent time in the West Indies and the Far East, and later rose
to the exalted rank of Admiral of the Fleet. Charles Austen served on
the North American station and in the West Indies, and was eventually
promoted to rear admiral. They both kept up a lively correspondence
with Jane and saw her whenever they came home on leave.[37] It was
from Charles that she had firsthand knowledge of women on warships. Charles had married Fanny Palmer, daughter of the attorney
general of Bermuda, in 1807, and when he became flag-captain to Sir
Thomas Williams on HMS *Namur,* he arranged for his wife and two
small children to live with him on board. This arrangement lasted for
some months and became a problem only when it was found that their
eldest daughter, Cassandra, suffered constantly from seasickness.

1

Seafaring Heroines

THE STORMS OFF CAPE HORN DURING OCTOBER 1856 WERE SO FEROCIOUS that one experienced sea captain retreated to the safety of Rio de Janeiro after his sails were ripped to shreds and ten of his crew washed overboard and drowned. Another ship, the *Neptune's Car* from New York, spent several weeks battling with the mountainous waves whipped up by the gale-force winds from the west. For every mile of progress painfully gained, the ship was beaten back two, so that Captain Joshua Patten considered bearing away and running before the storm to seek shelter in the Falkland Islands. He had spent eight days without proper sleep. He had taken double watches and had been almost continuously on deck, where it was so cold that ice had formed on the rigging.[1]

Before he was able to order a change of course he collapsed on deck. His young wife, Mary, was called up from below and was alarmed to find him lying prostrate with his face covered in sweat. Thinking that he must be suffering from pneumonia, she asked the seamen to carry him below and to lash him into his bunk to prevent him from being thrown out by the lurching rolls of the ship. With some desperation she looked through the books in the ship's library for advice on his condition. From one she gathered that he might be suffering from encephalitis, or brain fever, for which there was no remedy apart from rest. With her husband out of action, Mary had to decide what to do next.

Under normal circumstances the first mate would have taken over command of the ship, but this was not an option. The former first mate of *Neptune's Car* had broken his leg before the voyage, and the ship's owners had replaced him with an incompetent seaman who slept on duty and persistently disobeyed Joshua Patten's orders. He had been replaced as first mate by a man named Hare, who was competent enough to handle the ship but was unable to navigate. When the crew learned that Captain Patten was confined to his bunk, the man whom Hare had replaced attempted to incite a mutiny. Mary Patten, who had learned to navigate on a previous voyage, realized that she must take immediate action if the ship was to be saved from a mutinous crew and the onslaught of the storm. She ordered all hands to muster on the quarterdeck and prepared to address them from the raised poop deck at the stern of the ship. It is hard for us to imagine the scene and what must have been going through her mind—and the minds of the crew—at that moment.

The *Neptune's Car* was a magnificent clipper ship, very similar in size to the *Flying Cloud* and the *Cutty Sark*. In her hold she carried a valuable cargo of iron, sheet lead, and mining machinery for the California goldfields. She was 216 feet in length and under full sail carried a vast spread of canvas on her three great masts. In the gales they were facing off Cape Horn most of her sails were furled, and she carried just sufficient storm canvas to enable her helmsman to keep her on course. As the ship rolled through the heaving gray seas, the air was filled with a fine spray blown from the foaming wave crests. When the bows of the ship thumped into the body of the waves, clouds of white spume were flung in the air, drenching those on deck. Sometimes a larger than usual wave swept right across the main deck, so that much of the vessel appeared to be under water until she lifted on the next wave and tons of water streamed from her scuppers. Above the background roar of the sea was the constant, high-pitched howl of the wind in the rigging.

Mary Patten was a diminutive figure on the poop deck. Like most captains' wives of the period, she was wearing a long, dark skirt that reached to her ankles, and she clasped a shawl around her shoulders. At nineteen, she was younger than most of the captains' wives who went to sea. She was slender, with black hair and what one observer described as "large, dark, lustrous eyes and very pleasing features."[2] A few weeks earlier she had discovered that she was pregnant.

Facing her on the quarterdeck was a group of weather-beaten sailors. Exactly what she said to them as she clung to the rail we do not know, but her aim was to persuade them to remain loyal to her husband and to herself. She reminded them that the objective of the voyage was to deliver the cargo to San Francisco. She explained that if they put in to a foreign port en route, the ship's owners would suffer a heavy penalty. She made it clear that she was determined they get to San Francisco, and she asked for their support. To the older members of the crew she must have looked no more than a schoolgirl, and they were used to taking orders from men who had spent years at sea and learned their trade the hard way. But impressed by her determination and spirit, they agreed to follow her orders. It was a turning point in a voyage that was to make her a reluctant heroine.

Mary had been born in New England on April 6, 1837. A few days before her sixteenth birthday she had married Joshua Patten at the Old North Church in Boston. Her husband was twenty-six years old but was already an experienced seaman. She saw very little of him during the first two years of their marriage, but in 1855 he was given command of the *Neptune's Car* and it was agreed that she should accompany him on a voyage that took them around the world. The *Neptune's Car* had been built in Portsmouth, Virginia, and launched only two years earlier, so Captain Patten had already proved his ability to have been entrusted with such a magnificent ship. During the first part of their earlier voyage from New York to San Francisco, they raced the clipper ship *Westward Ho* commanded by Captain Hussey. Bowling along under the southeast trade winds, they recorded speeds of sixteen knots at times and on one occasion traveled an impressive 312 miles during the course of a day. After rounding the Horn and heading north up the coast of Chile, they were becalmed for eight days near the equator and lost ground. They arrived in San Francisco five and a half hours after *Westward Ho*, having completed the passage from New York in 100 days, 23½ hours. However, Captain Hussey was sufficiently impressed by the young Captain Patten's performance to challenge him to a race to China.

The passage across the Pacific was fast but was marred by a death:

One seaman was badly injured in a fall from the upper deck, and one of the lascar sailors fell overboard. The ship was brought into the wind and a boat launched to search for him, but he could not be found. In spite of this delay, the *Neptune's Car* succeeded in winning the race to Hong Kong, beating *Westward Ho* by eleven days. Captain Patten was awarded a charter to London, and the next stage of their circumnavigation passed without serious incident. On the final stage of their voyage, they ran into a mid-Atlantic thunderstorm. The foremast of the ship was struck by lightning, and several seamen who were working out on the yards fell to the deck. Mary took charge of the injured and organized a sick bay. She dressed their wounds and set broken bones, and her nursing efforts were so successful that none died as a result of their injuries.

The most valuable skill that Mary Patten acquired during that first voyage in *Neptune's Car* was the art of navigation. Her husband taught her about the winds and tides; he showed her how to calculate the ship's position with the aid of the sextant and the chronometer, how to work out the correct course to steer, and how to keep a daily record of the ship's progress in the logbook. This knowledge was to save the day when her husband fell ill on the second voyage.

The voyage began on July 1, 1856, when they set sail from New York bound for San Francisco. The big clipper ship sped south under full sail, the only problem being the behavior of the first mate. In addition to sleeping on duty, he sometimes ordered the sails to be reefed against the wishes of the captain. At this time they had no explanation for his mutinous behavior, and Patten solved the problem by making Mr. Hare first mate in his place. As they sailed farther and farther south, the shimmering blue seas of the tropics with the shoals of flying fish skimming over the surface were replaced by the cold gray rollers of the southern Atlantic. They sighted the occasional albatross, and storm petrels followed in their wake. By the time they were level with the River Plate, the westerly winds were sweeping off the Argentinian plains and the seas were swelling.

Mary's husband collapsed when they were battling the waves near Cape Horn. When she took over effective command of the ship, she had to decide whether to continue beating into the headwinds or to take an alternate course. She decided to head southeast in the hope of picking up a favorable wind when they reached latitude 60 degrees south. She ordered the crew to put the ship onto the starboard tack so that they ran before the seas rather than butting straight into them. The next day, the sun broke through the clouds, and Mary was able to take a noonday sight with the sextant. She went below to work out their position and found that they were 250 miles south-southeast of the Horn in Drake Passage, the 600-mile stretch of water that lies between the southern tip of South America and Antarctica.

The winds eased off, and they set more sail until a lookout spotted a white haze on the undersides of the clouds to the south. The experienced hands knew that this indicated the presence of field ice stretching up from Antarctica. The ship was hove to for the night and double watches were set to keep an eye out for icebergs. The next day brought them the favorable southeasterly wind they wanted. A fifteen-year-old boy with sharp eyesight was sent aloft to look for a safe passage through the ice, and following his shouted instructions, they cautiously proceeded westward. After four anxious days, they were clear of the danger from the ice and were able to head north into the warmer waters of the Pacific.

With calmer seas and sunny skies, the crew were able to wash and shave and to spread out their sodden clothes, mattresses, and blankets to dry. Captain Patten recovered sufficiently to come up on deck, and the mutinous first mate was reinstated. Unfortunately, the captain soon had another seizure, his legs buckled under him, and he was compelled to retire once again to his cabin. Mr. Hare, now second mate, then discovered that the first mate had once again disobeyed orders and had set the ship on a heading to Valparaiso. It was now obvious to the captain and his wife that the first mate must have bet his pay that one of their rival ships, the *Romance of the Seas* or the *Intrepid,* which had set off about the same time as *Neptune's Car,* would beat them to San Francisco. Captain Patten formally downgraded the first mate and told him that he would be reported to the American authorities with a recommendation that he be stripped of his first mate's certificate. The captain also got the ship's carpenter to fit a telltale compass next to his bunk so that he could ensure the helmsmen were always keeping to the correct course.

On October 17, they crossed the equator, but by this time the captain's illness had taken a more serious turn and he had lost his sight. Once again, Mary took command. She was now four months pregnant, but this in no way interfered with her duties. For the next fifty days she did not even allow herself the luxury of undressing but slept in her clothes and concentrated on getting the ship to her destination as quickly as possible. In early November they sighted the headland marking the entrance to San Francisco Bay, but the wind died and for ten days they were becalmed. At last, on November 15, the wind freshened and they headed into the bay. Mary insisted on taking the helm for the final stages and steered the salt-stained vessel into port. In the ship's log she noted that the voyage had taken them 136 days.

Word of Mary's heroic conduct spread rapidly around the port, and she was soon besieged by reporters who wanted her firsthand account of the voyage. However, she was far more concerned about her husband's condition because he was now deaf as well as blind. She arranged for them to travel home via Panama, and in the middle of February 1857, they arrived in New York on board the steamer *George Law*. Her husband was taken off the steamer on a stretcher, and Mary walked beside him to the Battery Hotel. One newspaper observed that she might have been mistaken for a schoolgirl had it not been for her careworn countenance "and her being near her confinement." The *New York Daily Tribune* sent a reporter to interview her at the hotel and found her entirely engaged in attending to her husband, who was lying on a couch, so weak it seemed he might expire at any moment. Sometimes he spoke to her lucidly but more often in a wild and incoherent manner. The reporter wanted to ask Mary about herself, but she politely brushed aside his inquiries: "She said that she had done no more than her duty, and as the recollection of her trials and sufferings evidently gave her pain, we could not do otherwise than respect her feelings."[3]

The Union Mutual Insurance Company, the underwriters for the *Neptune's Car* and her cargo, were so impressed by the part Mary had played in bringing their vessel safely into port that they awarded her the handsome sum of $1,000. In the accompanying letter, they commended the love and devotion that she had shown to her husband during his long and painful illness. They went on to say:

> Nor do we know of an instance on record where a woman has, from force of circumstances, been called upon, or assumed command of, a large and valuable vessel, and exercised a proper control over a large number of seamen, and by

her own skill and energy, impressing them with a confidence and reliance making all subordinate and obedient to that command.[4]

It was characteristic of Mary that in writing to thank them she pointed out that she had only done the plain duty of a wife toward a good husband who had been stricken down with a hopeless disease. She felt that they had overestimated the value of her services and that the ship would not have arrived safely at her destined port without the services of Mr. Hare, the second officer, and the full-hearted cooperation of the crew. Her modesty could not disguise her achievement, which was widely reported. The *Daily News* in London published an article that was extravagant in its praise, comparing her heroism with that of Florence Nightingale among the hospitals and Sarah Pellatt's reform work among the gold diggers of California. The ladies of Boston raised $1,400 for her benefit, and a blind gentleman in London sent her a check for $100 in recognition of her noble conduct.

Meanwhile, Mary and her dying husband moved from New York to Boston. There, on March 10, 1857, Mary gave birth to a baby son, who was christened Joshua after his father. Captain Patten died four months later at the Somerville Lunatic Asylum. When the news reached the waterfront, all the ships in Boston harbor flew their flags at half-mast. Mary never recovered from the rigors of the voyage. She contracted tuberculosis, and on March 18, 1861, a notice appeared in the *Boston Daily Courier:* "Mrs. Mary Ann Patten, widow of Capt. Joshua Patten, died yesterday of consumption. She had nearly completed her 24th year." She was buried beside her husband in Woodlawn Cemetery in Everett, Massachusetts.

In August of the same year, the owners of the *Neptune's Car* put an advertisement in the papers announcing that the ship was lying at a pier at the foot of Wall Street in New York and was ready to receive cargo. The advertisement reminded readers of her recent exploits:

> This ship is now rendered famous for having performed her last voyage under the most trying circumstances; when during the severe illness of her able commander Capt. Patten, she was successfully commanded and navigated for 51 days by his heroic wife, who, without assistance of any officers, succeeded in taking the ship safely into the port of San Francisco; and yet, under all these circumstances, making a quick passage.

•   •   •

THERE IS A DRAMA AND A POIGNANCY ABOUT THE STORY OF MARY PATTEN
that makes her exploits particularly memorable, but she was by no
means the only captain's wife who accompanied her husband to sea
and had to face the dangers and challenges of a deep-sea voyage. Joan
Druett has spent many years researching the lives of the women who
went to sea in merchant ships and whalers. She has tracked down the
diaries and journals of several hundred captain's wives and daughters
who sailed out of North American ports in the nineteenth century.[5]
Among their writings, she has found evidence of the extraordinary endurance and heroism of women who lived for months on board ships
traversing the Atlantic and Pacific or whaling in the Arctic. Although
very few of these women had to cope with a situation as demanding as
that faced by Mary Patten off Cape Horn, it is surprising how many
times women played a crucial role in a world generally regarded as ex-
clusively male.

There was, for instance, the remarkable story of Mrs. Clarke, the
wife of Captain Robert K. Clarke.[6] There is no record of her first
name, but at nineteen she married her husband and sailed with him on
all his voyages. In December 1885, they sailed from Manila on the
Frank N. Thayer, a fine windjammer of 1,647 tons. They were bound
for New York with a cargo of hemp and tar. Also on board was their
five-year-old daughter, Carrie. An outbreak of cholera among the
crew had compelled Captain Clarke to leave most of his regular hands
in a hospital at Manila and replace them with local Malay sailors. As
they headed out into the Pacific, one of the Malays fell ill and Captain
Clarke treated him with some rough-and-ready remedies from his
medicine chest, some of which were evidently unpleasant. Whether
this was the cause of what followed or whether the man was simply un-
hinged is not clear, but the sailor persuaded the other Malays to join
him in a bloodthirsty mutiny. During the night they attacked the
helmsman, cut his throat, and threw his body overboard. The first and
second mates were also slaughtered, and when Captain Clarke hurried
up on deck to see what was happening, he was cut across the chest so
badly that his left lung was exposed. Mrs. Clarke managed to grab two
loaded revolvers. According to one account, she handed a revolver to
her husband and he managed to shoot one of the mutineers; according

to another, Captain Clarke told her to defend herself with the revolvers and as a last resort to shoot her daughter and herself rather than fall into the hands of the Malays. The rest of the regular crew had retreated to the forecastle and had managed to launch one of the ship's boats. This was just as well, because the mutineers had set fire to the highly flammable cargo and smoke was billowing from the hatches. With the fire spreading rapidly the captain gave the order to abandon ship. Mrs. Clarke made sure that her daughter was in the lifeboat and ran back to the captain's cabin to get the sextant, chronometer, and charts. By the time she returned to the boat and the sailors had rowed them clear of the *Frank N. Thayer*, the fire had spread to the rigging. Mrs. Clarke bandaged her husband's wound and then stitched two blankets together to make a sail. Six days later, they sighted land and all made it safely to shore. What happened to the mutinous Malays is not known, but their chances of escaping alive from a burning ship in shark-infested waters were not good.

Another difficult situation was overcome by a girl who was considerably younger than Mary Patten had been during the voyage of the *Neptune's Car*. In 1850, the *Rainbow* sailed from Southampton bound for Aden, on the northeast coast of Africa. The ship was under the command of Captain Arnold, who had his sixteen-year-old daughter on board with him. The captain died when they were several days out of Southampton. The first mate was so drunk that he was incapable of taking any responsibility, so the second mate took command. Unfortunately, he had designs on the captain's daughter. She managed to evade his advances and ran to the quarterdeck, where she appealed to the crew to protect her honor. We learn that the British tars "with that manly feeling that sailors so often display" took charge of the ship and told the second mate that if he or anyone else attempted to molest Miss Arnold they would pitch him overboard.

Miss Arnold, who was old enough to realize that the men's mood might change if they got hold of the ship's supply of liquor, now persuaded them to throw every drop of spirits over the side. Astonishingly, they agreed to do so, and all the casks except one were emptied over the rail. One cask of spirits was retained in which to preserve the captain's body. For the remainder of the voyage to Aden, Miss Arnold slept in a screened cot near the wheel, and three members of the crew took turns watching over her to ensure that the lecherous second mate was unable to have his way with her. When they arrived at their destination, she reported the offense to the authorities, and the second mate and two other members of the crew were arrested and sent to jail.

During the course of her research, Druett has found several other, similar examples. In 1881, Captain George Morse of Bath, Maine, died of a bilious fever off the coast of Madagascar while in command of the ship *John W. Marr*. His wife, Jennie Parker Morse, put her husband's body in a cask of spirits, quelled a mutiny among the crew, and finding that she was the only person on board who could navigate, took charge. The ship reached New York safely under her command in December 1881. A similar situation faced Mrs. Howe in 1867 when her husband died at sea. He was captain of the *Ellen Southard* of Bath, Maine, and he died when the ship was a few days out of Hong Kong. Mrs. Howe took command of the ship but found herself up against a mutinous crew, including a number of Chinese sailors who proved so alarming that she felt it necessary to have a loaded revolver in hand at all times. As they headed across the Pacific toward San Francisco, the supplies of water fell dangerously low, and the crew became increasingly restless. In desperation, Mrs. Howe ordered the distress flag to be flown. This was spotted by the schooner *Wyanda* when they were some eighty miles west of the Farallon Islands, which lie at the approaches to San Francisco. The schooner immediately went to her assistance. Her captain was much impressed by Mrs. Howe's seamanship but was appalled by what she had been through. He told one newspaper "that he never listened to a more heartrending tale than that of Mrs. Howe, and he could not restrain his tears when she related her trials."[7]

An equally desperate situation was faced by the wife of a German sea captain in 1890. On April 1, the Bremen barkentine *Johanna* set sail from Mauritius under the command of Captain Meinders. The ship carried a cargo of sugar and was well provisioned, but she also carried a crew member who had contracted yellow fever. Within a few days seven men had died and been buried at sea, and several others had contracted the deadly disease. Frau Meinders had brought her young baby with her, and the captain therefore told his wife to stay away from the sick men in order to safeguard her life and the life of their child. When the cook died, Frau Meinders took over his duties in the galley. As more and more sailors died, Captain Meinders took the precaution of showing his wife how to steer the ship while he and the first mate worked the sails. Soon the only people alive on the ship were the captain, his wife and child, and the first mate. Then the captain contracted the fever, and when he became delirious, Frau Meinders had to lash him into his bunk. For the remainder of the passage, the first mate and Frau Meinders had to handle the ship on their own. They arrived in Fremantle, Australia, on July 9 after a nightmare passage of a hundred days. The first mate collapsed with exhaustion, and Frau Meinders took her husband and baby to the hospital in Perth, where she learned that he had a good chance of recovering.

What is clear from these and similar stories is that many ships were saved because the captain's wife had learned the rudiments of navigation. Whether it was the captain who initiated the lessons or the wife who asked to be taught is not always clear, but it was evidently a shared skill from which both derived considerable satisfaction. On August 13, 1853, Fidelia Heard embarked on her honeymoon voyage on board the Boston bark *Oriental*. Five days after their departure, she began learning the mysteries of navigation from her husband, Captain John Jay Heard. "I took my first lesson in navigation this afternoon," she wrote on August 18, "commenced learning to box the compass." On August 20 she noted: "looked through the quadrant for the first time & have been studying to find the difference of latitude and longitude. Hope to be able ere long to do it myself alone." A week or so later she was able to write, "The Capt. paid me a great compliment today by copying my ship's reckoning into his book."[8]

Eleanor Cressy, another captain's wife, was able to put her skills to impressive use. Her husband was commander of the famous clipper ship *Flying Cloud*, and on more than one occasion her astute navigation contributed to the record-breaking passages of the ship. However, it was her pinpointing of the location of a drowning seaman that made her famous. The *Flying Cloud* was heading for Madagascar in heavy weather, and Mrs. Cressy was working at the chart table when she glanced through the porthole and saw a man in the sea. She hurried on deck and yelled, "Man overboard!" The captain threw a life buoy to the seaman and ordered his men to launch a boat. They searched the area where they thought he should be but failed to find him, and the captain concluded that he was lost. Mrs. Cressy was not prepared to give up so easily. She knew the position where he had gone overboard, and she worked out the direction of wind and tide and the drift of the ship and encouraged her husband to persevere with the search. Captain Cressy decided to send two boats out, and sure enough, they found the sailor at dusk exactly where she had calculated he would be. He was weak but still alive, and he was taken back to the ship, where he made a full recovery.

It is easy to underestimate the achievement of these nineteenth-century captains' wives. In the last twenty or thirty years, women have raced yachts across the Atlantic, made single-handed voyages around the world, and taken part in the most grueling of ocean races. They have shown that they have the skill, the strength, and the courage to sail in some of the most dangerous waters of the world and survive the worst of storms. But they have been sailing relatively small yachts powered by light but strong Dacron sails, and equipped with nylon ropes, powerful winches, and radios that enable them to receive weather reports and to keep in touch with other ships as well as their home ports. A clipper ship like the *Neptune's Car*, which Mary Patten took around Cape Horn, was four times the length of a fifty-foot yacht. The tallest of her three masts was 120 feet from deck to mast cap, roughly the height of a ten-story building. We learn from her logbook that when she set off from New York in July 1865, she set her mainsails, topsails, topgallants, royals, and skysails. In addition to the five square sails on each of her masts, she would also have set a flying jib, outer jib, inner jib, and forestaysail on her bowsprit, several staysails from main and mizzenmasts, and a big gaff sail called a spanker from her mizzen. These sails were made of heavy canvas, and the largest sails on the mainmast were enormous, measuring some seventy feet across. In light winds all sail was set, but as the wind increased it became necessary to take in some sail. This meant sending a dozen members of the crew aloft to reef or furl them, a demanding enough job in light weather but extremely hazardous in gale-force conditions and driving rain. In addition to the vast array of canvas, the skipper was faced by a jungle of rigging. Apart from the massive shrouds and stays supporting the masts, there was a complex network of braces, sheets, and halyards to control the sails. When Mary Patten, Jennie Morse, Mrs. Howe, and the young Miss Arnold took charge of their ships, they relied on the experienced crew members to advise them on sail changes and to heave on the halyards and braces when necessary, but it was these lone women who carried the ultimate responsibility for the vast sailing vessels as they surged through the waves at sixteen knots or more. They had no radios with which to call for help, and if things got difficult when they were hundreds of miles from the nearest port, it was up to them—and them alone—to sort things out. It is little wonder that the underwriters of the *Neptune's Car* were so lavish in their praise of Mary Patten's achievement and particularly commended her for exercising control over the crew and bringing their large and valuable vessel safely into harbor.

8

Whaling Wives

"I AM VERY LONESOME," WROTE THE WIFE OF A WHALING CAPTAIN FROM Nantucket in 1808.

> Why should so much of our time be spent apart, why do we refuse the happiness that is within our reach? Is the acquisition of wealth an adequate compensation for the tedious hours of absence? to me it is not . . . In company I am not happy, I feel as if part of myself was gone. Thy absence grows more insupportable than it used to be. I want for nothing but your company.[1]

When a whaling ship set sail, the families left behind had to reconcile themselves to a very long wait before their men returned. Mary Brewster was eighteen when she married her husband in 1841. Within a few months of their wedding, Captain Brewster set off to command the whaler *Philetus,* and Mary did not see him again for two years. He came home to Stonington for two months and then went away on another voyage for more than a year and a half. When he returned in 1845, she decided she could not bear the separation any longer. Defying the wishes of her mother and all her friends and relations, she sailed with her husband on all his future voyages. Harriet Gifford, a whaling wife who lived in Falmouth, was one of the majority of women who did not join her husband at sea; she wrote in her diary on August 19, 1854, "We have been married five years and lived together ten months. It is *too bad, too bad.*"[2]

The reasons for the length of the voyages can be explained by the nature of the whaling business. While the captain of a cargo-carrying merchant ship was expected to deliver his cargo to its destination as quickly as possible, a whaling captain could not return home until he had filled the hold of his ship with enough barrels of whale oil to make his voyage worthwhile. The richest whaling grounds in the nineteenth century were in the Pacific Ocean. Most American whalers operated from ports on the East Coast, and in particular from New Bedford and Nantucket, which meant that the voyage began with a long haul south, through the Caribbean, along the coast of Brazil, and around Cape Horn. The whaling captain then headed north and began searching for whales in the vastness of the Pacific. When he found a whale he launched the whaleboats, open boats in which his men rowed after the enormous creature and endeavored to harpoon and kill it. The thrashings of the injured whale often resulted in one or more boats being capsized or smashed to pieces, and it was not unusual for men to drown during this perilous operation. Having captured the whale, the crew brought it alongside the whaling ship, where it was cut up and its carcass reduced to oil by boiling the blubber in a great tripot amidships. Some captains were lucky and tracked down enough whales within a few months to fill their holds with whale oil and set off for home. Others had to search the Pacific from New Zealand up to the Bering Strait before they had captured enough whales, and were consequently away from home for years.

Many wives were not prepared for the prolonged separation from their husbands, and as the whaling business expanded during the 1840s and 1850s, more and more captain's wives accompanied their husbands to sea. The Reverend Samuel C. Damon was a missionary in Honolulu, much used by whalers as a base for operations in the Pacific. In 1858, he noted that just a few years earlier it was exceedingly rare for a whaling captain to be accompanied by his wife and children, but it was now very common.[3] A Honolulu newspaper observed that one in six of all whaling captains was accompanied by his wife in 1853.[4] These women

were rarely called on to demonstrate the sort of heroism shown by
Mary Patten, Mrs. Clarke, and the other wives of clipper-ship captains,
but they nevertheless had to demonstrate considerable strength of character. The qualities required of whaling wives were physical and men-
tal endurance over a long period, the ability to occupy themselves for
days on end while the men worked, and an unswerving devotion to their
husbands, whose word was law when at sea. These qualities are vividly
demonstrated in the lives of two whaling wives whose journals have
been the subject of special study in recent years. Mary Lawrence kept a
journal that recorded her experiences during the course of a voyage on
the whaler *Addison* between 1857 and 1860, and Mary Brewster kept a
journal of her voyages on the *Tiger* from 1845 to 1851. Unlike the
equivalent men's journals, which tend to concentrate on the weather,
working the ship, and the battles with the whales, the women's journals
are more thoughtful and more reflective. They frequently recall family
and friends left behind at home. They comment on small things often
overlooked by the men: the chickens and pigs that were let loose to wander the deck after days of being penned up during a storm, or the curious selection of hats worn by Hawaiian islanders to church on Sundays.

The voyage of Mary Lawrence in the *Addison* makes an illuminating case study, because it was typical of so many whaling voyages and
because her experiences en route reflect those of dozens of other whaling wives. The voyage began and ended in New Bedford, lasted three
years and eight months, and consisted of seven separate cruises in
search of whales. In the Hawaiian ports of Honolulu and Lahaina the
Addison, in common with hundreds of other whaling ships, stocked up
on provisions and carried out repairs before setting out on the extensive cruises to the Arctic Ocean in the north or the whaling grounds
off New Zealand in the south.

Mary Lawrence was twenty-nine when she sailed from New Bedford with her husband and their five-year-old daughter, Minnie. She
was a small, bright woman with a ready wit and an indomitable personality. Like so many of the New England women who married sea
captains, she was a devout Christian and trusted in God to see them
through the dangers of the deep. In her journal she noted the storms
that lasted for days on end; she recorded that the weather turned damp
and foggy as they headed through the Bering Strait into the Arctic; but
she rarely complained.

She was born in 1827 in Sandwich, Massachusetts, and was one of the many children of Jonathan and Celia Chipman. In 1847, at the age of twenty, she married Samuel Lawrence, who was then mate of the *Magnolia*. Soon after their marriage, he was appointed captain of the whaler *Lafayette* of New Bedford and set off on a voyage to the Pacific that ended disastrously when his ship was wrecked off the Galápagos Islands. The ship struck a rock when they were close inshore at night and became a total loss. The captain and crew took to the boats and were picked up by other ships. Most of the cargo of whale oil was recovered, but it was a considerable setback for Lawrence's career: He had to spend several years as a mate before being offered the command of the *Addison*. His brother had previously commanded the ship and still had a part share in her ownership.

Having seen very little of her husband during the first nine years of their marriage, Mary Lawrence decided that she would accompany him on his next voyage and that she would take Minnie with them to sea. At no point in her journal does she ever question her decision or express regrets at exchanging the security of home and family for the unknown perils of a deep-sea voyage. They set sail from New Bedford on the morning of November 25, 1856. There was a fresh easterly wind, and they had a fine sail down the bay and out into the ocean. Before dark, Mary went on deck to take a last look at her native land before it vanished over the horizon. Her heart was sad at the thought that she might never again see the faces of her friends. The next day she embarked on her journal, and at the outset she explained her reasons for doing so:

> As this is my first experience in seafaring life, I have thought it advisable to attempt keeping a journal, not for the purpose of interesting anyone out of my own private family, but thinking it might be useful to myself or my child for future reference.[5]

On the second day the wind veered from the east to the west and blew a gale that lasted for ten days. For the first day of heavy weather Mary was seasick, and Minnie was sick for two days, but then they both recovered. They were fortunate; most whaling wives suffered horribly from seasickness for days on end. This was not because they were less adapted to seafaring than the men but because they were expected to remain below in their cabins, where they were disoriented by the rolling of the ship. Many wives also found the rancid stench of whale oil in the bilges contributed to their nausea. By contrast, the men were up on deck actively working the ship, which enabled most of them to recover from seasickness much more rapidly.

Although Mary had not recovered her appetite sufficiently to eat any of Grandma's turkey, which was served up to celebrate Thanksgiving on the third day out, she derived considerable pleasure from sitting on deck and watching the ocean, marveling at how their gallant ship rode the waves: "It is grand beyond anything I ever witnessed, sublimity itself." By December 8, the gale had moderated and soon they were sailing on a calm sea under a pleasant, warm breeze. Mary watched several dolphins following the ship, and when a flying fish flew up and landed on the deck, she was delighted that the steward cooked it and served it up for her breakfast. She thought it tasted like fresh herring. During the calm weather, she passed the time reading, writing letters to her friends, and listening to the singing of the sailors. On Sabbath days she usually dressed up a little more than on other days and spent most of her time on deck reading the Bible. Her daughter, Minnie, seems to have taken remarkably well to shipboard life. Occasionally, she was sad when she thought of the friends she had left behind, and once when Mary broke a wishbone with her, she wished she could see her aunt Susan, but most of the time she ran about the deck making friends with the crew. She treated the hens as pets and played with the two pigs, Juba and Wiggie, who were remarkably tame.

At intervals they would see other ships, and when another whaling ship hove in sight it was customary to come alongside and exchange news and pass on letters. On January 5, 1857, for instance, they encountered the Atlantic whaler *Dr. Franklin* of Westport. Her commander, Captain Russell, came on board the *Addison* and spent the evening with them. Before he sailed away, he presented Mary with two dozen oranges, which were much appreciated.

On January 13, Mary saw her first whale. She heard the sound of the whale nearby and went up on deck in time to see the creature blow and heave the monstrous flukes of his tail in the air. Captain Lawrence immediately ordered the whaleboats to be launched, and the men rowed in pursuit but after a few hours returned empty-handed. They were just sitting down to dinner when the cry of "There she blows!" caused all the men to abandon their meal. Mary decided to finish her dinner with Minnie, but her husband and most of the crew took to the boats and headed for where the whale had been spotted. Mary waited anxiously and thought her worst fears had been realized when one boat returned with its planks stove in. She heard someone shout, "Another boat stove!" and she looked and saw an empty boat. "I had not the heart to ask whose boat it was but went down into the cabin. I could stand it no longer." And then she thankfully heard Samuel's voice as he came alongside. She learned that his boat had been stove in by the whale and all on board thrown into the water, but they had been picked up by the other two whaleboats. They lost the whale but were lucky to lose no men.

The weather turned cold and stormy as they approached Cape Horn, but by February 2, they had sailed through Drake Passage and were heading north into the Pacific. By March 9, they were level with the Galápagos Islands on the equator, and as they headed northwest, a favorable breeze swept them along at a rate of 200 miles a day. On March 31, Mary noted in her journal that apart from her daughter, Minnie, it was over four months since she had spoken to one of her own sex, and she wondered whether she would remember how to speak to a lady when she next met one. By April 12, they were within three days' sailing of the Hawaiian Islands, or the Sandwich Islands as they were then called, the name given them by Captain Cook.

Mary was excited at the thought of setting foot on foreign soil for the first time in her life and watched the approaching landfall with keen interest. They sailed past Hawaii, the largest of the island group, and headed for the island of Maui and the town of Lahaina. Mary thought the high, barren mountains, with their summits in the clouds, and the trees and houses on the lower slopes were all so different from anything she had ever seen before. The *Addison* dropped anchor on April 17, 1857. There were only two other ships lying at anchor in the sheltered bay of Lahaina.

The customs officer came on board, and Captain Lawrence accompanied him ashore to find a place for them to stay. He arranged for them to lodge in a straw-roofed house that had been built for the American consul. It was beautifully situated on the shore among trees, with shady walks laid out with flowers. A long sitting room extended the length of the house, and from its windows there was a spectacular view of the waves breaking on the beach. There were paintings and engravings hanging on the walls, straw matting on the floor, and furnishings including Chinese-style chairs, a sofa, and various tables. Their first visitor was a little girl named Lizzie Bigelow, who called to see Minnie. She was followed by her mother and a Mrs. Brayton. Mary later noted in her journal, "We were delighted to enjoy female society once more."

The next morning they went to church and heard Mr. Bishop, the seamen's chaplain, preach on the appropriate text, "And they left their nets and followed him." Mary was surprised by how few people were in the congregation but was thankful that they were able to worship the God of their fathers in a strange land. In the afternoon they went along to the native church, where the singing was excellent. Mary was amused by the Sunday fashions of the Hawaiian women and bore their curious stares with good grace. She was not so amused by the everyday appearance of the local people:

> Many of them go without clothing; both sexes bathe in the water entirely naked, unabashed. As I am writing, two men are close by my door without an article of clothing, Minnie says, "I have to turn my head the other way." There are but very few that can be depended upon, even members of the church.[6]

Mary's pious upbringing and her Protestant work ethic caused her to deplore the Hawaiians' easygoing ways. She judged them to be low, degraded, indolent, and much given to stealing. In her journal, she confessed that many scenes she encountered made her blush, and she was particularly upset to hear even young children using English swear words. She blamed the influence of the foreign sailors, but like the majority of Westerners who encountered the Pacific Islanders during that period, she was completely ignorant of the very different customs and beliefs that governed their lives.

In spite of her disappointment with the uncivilized behavior of the Hawaiian people, Mary much enjoyed the ten days they stayed at Lahaina. She found the climate delightful and would happily have spent many more weeks there, but Captain Lawrence was impatient to be off. The friends they had made among the foreign residents came to see them before they left and brought them presents. Mary was given chocolate, walnuts, tamarinds, a box of cologne, and other luxuries, and Minnie was given baskets, toys, and books.

On April 27, they sailed for the nearby island of Oahu, and the next day they dropped anchor off the town of Honolulu. They spent a day ashore seeing the sights and meeting a number of American families before setting sail on the second cruise in search of whales. From the Hawaiian Islands, they headed northward to the Kodiak whaling grounds in the Gulf of Alaska. The weather grew steadily colder, and the days became damp and foggy. They met up with several other American whaling ships, all of which had experienced very rough weather. On several occasions they sighted whales, and lowered the boats and chased them, but without success. And then on June 6, after a day of very thick fog, they almost ran down a whale. Captain Lawrence turned the ship around and lowered the boats. By seven o'clock in the evening, a large whale had been caught and was lying alongside the ship. It was reckoned that it would produce 135 barrels of whale oil. Mary missed much of the excitement because she had been suffering from a severe headache and was so sick that she could not even sit up in bed. She heard the men engaged in cutting up the whale's carcass and swinging the pieces on board but was disappointed that she could not see what was happening.

Five weeks later they were again successful, capturing a female whale and her calf. Whether it was because she had been so sick on the last occasion or whether she found the capture and cutting up of the whales too unpleasant to watch, she dismissed the whole operation in a couple of sentences and was much more concerned about a pretty brown-and-yellow bird that flew on board from nearby Mount Fairweather. She converted one of her work baskets into a cage, gave the bird some flaxseed and rice to eat, and hoped it would sing. Sadly, the little bird died two days later.

On July 22, they left the Kodiak whaling grounds and headed west for Bristol Bay. All the whale oil had been collected and stored, and they now had 600 barrels. By mid-August they were negotiating the Unimak Strait, a passage ten miles wide between the islands off southwest Alaska, but were becalmed before they were safely through. They could see great mountains in the distance, their snow-covered peaks rising above the clouds. To prevent the ship from being swept ashore by the current, they dropped anchor, and some of the men took a boat ashore and collected some strawberries, blackberries, and huckleberries, and a large bunch of flowers for Mary and Minnie. They were both delighted by the fragrant flowers and decorated the cabin with them.

After a month of searching for whales in Bristol Bay, they headed south. They frequently found themselves in damp, clammy fog so thick that nothing could be seen beyond the ship's rail. On one occasion the boats were out searching for whales when the fog enveloped them, and they had to fire guns on the *Addison* and blow horns so that the men in the boats could find their way back to the mother ship. Food stocks were getting low, but they managed to catch large numbers of cod and flatfish, of which Mary noted, "We are now living on fresh fish, which are very nice."

The passage back from the whaling grounds took them three weeks, and on October 14, 1857, they returned to the Hawaiian Islands and dropped anchor off Honolulu. As on the previous stay in Lahaina, Mary's days were filled with social visits. Most of her acquaintances were expatriate Americans or whaling captains and their families. She visited the Sailors' Home and was invited on board the *St. Mary*, an American man-of-war lying in the harbor. On November 13, 1857, they set off on the third cruise of the voyage. This time they headed south to the New Zealand whaling grounds. As they crossed the equator, Mary noted in her journal that one year had passed since they had left New Bedford and that they had sailed a total of 35,985 miles. On this cruise they made a great sweep across the South Pacific to Sunday Island, and down level with New Zealand, across to Pitcairn Island, and then north to the Marquesas. They were back in Honolulu on March 7, 1858, after four months at sea.

More social visits followed, and after a stay in port of three weeks they set off on March 28 for another cruise, this time to the far north across the Bering Sea, through the Bering Strait to the Arctic Ocean.

The fifth cruise took them to Cape Lucas in California, and the sixth was a repeat of the fourth, taking them up into the Arctic Ocean again. Finally, on December 5, 1859, they set off on their seventh and final cruise, which was to take them home via New Zealand. Mary set off with a sad heart because she had learned that her father had died while she was away: "Home will hardly be home—that vacant chair. How my heart aches to think of it, and I shall not realize it fully until I get home. It will be a sad meeting should we live to reach home."[7]

They spent another Christmas at sea. On Christmas Eve they met up with the bark *Lagonda,* commanded by Captain Willard. Minnie hung up her stocking and the next day found in it some candies, a pair of ivory candlesticks that had been turned on the lathe by her father, a book from her mother, and a portmanteau from Captain Willard.

New Year's Day 1860 was spent anchored off the beautiful South Sea island of Aitutaki. Mary described it as being like a perfect garden, rich in vegetation, with pineapples, oranges, limes, bananas, plantains, breadfruit, yams, and custard apples in abundance. They met an English missionary, Mr. Royle, and his wife. They had lived on the island for twenty-one years and had six daughters, the youngest of whom made a pleasant playmate for Minnie. They proved to be a delightful family, and Mary was much impressed by their schoolhouse and chapel, which were both neat and commodious. But such meetings were all too brief, and after no more than a day ashore they were back at sea. However, they were fortunate to meet another whaler with children on board. On January 8, they sighted the *Rambler,* commanded by Captain Willis. They went aboard and passed a happy day together. Mary wrote, "This meeting with families at sea is very pleasant for all concerned, particularly so for the children."

They sailed on around the South Island of New Zealand and headed east for Cape Horn. By mid-April they were clear of the Horn's cold and stormy waters and heading northward. As they approached home, Mary engaged in an energetic round of cleaning, washing, and sewing. She scoured the dishes in the pantry, polished the spoons, cleaned all the drawers and lockers, and then began packing. On one day she packed five trunks, a barrel, and two boxes. Their final approach to New Bedford was severely delayed by a northwesterly gale that they had to beat into. The gale was accompanied by an extraordinary display of lightning: "I never saw such lightning before. The flashes would extend almost entirely around the horizon." They tacked slowly northward under shortened sail. "This is really discouraging. It makes us feel very badly to be so near home and making no headway. . . ."

The gale was followed by a dead calm that was equally frustrating. But at last, on June 13, the wind freshened and they made the final approach. The pilot came on board at nine o'clock in the morning at Montauk. The next day they dropped anchor in the Acushnet River off New Bedford.

•　　　•　　　•

MARY LAWRENCE'S JOURNAL IS A FRESH AND VIVID ACCOUNT OF ONE woman's experiences during an extended whaling voyage. It is more factual than introspective: We see what she sees but rarely what she feels. She hardly ever complains and she never questions her role in the ship, presumably because she intended the journal to be read by her husband and family later. Consequently, we are left wondering exactly what it must have felt like to be a woman alone in a man's world, a world that was alarmingly different from the one she had left behind.

The captain's wives who remained at home had the security of familiar surroundings and a well-worn routine. Their days were filled with a multitude of tasks, some of which might be monotonous and dreary, but at least they had some control over their lives. They might have missed their husbands, but they had the consolation of family and friends around them. They had the support network of parents and grandparents, aunts and uncles, brothers and sisters. They were able to call on other women for advice or help or simply to have an enjoyable chat.

The captain's wife at sea was cut off from all this. She was isolated in a confined space in which she had no defined role. It was extremely rare for a woman to take over command of a ship in an emergency as Mary Patten had. In normal circumstances, the captain's wife had little or nothing to do with the day-to-day running of the ship. She might mend the cabin boy's shirt, or act as a nurse to an injured crewman, but there was little else for her to do of a practical nature. The cook and the steward looked after the captain and the other officers, and so she found herself a mere onlooker in a world ruled by her husband. Her presence was often resented by members of the crew who regarded her as a spy who would report their behavior to the captain. "The carpenter has put a long window in the forward part of the house so Mrs. Hamblin can set down and look what's going on on deck, who goes over the bows or to the urine barrel," wrote Abram Briggs.[8] And John Perkins, a seaman on the whaling ship *Tiger,* provides us with a picture of the isolated position of Mary Brewster, who traveled with her husband on a four-year voyage: "The Captain's lady sits on deck sewing every pleasant day. There is nothing remarkable in her appearance. She never speaks to any of the other officers when on deck but her husband."[9]

With no useful tasks to perform, many wives found that life at sea could become extremely tedious. As Eliza Brock of Nantucket wrote on Sunday, July 31, 1853, "It is a long lonesome day to pass upon the Stormy deep, all I can do is to read, write and sing a hymn now and then, and in thinking of my far distant home and friends."[10]

The whaling wife's isolation was enhanced by the fact that she was mostly confined to the stern of the ship. She shared the captain's accommodations, but while he was free to roam the ship at will, she was expected to remain within her allotted area. In most whaling ships, this consisted of three rooms: the captain's stateroom, the captain's sitting room, and the main cabin. The stateroom was where they both slept, and it had a small alcove adjoining it that contained a water closet, a washbasin, and a locker. The captain's sitting room was a narrow room across the width of the stern that was lit by the stern windows. This was his dayroom and office and was the coziest room as far as his wife was concerned. It might be furnished with a sofa, an easy chair or two, a carpet on the floor, a barometer and perhaps a picture on the walls, and a space for the books that were her principal source of entertainment. The main cabin was the dining room for the captain, his wife, and the ship's officers. This was dominated by a dining table with the captain's chair at one end and chairs or benches for the three or four mates who were the officers. The rest of the ship was effectively out of bounds. Henrietta Deblois was able to give a detailed account of the captain's accommodations in her journal, but she noted, "For'ard is the Forecastle where the seamen live. I cannot take you there as I have not been there myself but am told it is very nicely fitted up."[11]

In addition to the confinement of her quarters, the boredom, and the feelings of inadequacy and inferiority due to the lack of a useful role on board, almost all captains' wives desperately missed female company. We have seen Mary Lawrence comment on this at intervals, but her isolation was somewhat relieved by the presence of her young daughter, Minnie. For many wives the absence of other women was almost more than they could bear. Emma McInnes confessed to crying like a baby when she missed the chance to speak to a woman on another ship, and Eliza Williams described an occasion when she saw a captain's wife on a passing ship staring at her with a telescope: "She was looking at me, I imagine, anxious with me to see a Woman; she had the glass up to her eyes, I could see."[12]

The only person a woman could confide in was her husband, but he was often preoccupied with running the ship and was not always sympathetic to things that were troubling her. As Dorothea Balano pointed out, "I can't turn to anyone for understanding, let alone help, because all the creatures on board are completely and absolutely in his power."[13]

In fact, most of the wives who made the difficult decision to accompany their husbands to sea appear to have been so devoted to them that they were prepared to put up with all kinds of hardships. "I am with my Husband and by him I will remain. No seas can now Divide us. He can have no trouble, no sorrow but what I can know and share," wrote Mary Brewster, who concluded, "I have need of nothing more and gladly willingly resign all friends and home and native land."[14]

Hannah Burgess declared that she loved her husband more than she could express: "It is true that for love the human heart will make almost any sacrifice, and it was this alone that prompted me to leave the scenes of my youth, the kind parents, and loved friends, to wander with my Husband, and with him share the joys and sorrows that fall to the lot of a Mariner."[15]

The single-minded devotion that seems to have been shared by so many whaling wives helped them to put a brave face on storms and on the seasickness that invariably accompanied rough weather at the beginning of a passage. Mary Brewster was so sick during the first month of her first voyage that she was confined to her bed almost continuously and was unable to write a word in her journal. When at last she felt well enough to sit up, she wrote a little, then vomited, then rested at intervals until the weather improved. But eventually she gained her sea legs and was able to face a storm without fear. She went up on deck to find the wheel lashed, all sail taken in, and huge waves breaking over the bows: "Never since I had been out had I seen such a time or witnessed such a sublime sight." Harriet Allan experienced a severe gale in November 1869. The hatches were battened down, and the men had to cut away the foretopgallant mast. She braced herself in the doorway and watched the waves, which seemed mountains high. The noise of the wind and the sea was so tumultuous that it was impossible to hear herself speak, and yet, like Mary Brewster, she did not feel any fear: "I had confidence in the little ship and her captain and the strange wild excitement, even fascination, of the scene, banished fear."[16]

The whaling wives who stayed at home were not able to share the perils and adventures of the long voyages with their husbands; nor did they have to suffer the seasickness, the confined quarters, and the isolation of being the lone woman among a crew of men. But they did have troubles of their own. Apart from the loneliness and grief that many women experienced when their husbands were away, many suffered financial hardship. In April 1844, Phebe Cottle of Nantucket wrote to the shipowners Charles and Henry Coffin: "I am sorry to be obliged to again call for assistance but my rent has become due and my wood is out and I am in need of many articles for my family that I cannot do without."[17] She explained that she was forced to give up work because her mother was sick and asked for the sum of $30 or $40. The following year, the pregnant wife of John Codd, who was on a whaling voyage in the Pacific, wrote to the same shipowners for a loan of $50: "I do not feel you have treated me well; My husband did not think you would let his family suffer for the necessaries of life, when he shipp'd in your employ. I am out of food and fuel, and unless you can do something for me must write by every Ship for him to return and take care of his family."[18] When Sarah Tripp of Tiverton had heard no news of her husband for two years, she despaired of his ever returning and appealed to the town council for help. The general assembly agreed that she and her four small children were "in a poor, low, & deplorable state & condition," and gave her permission to sell some of her husband's land in order to support herself and her family.[19]

Faced with having to fend for themselves, many whaling wives found jobs and took on responsibilities that would normally have been considered the husband's concern, such as managing budgets, settling accounts, and buying and selling land and property. Center Street in Nantucket became known as Petticoat Row because so many of the shopkeepers were women, and in New Bedford the women earned money by taking on various types of piecework. Eliza Stanton earned $27.17 from some outfitters in town for sewing shirts for sailors, and Sarah Cory, who worked as a seamstress for a clothing store, wrote to her husband, who was at sea, "I have so much sewing all the time I don't hardly know what to do some times but they won't take no for an answer and I am obliged to do it."[20]

Many women earned a living by taking in boarders. Sylvia Sowle took in four ship's carpenters as boarders for a few months, while Julia Fisk, the wife of a whaling ship captain, ran a resort-style boardinghouse that catered to dozens of guests at a time.[21] In the rural areas, women like Caroline Gifford of Dartmouth and Hannah Blackmer of

Acushnet kept farms going with the help of their children and neighbors. Abby Grinnell of Tiverton, Rhode Island, was able to report to
her husband at sea that her corn was very large, the barley very good,
and the oxen had done so well that they were fat enough for beef. But
not all whaling wives were able to cope so well, and all too many found
it a real struggle to bring up a family on their own. No doubt Myra
Weeks spoke for many when she wrote to her husband in 1842: "I think
it is rather lonesome to be shut up here day after day with three little
children to take care of. I should be glad to know how you would like
it."[22]

The whaling wives were not the only ones who were lonely. Many
of the men who went to sea in whalers sorely missed their homes and
families. In the privacy of their cabins, the whaling captains wrote in
their journals and poured out their feelings in their letters to their
loved ones. In 1871, Captain Charles Allen wrote a letter that began,
"Dear Daughter Emma, as I have been sitting here in my cabin alone
and lonely, the thought rushed into my mind: Is this all of life? My
heart answered No."[23] Another Captain Allen, writing to his sister
Hannah in 1859, echoed his thoughts: "But I am so lonely at times for
my dear wife I can hardly content myself, and even think that it is so,
that I am alone, that she has gone to heaven."[24]

For the ordinary seamen in the spartan accommodations before the
mast, there was no privacy. In whaling ships, as in most merchant
ships, the seamen lived in cramped conditions and were expected to be
tough and self-reliant. It was a male, macho culture in which feminine
values played no part and sensitive feelings were masked or sup-
pressed. Sailors who were homesick were likely to be ridiculed by their
shipmates. When a young sailor on board the *Sunbeam* was found
weeping on his sea chest, clutching a bed quilt given him by his grandmother, he became the target of practical jokes.[25] Marshall Keith of the
Cape Horn Pigeon cried all afternoon after being reprimanded by his
captain for spending too much time thinking about his wife.

Yet in spite of the culture that prevailed on board ship, we find that
sailors of all rates placed great value on the letters, presents, and keepsakes from home. As they sailed across oceans, these keepsakes were a
potent link to the women they had left behind. Food and clothing seem
to have been the most usual items. Ruth Post asked her husband, "do
let me know if your butter and cheese and dried fruit turned out

well."[26] Edmund Jennings took Aunt Dyer's cake to sea with him. Samuel Brayley went loaded with his wife's cranberries and his mother-in-law's quince, and later wrote to his wife to inform her that "Grandmother Douglas' cotton stockings wear well, but then here is not more than half enough for the voyage; I wish you would send me a dozen pair more." He went on to tell her, "I cannot wear those that you knit; it seems sacrilege. How much I prize every thing that is the work of thy dear hands."[27]

While captains and officers could keep such things in drawers and lockers in their cabins, the ordinary seaman kept all his possessions in his wooden sea chest. He used this chest as a seat, he played cards on it, and he took it with him from ship to ship. In addition to the letters and presents from home, it contained his shoregoing clothes, a picture or two, and his ditty box containing buttons, needles, and thread. Many seamen also kept a Bible. Samuel Leech said that he spent many weary hours reading, "and sometimes I perused the Bible and Prayer Book which my mother so wisely placed in my chest on the eve of my departure."[28]

The letters and reminders of home helped to keep the men going on their voyages, but for many of them, particularly the older men, they were no substitute for the loved ones they had left behind. All they wanted was to get back to their homes and families. "I think some times if I ever get home alive and well I will never leave you again," wrote William Ashley to his wife, Hannah.[29] He told her that whaling was all very well for single men, but it was not healthy for married men. Soon after writing this he obtained his discharge, left the whaling voyage before it had ended, and returned to Hannah and the farm, where he settled down and never went to sea again.

9

Men Without Women

ON JULY 2, 1761, A COURT-MARTIAL WAS HELD ON BOARD THE *PRINCESS Royal,* an aging 90-gun warship lying at the Nore, near the mouth of the Thames. On trial were George Newton, a seaman belonging to HMS *Ocean,* and Thomas Finley, a boy belonging to the same ship. They were charged with committing "the unnatural and detestable sin of sodomy."[1] The president of the court was Admiral William Boys, commander in chief of the ships and vessels in the Thames and Medway. Alongside the admiral in the great cabin of the warship were four naval captains whose task it was to assist him in his deliberations and to determine whether the two prisoners were innocent or guilty of the crime punishable by the 29th Article of War.

When the prisoners had been brought into the court by the provost marshal, a letter from their commander, Captain Langdon, was read aloud. The court then proceeded to question the witnesses for the prosecution. The first witness was a black seaman named Charles Ferrett. George Newton immediately objected to Ferrett's giving evidence, because he said that a black man should not swear against a Christian. When Ferrett was asked whether he had been christened, he said that he had been baptized at Portsmouth when he was a member of the crew of the *Maidstone*. He could not remember who was present at the time but recalled that Commodore Keppel was one of his godfathers. Under further questioning he confessed that he could not read or write, but he said that he was a free man and received his own pay. He was then admitted as a witness and was sworn in. The admiral asked him to tell the court about the crime of sodomy of which the two prisoners were accused. This is what Ferrett had to say:

> The prisoner George Newton, when he came on board the *Ocean*, he had no bedding; I took compassion on him and let him lay with me, having spread my bed clothes upon the deck to serve us both. One night I was asleep, and hearing somebody blowing and puffing alongside of me, close to my knee and shaking me which waked me; I never stirred him but put my left hand up, and got hold of both his stones fast; the other part was in the body of the boy; I asked him what he had got there, he said, cunt. Then I said you are worse than any beast walking in the field.

When asked what time of night this happened, he said it was about three or four in the morning.

> Was there any light?
> There was not any. It was dark.
> If it was dark, how can you know it was that boy?
> I kept the boy in my berth until it was fair daylight, and then I
>   found it to be the boy, the prisoner Finley.

He was asked how he could be sure that it was the prisoner George Newton committing the sin of sodomy if it was dark. He replied, "There was no other persons lay by me, only one man, that lay in a hammock over my bed, in the same berth."

He was asked whether he was sure of what took place.

> I felt the prick of George Newton, in the boy Finley's arse.
> What did you do then?
> I made a great noise. The ship's cook was coming at that time, but
>   his wife stopped him, as he told me afterwards.

When Ferrett was asked whether there had been any falling-out between him and the prisoners, he said there had been none. At this point George Newton was allowed to question the witness. He asked

Ferrett whether he had ever heard him use any indecent expression which might suggest that he wanted to commit the sin of sodomy. Ferrett said that he had sailed with him three years on the *Harwich* and never knew him to be guilty of a crime of this nature.

The black seaman withdrew, and George Dawson, the ship's cook, was sworn in. He was asked to relate what he knew of the prisoners' actions on board the *Ocean*. He said that he had heard the black man call out that the prisoner had his yard in the boy's fundament and that he was worse than the brute beasts in the field. He said that it was about two o'clock in the morning, and he confirmed that it was dark.

> Did you see the boy at that time?
> When I got up I saw the boy, he had been secured in the berth all
>   night by the black man, Ferrett.
> Do you know, or think that the black man was drunk?
> I cannot say whether he was drunk. I saw the black man about six in
>   the morning. He was not drunk at that time.

The cook withdrew, and George Gubbs, the seaman who had been lying in the hammock above Ferrett and Newton, was called as the next witness. He repeated the same story as the cook, as did the fourth witness, Isaac Wright.

Captain Langdon, the commander of the *Ocean,* was then called and was sworn in. He told the court that he had gone on board his ship and been informed by the first lieutenant that he had put a man in irons on a charge of buggery. The captain said that he had ordered Newton to be brought before him and his officers on the quarterdeck. He had asked him how he came to be guilty of so heinous and unnatural an offense. Newton had denied the charge, so he sent for the boy, who confessed that the man was guilty and had buggered him several times. The captain said that he had ordered them both to be confined in irons and had written to his commanding officer requesting a court-martial. When asked whether the boy's confession was voluntary or whether it had been extracted from him by threats or punishment, the captain said that the confession was voluntary.

The next witness was Lieutenant William Orfeur, who said that he had received a complaint from the ship's cook, from Ferrett, and from Gubbs and Wright that the prisoner George Newton had committed sodomy with the other prisoner. He had questioned Newton, who said that he was very drunk and that he did not know he had done any such crime, and that he had never been accused of such a thing before.

The admiral asked the lieutenant, "Do you remember to have heard the boy declare he had ever been guilty of this sin before; or had been accustomed to suffer men to commit sodomy with him?"

"He said that he had run away from his friends, and had been accustomed to run about the Bird-Cage Walk in St. James's Park; but on what account he did not say."

George Newton now called various witnesses in his defense. They included the master, the mate, and several other seamen. They all testified that he had never been guilty of sodomy before and that on the *Harwich* he was esteemed a regular man like any other. The final witness was the boy's father, John Finley of the parish of St. James's, London. When he had been sworn in, the admiral put the following question to him:

> Your son has called upon you to give the Court a character of him. What course of life had he followed?
> He has always behaved dutifully to his mother and myself. He used to attend upon butchers. He had an inclination to go to sea, and was entered by one Mr. Barratt.

At this point Thomas Finley fell upon his knees and begged for mercy and said he would never do the like again. George Newton professed his innocence, and the court was then cleared. Upon considering the charges against the two prisoners, the president and the four naval captains had no doubt that the charges were proved against them and that they were both guilty under the 29th Article. The president then announced the punishment that would be inflicted on them:

> George Newton, seaman, and Thomas Finley, boy, shall suffer death, each being hanged by the neck until they are dead, at such time, and at the yard arm of such of His Majesty's ships as the Lords Commissioners of the Admiralty shall direct.

In the volume of court-martial documents at the Public Record Office in London in which the above details are recorded, there is a scrawled note by a clerk noting that on July 17 it was ordered that they both be executed on board the *Princess Royal* at the Nore on Monday, July 27.

In the modern Western world, the hanging of two people for sodomy would be regarded by most people as barbaric. What is particularly shocking in this case is that the boy was executed, as well as the man, because he was over the age of fourteen. Moreover, it seems likely that George Newton was normally heterosexual. When asked by Ferrett what he had there, he replied "cunt," which suggests that he was driven by sexual needs to use the boy in the place of a woman. His protestation to the lieutenant that he was very drunk may explain why he risked committing a crime that was likely to have fatal consequences. But as far as the Royal Navy was concerned, homosexuality was not to be tolerated under any circumstances, and all sailors were aware of this. Every Sunday on every ship at sea the captain read out the Articles of War to the assembled crew. Article 29 clearly stated, "Unnatural offences to be punished by death," and sodomy was on a level with other offenses carrying the death penalty, such as mutiny, desertion to the enemy, and running away with the ship.

Naval officers were more likely to get away with homosexual acts than the ordinary seamen. Unlike the seamen, who lived and slept alongside each other with no privacy whatsoever, the officers had the benefit of small cabins, and in some instances where an officer was accused of homosexuality the case never came to trial. But where the evidence was sufficiently damning they could expect no mercy. The case of twenty-two-year-old Lieutenant William Berry is a good example of this, and has the added interest that a key witness was a female member of the crew who was dressed as a boy.

William Berry was a lieutenant on the sloop *Hazard,* and during the course of August 1807, he allegedly committed several homosexual acts with Thomas Gibbs, who was rated as a boy of the second class on the same ship. On August 23, Lieutenant Berry called the boy to his cabin and ordered him to hang a tablecloth alongside his bed as a screen, to lock the door, and to put his handkerchief over the keyhole. He then dragged the boy onto his bed and buggered him. When the boy protested that he was hurting him, Berry thumped him on the shoulder and told him to be quiet. Afterward, Berry told him to button up his trousers and to go away and say nothing to anybody. The boy went out crying and told John Hoskin, the gunroom steward, what had happened. Hoskin was aware that the boy had been abused by the lieutenant on at least a dozen prior occasions, but this time he decided that something must be done about it. He told the purser and at half past eleven that night Captain Charles Dilkes, the commander of the *Hazard,* called Gibbs to his cabin and asked him to explain what had happened between him and Lieutenant Berry. Gibbs recounted his story, and in due course the captain reported the matter to his commanding officer and Berry found himself facing a court-martial.

The court-martial took place on board HMS *Salvador del Mundo* at Plymouth on October 2, 1807.[2] The president of the court was Admiral Sir John Duckworth, and the principal witness for the prosecution was Thomas Gibbs. The boy told the assembled company what had taken place in the lieutenant's cabin in graphic detail. He was followed by Captain Dilkes, who said that Gibbs had been guilty of theft on a couple of occasions, but he did not believe him to be a liar. The next witness was a female sailor. She was described in the court-martial proceedings as "Elizabeth alias John Bowden (a girl) borne on the *Hazard's* books as a Boy of the 3rd class," and according to the *Naval Chronicle,* she appeared in court in a long jacket and blue trousers. Elizabeth Bowden came from Truro in Cornwall; following the death of her parents, she had gone to look up her elder sister, who lived in Plymouth. Failing to find her sister, she had decided to disguise herself and volunteer for the navy. She had joined the crew of the *Hazard* in February 1807 and had served for six weeks before it was discovered that she was a fourteen-year-old girl. Instead of sending her ashore, the captain gave her a separate apartment to sleep in and allowed her to remain on board as an attendant to the officers.

Standing in the great cabin of the *Salvador del Mundo,* Elizabeth Bowden was asked whether she had ever looked through the keyhole of Lieutenant Berry's cabin door and seen the boy Thomas Gibbs behaving in an indecent manner with the prisoner. She replied that she had, once, shortly before the ship came into Plymouth:

> I looked through the keyhole and I saw Thomas Gibbs playing with the prisoner's privates—I went up and called the gunroom steward and told him to come down and look through the keyhole and see what they were about—he did come down but did not look in and called me abaft told me to sit down.
>
> Have you frequently observed Thomas Gibbs go into the prisoner's cabin and the door shut, and the prisoner at the same time in the cabin.

Yes.

Did Thomas Gibbs ever relate to you or in your hearing what
    passed between him and the prisoner—and what induced you to
    look through the keyhole.

Gibbs has never told me anything that had happened—he was
    called in several times and I thought I would see what he was
    about.

The next witness was Charles Gregson, the ship's surgeon, who
repeated the boy's graphic account of the indecent act that had taken
place on August 23, adding that the boy had been forced to have oral
sex with the prisoner on two occasions and "that he had cut up his fishing lines and flogged him upon his bum—and after that Mr. Berry had
played with his cock and he had done the same with Mr. Berry." When
asked whether he had conducted a physical examination of the boy, the
surgeon said that he could not find any mark of any injury on the boy,
although the boy had complained of feeling sore.

The final witness for the prosecution was John Hoskin, the gunroom steward, who told the court of the various sex acts that the boy
had reported to him. He was asked whether he believed the boy to be
a liar. He replied:

I know the boy to be a liar—but I believe him to have spoke the
    truth in this instance.

Why the truth in this instance?

I frequently saw him come out of Mr. Berry's cabin, apparently
    very red and high coloured more than he usually is.

In his defense Lieutenant Berry called a relation, William Sandell,
an apothecary and male midwife from London, who said that Berry
had consulted him in the past because he had problems with impotency
and that he believed it would have been impossible for him to have
committed an act of sodomy. The *Hazard*'s surgeon said he had examined Berry and believed he was capable of an erection, but stressed he
could not be certain of this "as it involves some nice and intricate parts
of physiology."

The court considered the evidence and came to the conclusion that
Lieutenant Berry was guilty of sodomy and the other charges of uncleanness and was therefore condemned to be hanged. The sentence
was carried out on October 19, 1807, and Berry was hanged from the
starboard fore-yardarm of the *Hazard*.

Hanging was not the only sentence meted out to those condemned under the 29th Article. At a court-martial in December 1754, Thomas Landerkin of HMS *Porcupine* was found guilty of having committed uncleanness and was sentenced to receive twenty lashes with a cat-o'-nine-tails on his bare back alongside every ship and sloop in commission at Plymouth. The floggings were to be inflicted at two different times, and he was ordered to be dismissed from the service afterward.[3] Robert Paton, the boatswain of HMS *Volage*, received a variation of this punishment, which involved the maximum public humiliation. In February 1800, he appeared before a court-martial at his own request for attempting to commit an unnatural crime. He was found guilty and was sentenced to receive 200 lashes and to be drummed ashore with a halter about his neck "in as disgraceful a manner as possible." He was also stripped from his post as a boatswain, lost all pay due to him, and was ordered incapable of ever serving in the Royal Navy in any capacity.[4]

Considering that the navy cooped up thousands of young men for months on end without access to women, it is surprising how few homosexual incidents resulted in prosecutions. When one looks through the massive leather-bound volumes in the Public Record Office that contain the summaries of naval courts-martial, one rarely finds cases of "unnatural crimes" among the multitude of other offenses. During the course of the Seven Years' War of 1756 to 1763, for instance, there were only eleven courts-martial for sodomy, four of which led to acquittals. Since there were some 70,000 or 80,000 men serving at sea during the war, one can only conclude that homosexuality was either overlooked, was not reported because of the savage punishments, or was very rare indeed. In 1795, no cases of sodomy appear among the offenses listed in the summary of courts-martial. In 1800, when the naval war against Revolutionary France was at its height, there were 272 courts-martial.[5] Analyzing the various offenses for which the accused men were charged, we find that 64 courts-martial were held for men charged with desertion; 34 for drunkenness and neglect of duty; 25 for mutinous behavior and seditious language; 21 for robbery, fraud, and embezzling stores; 20 for attempting to desert; 18 for being absent without leave; 14 for riotous and disorderly behavior and bad language; 13 for captains and officers charged with the loss of their ship; and then came such offenses as striking a superior officer and sleeping on watch. There were four cases of sodomy that year.

Thomas Hubbard and George Hynes, both of HMS *St. George*, were found guilty and hanged; Robert Paton of HMS *Volage* we have already noted; and Joshua Thomas was charged with the unnatural sin of sodomy on a beast but was acquitted.

The fact is that the vast majority of seamen, when not actively engaged in working the ship, seem to have spent far more time thinking about women than about men. They wrote letters to women, they sang sea chanties and ballads about women, they tattooed their bodies with the names of women, they scratched pictures of women on whales' teeth and walrus tusks, they collected souvenirs in foreign ports to take back to their women, and they treasured mementos from the women they had left behind at home. And they thought about their women when they went into battle. Captain Collingwood, the friend of Nelson and his second in command at Trafalgar, wrote to his father-in-law shortly after the Battle of the Glorious First of June in 1794 and gave him a report of the action. He said that the night before the battle was spent in watching and praying and preparations for the next day, "and many a blessing did I send forth to my Sarah, lest I should never bless her more." At dawn on June 1, the British fleet bore down on the French fleet under cloudy skies with a fresh breeze from the southwest. As the two lines of ships came within range, the French ships began firing their broadsides. Collingwood was flag-captain of the *Barfleur* and was on the quarterdeck with Admiral Bowyer as the thunder of the French guns boomed out across the ocean. "It was then near ten o'clock. I observed to the Admiral, that about that time our wives were going to church, but that I thought the peal we should ring about the Frenchmen's ears would outdo their parish bells."[6]

Collingwood married Sarah Blackett in 1790, and in the four years before the battle she gave birth to two daughters. Collingwood was devoted to them but was fated to spend most of his married years at sea, blockading the French ports. He was a courageous and able commander who put his service to his country before all else, but his letters betray his continual regret at being apart from his loved ones. "Would to God that this war were happily concluded!" he wrote in May 1800. "It is anguish enough to be thus separated from my family; but that my Sarah should, in my absence, be suffering from illness, is complete misery." By October of the same year he was longing for peace to bring an end to the endless patrols off the French coast: "I have come to another resolution, which is when this war is happily terminated, to think no more of ships but pass the rest of my days in the bosom of my family, where I think my prospects of happiness are equal to any man's."[7]

In February 1802, during the negotiations for the Peace of Amiens, Collingwood was able to return home to spend a few precious months with his family in their house on the banks of the beautiful River Wansbeck. He spent an idyllic summer planting and cultivating the garden and getting to know his daughters, aged nine and ten. In the spring of 1803, the war was resumed and he was called back to sea. He never saw his home again. In August 1805, exactly two months before the Battle of Trafalgar, he was aboard the *Dreadnought* off Cádiz. As his squadron kept watch on the movements of the enemy fleet, his home was constantly in his thoughts. "Pray tell me all you can think about our family," he wrote to his wife, "and about the beauties of your domain, the oaks, the woodlands, and the verdant meads."[8]

After Nelson's death at Trafalgar, Collingwood had to take over temporary command of the British Mediterranean fleet. The administrative burden that this placed on his shoulders was daunting. "How I shall ever get through all the letters which are written to me, I know not," he wrote to Sarah in December 1805. "I labour from dawn till midnight, till I can hardly see; and my hearing fails me too. . . ."[9] His hopes of getting home were dashed when he was formally appointed to the command. A deeply conscientious man, he wore himself out with his unflagging attention to his duties. In February 1810, he was on board his flagship, the *Ville de Paris,* when he became so seriously ill that he was persuaded to hand over his command to Rear Admiral Martin so that he could return to England to recuperate. His ship cleared the harbor on March 6, 1810, and set sail for home, but he died the next day. A postmortem examination was carried out, and the surgeon concluded that his death was caused by a contraction of the pylorus, brought on by the confinement on board ship and by his continually bending over a desk while engaged in his correspondence.

Letters from other naval officers at sea betray their constant preoccupation with home and family. George Rodney, who achieved fame late in his life as commander of the victorious British fleet at the Battle of the Saints, married Jenny Compton when he was a thirty-three-year-old captain. She was the second daughter of the sixth Earl of

Northampton. The marriage took place in London in January 1753, and the following year they acquired a town house on Hill Street near Hyde Park. Their letters reveal the warmth of their love for each other and their unhappiness at the separation caused by naval life. Rodney told her that ambition had lost all its charms and that to have a wife and children meant more to him than anything else, "for whatever I am about or doing, I think of nothing but Hill Street, and the dear pledges I left there with you."[10] Jenny replied that nothing could make up for her sufferings while he was away: "without you life is not worth my care, nor would millions make me happy." She concluded, "I hope you will then, as soon as you possibly can, give up that vile ship that causes us so much pain."[11]

Rodney could not abandon his naval career, but he did apply to Lord Anson for a transfer from HMS *Fougueux*, which was due to be ordered to sea, to the 90-gun ship *Prince George*, which he believed would be stationed at Portsmouth for the foreseeable future. Anson approved the transfer, and Rodney took lodgings in Portsmouth so that Jenny could join him. They were together only briefly, for within weeks he received orders that the *Prince George* was to join the Channel Squadron under Sir Edward Hawke. Jenny was distraught at their parting and later wrote to apologize for not being able to control her emotions. She explained that "when the time approached that you (who are far more dear to me than my own life) was to leave me, I could not support it with the patience I am afraid I ought."[12] By August 1755, Rodney's ship was off Cape Finisterre on the northwest tip of Spain. In the great cabin of the *Prince George*, he sat down at his desk and wrote "to tell my dearest Jenny that thank God I am very well but not in the least satisfied with being at sea." He told her that their two little boys were ever in his mind, waking and sleeping, and he thanked God for bestowing on him a woman of virtue whose love meant more to him than the whole world. During the next sixteen months they met briefly when his ship put in to Portsmouth, but then in December 1756, Jenny became seriously ill. Rodney took a leave of absence and was by her side when she died on January 29, 1757, at their house on Hill Street. They had been married only four years.

The correspondence between Rodney and his wife, Jenny, provides a glimpse of the travails that have faced naval families over the centuries. It is vivid, but it is fragmentary. By comparison, the correspondence between Admiral Boscawen and his wife, Fanny, provides a more detailed and illuminating account of their lives for certain periods when he was serving at sea. Her letters were published in 1940 in a biography entitled *Admiral's Wife*, and they will be examined in chapter 14, which looks at the fate of the women left behind. Boscawen's letters to his wife from the years 1755 and 1756 were published in 1952.

Boscawen never achieved the fame of Rodney, Hawke, Nelson, and other British admirals who commanded ships in celebrated naval victories. Much of his early naval career was spent in the West Indies. He later headed an expedition to North America that led to the capture of the fortified town of Louisbourg, situated at the entrance to the Gulf of St. Lawrence, in 1758, and the following year, as commander in chief in the Mediterranean, he inflicted a crushing defeat on the French fleet at Lagos Bay, Portugal. During the course of his naval career he accumulated enough prize money to be able to acquire Hatchlands Park near Guildford. At first he and his wife lived in the old Tudor house on the estate, but later they built an imposing redbrick mansion and commissioned Robert Adam to carry out the internal decoration of the principal rooms. The planning of the spacious grounds was a major preoccupation of Boscawen while he was at sea, and his wife was much consumed with running the estate.

Fanny Boscawen was perhaps the most intelligent of the many accomplished women who married naval officers in the eighteenth century. She was born at St. Clere in Kent in 1719. Her father was a member of Parliament and high sheriff of Kent, and her mother was a descendant of John Evelyn, the diarist. Fanny first met Boscawen when he was home on leave in 1738 and was staying with his elder sister in Kent. He was then a twenty-seven-year-old captain, and she was eighteen. They continued to meet in Kent and were married in December 1742. She became a well-known figure in London society and was a friend of David Garrick, Sir Joshua Reynolds, and Dr. Samuel Johnson. In his *Life of Johnson*, James Boswell wrote, "her manners are the most agreeable, and her conversation the best of any lady with whom I ever had the happiness to be acquainted." She became a close friend of Elizabeth Montagu, and together they founded the "Blue-Stocking assemblies," the object of which was to replace the game of whist with good conversation.

Fanny had no illusions about her looks, and there is a moving passage in one of her letters to Boscawen in which she writes, "Beauty and I were never acquainted. But may I not hope, dear husband, that you will find charms in my heart, the charms of duty and affection, that will endear me as much to you as if I were in the bloom of youth and beauty."[13]

Her charms did indeed endear her to Boscawen, who was devoted to her. "Don't conceive I live one day without thinking of you," he wrote from on board the HMS *Torbay* some 300 miles out from England. "Rest assured, my dearest love, that I am well, that I love you, and think of you constantly. . . ."[14] He treasured the letters that she wrote to him when he was at sea; he arranged them in order and read them over and over again. Fanny was a wonderful writer. She kept Boscawen in touch with the activities of their children, described her friends, and detailed her life in London and on their country estate at Hatchlands with a revealing frankness.

Boscawen in turn kept her in touch with his life at sea. At one point he wrote to her every day, but she complained that his letters contained little else but the trite accounts of wind and weather. He explained that often there was little else to write about and that the workings of the ship were scarcely intelligible to anyone who was not a seaman. Most of his time was spent exercising the squadron under his command, carrying out gunnery exercises, and seeing which ship sailed the fastest. He did his best to match Fanny's lively descriptions of her social life, but his account of his daily routine was restricted to a few sentences. "We rise before six, breakfast at eight, dine at one, and sup at eight again and all very regularly. My mess at dinner consists of six, and breakfast and supper only Colby and Macpherson."[15] He said that conversation was limited and mostly amounted to a repetition of old voyages, interspersed now and then with accounts of fox hunts by Captain Colby, who was a sportsman. Boscawen seemed to have lived well on most of his voyages. Sometimes there was venison on the menu, sometimes turtle or fresh fish, and he was fortunate to have a baker who produced hot French bread every morning, on which he spread orange marmalade for his breakfast. Fanny had supplied him with some books, but he seems to have spent little time reading. He told her that he found the *History of Gustavus Vasa* to be entertaining, but he did not enjoy the French books she had given him.

A notable feature of Boscawen's letters is his aforementioned pre-occupation with his country estate. "A gentle rain all yesterday evening made me think of Hatchlands Park," he wrote to Fanny in 1756, and he was constantly giving her detailed instructions to pass on to Mr. Woodrose, the estate manager. "Pray exhort Woodrose to roll and weed. By this I think he must have completed his sowing and pray don't forget to buy me 12 load or thereabout of clover hay if it is cheap."[16] He also wanted the three roads in the park to be leveled, the ditch around the grotto to be cleaned, and all the ground at the lower end of the park to be plowed, leaving a broad walk under the grown trees. But always his thoughts came back to his beloved Fanny. "I am heartily tired of this prison kind of life," he wrote from on board the *Invincible* in May 1756, "and what I think is extraordinary, the older I grow, and the more used I am to it, the more tiresome I find it. I wish myself with you every hour, and dream of you every night."[17]

We know more about the feelings of admirals and naval captains than we do about the other ranks, because much more of their correspondence has been preserved. It is also a fact that senior naval officers tended to be considerably older than most ordinary seamen and therefore were more likely to have wives and children. The majority of the sailors of the lower deck in the navy were young men in their twenties. Many had gone to sea out of a spirit of adventure or because they wanted to see the world. Often they came from seafaring families, and it was taken for granted that they would go to sea to earn a living. During times of war, surprisingly large numbers of young men joined the navy for patriotic reasons or were prepared to tolerate the hard life, even if they were victims of the press gang. A common sailor, who had been pressed into the navy and was in Vernon's fleet at the capture of Portobelo, told his wife that it was with an aching heart that he had been taken from her by a gang of ruffians but that he was pleased to be fighting for his country against the impudent Spaniards: "I am and so is every man of us resolved either to lose our lives or conquer our enemies, true British spirit revives and by God we will support our King and country so long as a drop of blood remains."[18]

But many sailors would have agreed with Boscawen that life aboard a warship was "a prison kind of life." And unlike the senior officers, they did not have the luxury of a large cabin with fine furniture,

French bread for breakfast, and splendid wines with their dinner. The younger seamen missed their mothers and sisters, and those who were married missed their wives. Since a large number of sailors were illiterate, it was difficult for them to keep in touch with their loved ones by letters. Samuel Leech, a sailor on HMS *Macedonian* during actions against American ships in the War of 1812, acted as a scribe for those of his shipmates who could not read and write, but there must have been many men who lost touch completely with their families while they were away at sea. For them it was a matter of surviving the hard life as best they could. Leech described the informal concerts that would take place on deck during calm weather at sea. Scores of men would gather around a gun, and one of their number would seat himself on the gun and sing a selection of favorite songs. Another man would stand up and tell a few stories, and another would crack jokes. Leech thought that a casual visitor to a man-of-war might assume from the songs, the dances, and the revelry of the crew that they were happy, but it was his belief that these interludes only made life tolerable: "By such means as this sailors contrive to keep up their spirits amidst constant causes of depression and misery."[19]

William Nevens, the American sailor from Maine, entitled his memoirs *Forty Years at Sea . . . Being an Authentic Account of the Vicissitudes, Hardships, Narrow Escapes, Shipwrecks, and Sufferings in Forty Years Experience at Sea*. It will be recalled from chapter 2 that he had gone to sea at seventeen, made a number of voyages in a merchant ship to the West Indies, and been taken by the press gang in Barbados and forced to join the crew of a British warship; he had escaped by swimming to another vessel and ended up in Boston, where he married an English girl from Liverpool. She was nineteen and he was still only twenty-three. Like the majority of seamen, he saw very little of his wife over the next few years because he was earning a living at sea. While he was away on one of his voyages, he learned that his wife had died, leaving him with a baby boy of ten months. In his memoirs, which were published in 1850 after he had lived through numerous hazards and risen to become captain of a merchant ship, Nevens looked back on his years of marriage. He realized that many people would say that a sailor should not take on the responsibility of a wife but pointed out that only a sailor could appreciate what it meant to have someone he loved who would be there for him when the voyage was over. Of his own wife he wrote, "Although the most of my time had been spent away from her since our marriage, yet whilst she lived I felt that I had something to bind me to society, a kind and sincere friend, a trusty counsellor, an agreeable companion. With what eagerness did I seek her ardent welcome when returned from a long voyage."[20]

10

Women and Water, Sirens and Mermaids

WHEN CAPTAIN COLLINGWOOD LEARNED THAT THERE WAS A WOMAN aboard one of the ships in his squadron, he ordered her to be sent home at once. "I never knew a woman brought to sea in a ship that some mischief did not befall the vessel," he wrote to Admiral Purvis.[1] It was a view that had been shared by seamen for centuries and is still prevalent among some sailors and fishermen today. Linda Greenlaw, the captain of the fishing boat *Hannah Boden* and one of the most consistently successful fishermen operating on the Grand Banks of Newfoundland in recent years, has said that for a long time she had to endure the Jonah-like forebodings of an old fisherman on the quay at Gloucester, who made it clear that every time she set off for the fishing grounds he expected some disaster to befall her boat.[2] For eight years he watched her comings and goings and was always surprised when she returned safely to port.

As with so many sailors' superstitions, it is hard to discover the origins of the belief that a woman on a ship brings bad luck, and even harder to find any factual basis for it. Columbus, Magellan, and Drake might not have taken women on their epic voyages, but the ships of the Pilgrim Fathers were loaded with women and survived the Atlantic crossing, as did the hundreds of emigrant ships that followed in their wake. We have already seen that the British navy was prepared to turn a blind eye to the wives of warrant officers living on board; and the wives of captains, diplomats, and colonial governors frequently traveled overseas without bringing any harm to themselves or their fellow passengers. Those naval officers who did object to the presence of women on their ships seem to have regarded them as a nuisance rather than a source of bad luck—an attitude summed up by Nelson's remark before setting sail in 1801: "On Sunday we shall get rid of all the women, dogs and pigeons, and on Wednesday, with the lark, I hope to be under sail for Torbay."[3]

What is curious about the sailors' superstition is that it is flatly contradicted by the long-held belief that water is the female element and that women have powers over the sea that are denied to men. This belief dates back to ancient Greece and beyond. Evidence has been found at Knossos to indicate that the Great Goddess of the Cretans not only symbolized fertility but also regulated the course of the sun and stars and protected seamen on their voyages. When the Egyptian goddess Isis was adopted by the Greeks, she became the goddess of seafarers, and Greek ships were often named after her. Aristotle and the medical writers of his time believed that women were physically wetter than men. Their soft, spongy flesh retained more fluid from their diet, and the purpose of menstruation was to remove the excess fluid from their bodies. Pliny the Elder, in his monumental *Natural History*, which was published in A.D. 77 and summed up the thinking of the generations of writers and philosophers who had preceded him, said there was no limit to the marvelous powers attributed to females:

> For, in the first place, hailstorms, they say, whirlwinds, and lightning even, will be scared away by a woman uncovering her body while her monthly courses are upon her. The same, too, with all kinds of tempestuous weather; and out at sea, a storm may be lulled by a woman uncovering her body merely, even though not menstruating at the time.[4]

This belief that the naked female body could calm storms may account for the large number of ships' figureheads that feature a woman with one or both breasts bare.

The power that women were believed to have over water is most clearly demonstrated in the link between the Virgin Mary and the sea. In Catholic countries she was, and still is, widely regarded as the patron saint of sailors and fishermen. On the hills and cliff tops overlooking innumerable ports and fishing villages around the coasts of France, Spain, Portugal, and Italy can be found churches dedicated to the Virgin. Inside many of these are altars and chapels specially dedicated to seamen, and over the centuries it has been the custom for seafarers to offer prayers to the Virgin before setting out on a voyage. It was usual on the ships of Catholic countries (and on English ships before the Reformation) to have a shrine to the Virgin on the poop deck. Christopher Columbus was only one of many seafarers to name his ship *Santa María* in the belief that the Virgin Mary would guide him safely across the ocean. In the Spanish Armada of 1588, there were five ships named *Santa María* and four called *La María*.

The very name of the Virgin Mary was derived from the Latin name for water, the symbol of her purity, and her blue cloak represented the sea, the sky, and eternity. In Italian Renaissance paintings, she was often depicted against a distant lake or a glimpse of sea, usually a calm sea representing tranquillity. In Leonardo da Vinci's *Annunciation*, in the Uffizi Gallery in Florence, there is a sunny and peaceful harbor in the distance beyond the figure of the young Virgin Mary, symbolizing her role as the Port of Salvation. Mary was also associated with the moon and the stars and became known as *Stella Maris*, the Star of the Sea. The moon controlled the tides, and the stars were used for navigation; thus, Mary was seen as a crucial mediator between the seafarers and the elements when they ventured out to sea.[5]

Four hundred years after Leonardo da Vinci painted *The Annunciation*, we find Sigmund Freud pointing out the association between women and water in the lectures he delivered at the University of Vienna during the winter terms of 1915 and 1916. He was nearly sixty, and the lectures summed up much of his life's work on the interpretation of dreams. In his tenth lecture, on the symbolism in dreams, he observed that birth was represented in dreams by water. He reminded his audience that not only are all mammals, including man's ancestors, descended from creatures that lived in water, "but every individual mammal, every human being, spent the first phase of its existence in water—namely as an embryo in the amniotic fluid in its mother's uterus, and came out of that water when it was born."[6]

Freud also maintained that the female genitalia were symbolically represented in dreams by objects which enclosed a hollow space such as cavities, hollows, bottles, boxes, chests, cupboards, and rooms. Ships also fell into this category, and he made the interesting point that the link between ships and women was confirmed by etymologists "who tell us that 'Schiff' [the German word for ship] was originally the name of an earthenware vessel, and is the same word as 'Schaff' [a dialect word meaning 'tub']." This is not such an obscure argument as it might appear when it is recalled that for centuries ships have been regarded as feminine and referred to as "she" or "her" by sailors. Most of the early written references in English to a ship being a "she" appear in sixteenth-century documents, but there are one or two earlier references. By the eighteenth century, the majority of English-speaking seafarers referred to ships as female, although the terms "man-of-war," "merchantman," "Indiaman," "Guineaman," and similar masculine terms continued to be used for certain types of ships. There have been numerous explanations put forward as to why a ship should be regarded as feminine, some more convincing than others. Some will say it is because the ship is beautiful, or capricious, or full of curves; some will point out the anatomical similarities—that a ship has a head, cheeks, ribs, a waist, a belly, a bottom, and knees; some will say that a ship is like a mother and offers womblike protection to those on board; it has also been suggested that sailors think of ships as feminine because there is often a female figurehead on the bow.

At first sight there would appear to be an obvious link between the concept of a ship being feminine and the female figurehead. If a woman had special powers over the sea, it made sense for the figurehead to depict a woman, and ideally a naked or seminaked woman, since an unclothed woman could allegedly calm storms. In fact, female figureheads did not become popular until the nineteenth century, and it is only because the majority of the figureheads that have been preserved date from the 1780s onward that it is commonly assumed that most figureheads depicted voluptuous women. The reality is that in earlier centuries, most figureheads depicted male subjects, animals, birds, or monsters. Egyptian vessels displayed the sacred symbols of the gods, such as the falcon, the ibis, and the lotus flower. The ships of classical Greece usually had the head of a ram or a wild boar at the prow, and a large eye, the *oculus*, painted on each side of the bow. Viking ships had serpents or dragons.

The warships of the maritime countries of medieval Europe were decorated with heraldic designs, and the figureheads were often of animals. English ships of the Elizabethan period had lions, tigers, unicorns, eagles, and St. George and the Dragon.

It was during the course of the seventeenth century that carved decorations on the bows and sterns of warships proliferated. The carvings were loaded with symbolic imagery that was intended to express the power of each nation and to glorify the head of state. The French ship *Le Grand Louis,* commissioned by Cardinal Richelieu in 1600, featured a figurehead of Jupiter riding on an eagle. The *Wasa,* built for King Gustav Adolf of Sweden and launched from the royal dockyard at Stockholm in 1628, had a lion figurehead and nearly 500 carved figures. Like the *Mary Rose* of the previous century, the *Wasa* sank during her maiden sail in full view of the watching crowds. Preserved in the mud for three centuries, she was raised in 1961, and she has since undergone extensive restoration and has been the subject of meticulous research. No fewer than 453 of the sculptured figures have been recovered, and analysis of these has revealed a great deal about the ideas that lay behind the ship carvings of this period. The central theme of the decoration is the glorifying of the king, whose portrait is the focus of the stern carving. The rudder is decorated with a large lion trampling on a grotesque head, one of several images intended to symbolize Sweden defeating her enemies. The majority of the *Wasa*'s carvings are male figures, mostly armed warriors, Roman emperors, mythological figures like Hercules, and wild men with clubs symbolizing strength and aggression. The only female figures are a few caryatids representing nereids and a dozen relatively small mermaids.[7]

A similar decorative scheme was adopted on the magnificent British warship the *Sovereign of the Seas* (also called the *Royal Sovereign*). This 100-gun ship was designed by the famous shipbuilder Peter Pett and built at the royal dockyard at Woolwich. She was launched in 1637, and we are fortunate to have a detailed explanation of her decoration from Thomas Heywood, a designer of masques who planned the overall scheme. He leaves us in no doubt about the message he wished to convey in the symbolism of the various figures:

> Upon the beak head sitteth Royal King Edgar on horseback trampling upon seven kings. Upon the stem head there is a Cupid, or a child resembling him, bestriding a lion, which im-

porteth that sufference may curb insolence, and innocence restrain violence; which alludeth to the great mercy of the King,
whose mercy is above all his workes. On the bulkhead right forward stand six severall statues in sundry postures; their figures
represent Consilium, that is Counsell; Cura, that is Care; Conamen, that is Industry; Counsell holds in her hand a closed or
folded scroll; Care a sea compass; Conamen, or Industry, a lint
stock fired. Upon the other side, to correspond with the former,
Vis, which implyeth Force or Strength, holding a sword; Virtus,
or Virtue, a spherical globe; and Victoria, or Victory, a wreath of
Lawrell. The moral is that in all high enterprises there ought to
be first, Counsell to undertake, then Care to manage and Industry to performe; and in the next place, where there is an Ability
and Strength to oppose and Virtue to direct, Victory consequently is always at hand to crown the undertaking.[8]

By the end of the seventeenth century, the carved work on British
ships had become so elaborate and so expensive that the Navy Board
issued an order in June 1703 that restricted the amount of carving and
required all but the largest warships to have a figurehead in the form
of a lion. Elaborate figureheads continued to be installed on the large
three-deckers, and these usually consisted of a male rider on horseback
surrounded and supported by various allegorical figures.

Although most eighteenth-century figureheads on British, French,
Dutch, and Scandinavian warships were either heraldic beasts, decorative coats of arms, or male horsemen, there were exceptions. F. H.
Chapman's great book of ship designs of 1768, *Architectura Navalis*,
shows a number of female figureheads, notably that of the French
frigate *La Sirenne*, 34 guns, which had a winged female figure representing a siren; and various merchant ships are shown with female figures, one with a sword and scales representing Justice, and others that
appear to be goddesses. British royal yachts often had a female figurehead, usually a sculpted portrait of the queen or princess after whom
the yacht was named. The yacht *Royal Caroline* of 1749, for instance,
had an elaborate gilded figure of Queen Caroline, the wife of King
George II. The importance attached to the decoration on such a vessel is revealed by the costs. The decorative carving on the *Royal Caroline* cost no less than £1,100, while the figurehead required 120,000
sheets of gold leaf at a cost of £950. The combined cost of the carving and gilding in today's terms would be in the region of £140,000.[9]

Female figureheads began to come into their own in the 1780s, and during the course of the nineteenth century they became as popular as male figures, particularly on merchant ships. Warships continued to have kings, warriors, naval heroes, and Greek gods, but these were now joined by a range of goddesses, such as Diana, Thetis, and Minerva, as well as by sirens, sea nymphs, and mermaids, and by allegorical figures representing positive attributes such as Fame, Fortune, and Victory. French female figureheads were particularly impressive and reflected the quality of French monumental sculpture. There are some fine examples in the Musée de la Marine in Paris, notably the vigorously sculpted figure of a female warrior from the *Poursuivant,* the imperious and statuesque carving of the sea nymph wife of Neptune for the *Amphitrite,* and the exquisitely beautiful mermaid on the bows of the small state barge built for Marie Antoinette and designed for use on the Grand Canal at Versailles.

Similar subjects appear among the work of the Swedish craftsman Johan Tornstrom, who was one of the most gifted of all carvers of figureheads. His first major work was the figurehead for the frigate *Camilla* of 1784, depicting a seminaked woman with one raised hand pointing an arrow at her breast. During the course of the next thirty years, he carried out a range of commissions, many of them for ships built to the designs of the master naval architect Frederick Chapman. One of his most impressive carvings is an armed and helmeted female warrior, presumably representing Athena or Minerva, for the ship *Aran.* In stark contrast is the sorrowing figure of the tragic wife of Orpheus that came from the Swedish frigate *Eurydice,* and in a very different mood, the shameless whore from the bows of *La Coquette* who cups her hands under her exposed breasts.[10]

The owners of nineteenth-century merchant ships were also fond of figureheads of goddesses and allegorical images. The following notice in *The Boston Gazette* of October 10, 1811, is worth quoting in full, because it indicates that the symbolism of the carvings, even on relatively small vessels, continued to be significant and was certainly appreciated by the newspaper's reporter:

> Last Tuesday was launched from Mr. William Merrill's yard in Newbury, a brig named *Pickering.* She has for a figurehead the Goddess of Liberty. On her stern are represented Truth and Justice, holding a Wreath over the head of a Bust of the illustrious

Patriot, whose name she bears. At the side of them is Peace and Plenty. The vessel is about 250 tons, and one of the most beautiful we have ever seen; we understand she is owned in Gloucester, by Messrs. Sargent & Co. Very often have we seen vessels with the names of great men, but we have seldom met with one, combining so much beautiful hieroglyphical allusion. Its design and execution confer equal honor on the owners and workmen, while it conveys a delicate and deserved compliment to Mr. Pickering.

Not all shipowners were as concerned about the hieroglyphical allusions of their figureheads. In 1798, the Scottish firm of Scotts of Greenock wrote to the London ship carver Henry Hopkins and simply ordered "a fashionable lady head in the present taste."[11] Hopkins was told it must be five feet long, and when it was complete, he was ordered to send it by the first Berwick smack to the port of Leith near Edinburgh. The same shipyard wanted a figurehead for an East Indiaman in 1849. The ship was to be called *Seringapatam,* and the ship carver Archibald Robertson was told to fashion a seven-foot-high male figure in eastern costume. However, if he thought an eastern female figure would be more showy and look better, he was told to carve it in that style instead.

In addition to goddesses, Indian maidens, and females representing abstract concepts like Faith, Hope, and Charity, many of the figureheads on merchant ships were portrait sculptures of women known to the shipowner. In 1840, for instance, the Devonshire shipowner Joshua Quinton ordered for his schooner *Mary Ann* a carving that depicted the nanny who had saved his children from drowning. The figureheads of many merchant ships depicted the wife or daughter of the shipowner. Among the many fine figureheads in the Mariners' Museum at Newport News, Virginia, is that of the schooner *Irma Bentley,* which was built by George Bentley at Port Greville, Nova Scotia, in 1908. One of the fifteen children of George Bentley identified the figurehead and informed the museum that it was a portrait of the shipowner's daughter, Irma, when she was four or five years old. Irma Bentley subsequently visited the museum and was able to provide a complete history of the carving. She said that she had accompanied her father on many of his voyages to the Caribbean and beyond and was chosen for the figurehead because she was a good sailor and was never seasick.

A survey of the carved figures on the bows and sterns of ships from the seventeenth century to the end of the nineteenth century shows that there were four female images that were consistently favored by the men who commissioned decorative carvings. The first was the figure of an armed and helmeted female goddess or warrior, usually representing Athena or Minerva. The second was a sea nymph or nereid: These frequently appeared among the mass of carvings on the sterns of ships or as supporters to figureheads, and tended to be used as the subject of a figurehead only when the ship was named after a particular nereid such as Arethusa or Galatea. The third female figure was the siren, originally a bird woman in Greek mythology but usually shown on ships as a mermaidlike figure with the addition of wings and a double fish's tail. And the fourth figure that appeared almost as often as a figurehead as she did among the stern decorations was the mermaid herself.

Armed goddesses were popular subjects for figureheads on warships, because they combined an impressive warlike appearance with the sterling qualities of the goddess Athena and the mystical powers that women were believed to have over the element of water. The appeal of this image is underlined by the fact that it was adopted by Great Britain as the personification of her role as a maritime power. With the addition of a trident in one hand and the flags of England and Scotland painted on her shield, the Greek goddess Athena became Britannia. The original figure of Britannia can be traced back to the images of a captive female warrior that appeared on coins struck by various Roman emperors to represent the conquered island of Britain, but during the course of the seventeenth century, a version of the helmeted Athena figure was increasingly used as a patriotic symbol.[12] The visual image was given an additional boost by the stirring tune that Thomas Arne composed for the poem which was to take on the guise of a national anthem for the Royal Navy. "Rule, Britannia!" was written by James Thomson as the finale for a masque that was commissioned by the Prince of Wales and performed at his summer residence in 1740. The words reflect the aspirations of a pugnacious island race that had suffered conquest by Romans, Vikings, and Normans in the distant past, had fought off the Spanish Armada, and was determined not to be conquered again:

> When Britain first, at Heaven's command
> Arose from out the azure main,

This was the charter of the land
And guardian angels sang this strain
"Rule, Britannia! Britannia, rule the waves,
Britons never, never, never will be slaves."

English caricaturists such as James Gillray and George Cruikshank frequently used Britannia as the personification of Britain. In
their savage cartoons that were drawn during the course of the wars
against Napoleonic France, Britannia looks more like a large washer-
woman in fancy dress than a Greek goddess, but she later assumed a
more serious aspect. Whenever she has appeared on British coins and
banknotes (she is currently found on the reverse of the 50-pence
piece), she is closer to the original image of Athena.

The sea nymphs on the bows and sterns of European ships were
mostly derived from Greek mythology. In Greek legend there were
two families of sea nymphs. There were the oceanides, who lived in
the oceans, and the nereids, who were the fifty daughters of the sea
god Nereus and Doris and who lived in the Mediterranean. According
to Apollodorus of Athens, there were no fewer than 3,000 oceanides.
The best known of them was Calypso, who ruled over the island of
Ortygia in the Ionian Sea. In Homer's *Odyssey*, she kept Odysseus a
prisoner in a cavern on the island for seven years before she was ordered by Zeus to release him.

The nereids were fair virgins with golden hair who could sometimes be seen frolicking among the waves in the company of tritons,
who were half-men and half-fish. On ship decorations, the nereids are
often shown riding dolphins, with usually a few tritons in attendance.
Many warships were named after particular nereids, the most popular
being Arethusa, Galatea, and Thetis. In the Greek myths, Arethusa
was pursued by an amorous hunter and escaped by changing into a
spring on the island of Ortygia. Galatea was courted by Polyphemus,
the one-eyed cyclops, but fell in love with Acis, a young herdsman, and
was changed into a river. Thetis was so beautiful that she was courted
by Zeus and Poseidon before she settled down and married Peleus,
king of Thessaly. Five British warships were named *Calypso*. Five
British warships, and several French ships, were named after Arethusa.
There were five warships called *Galatea*, and no fewer than nine
British warships operating between 1717 and 1855 were named after
the sea nymph Thetis.

Like the nereids, the sirens originated in the Greek myths.[13] They
were among the hybrid creatures such as centaurs and sphinxes, half-
animal and half-human, who lived on the boundaries of the known
world and were likely to be encountered by the more intrepid travelers and explorers. It was said by some that the sirens were demons of
death: And like the soul birds of ancient Egypt, they were souls who
were sent to catch souls. The song of the sirens was impossible to resist, and lured seafarers to shipwreck and death. According to some accounts, it was the beauty of the song that attracted men. It was
described as being like the music of the spheres. Other accounts maintained that it was the contents of the song that was its attraction. It was
a source of knowledge: It told men what they most wanted to hear, and
in particular, it foretold the future.

The earliest written description of the sirens appears in the
Odyssey. Circe warned Odysseus about the sirens while he was staying
on her enchanted island:

> Your next encounter will be with the Sirens, who bewitch every-
> body that approaches them. There is no homecoming for the
> man who draws near them unaware and hears the Sirens' voices;
> no welcome from his wife, no little children brightening at their
> father's return. For with the music of their song, the Sirens cast
> their spell upon him, as they sit there in a meadow piled high with
> the mouldering skeletons of men, whose withered skin still hangs
> upon their bones.[14]

Circe advised Odysseus to plug the ears of his crew with beeswax
and have them bind him to the mast so that he could hear the sirens'
song but be unable to approach them. As his ship neared the spot
where they lived, Odysseus heard their lovely voices coming across
the water and was filled with such longing that he signed to his men to
set him free, but they ignored him and rowed resolutely on until they
were out of danger. Homer does not describe the appearance of the
sirens in the *Odyssey,* but in Greek and Roman art and literature they
are always depicted as bird-women, sometimes as women with wings,
more often as birds with women's heads. According to tradition, they
lived off the coast of Italy on the island of Capri.

Sharing some of the attributes of the sirens but altogether more
beguiling were the mermaids. Their origin is difficult to determine be-

cause they appear in various forms in the myths of many countries. In Russian folktales, a maiden who drowned was likely to become a Rusalka. In the southern regions around the Danube, the Rusalki were beautiful in appearance and so bewitched their victims with their sweet songs that death in their arms was peaceful. In the cold northern regions, the Rusalki were frightening to behold; their eyes shone with a green fire, their hair was unkempt and uncombed, and their skin was like that of the bodies of the drowned. Scandinavian legends tell of the goddess Ran, the ravisher, who caused storms at sea and captured dying sailors in a huge net. She entertained the drowned men in a great hall beneath the sea and fed them on fish delicacies. Her nine daughters were temptresses who reached out their arms and dragged young men to the seabed.

The mermaid who appears in the art and literature of Western Europe is invariably beautiful, but she too is associated with death. Invented by men, she became a symbol of men's ambivalence toward women. She is a temptress like Eve, and her fishy tail is a reminder of the serpent in the Garden of Eden. Like Aphrodite, who was born from the sea in a scallop shell, the mermaid has long, flowing hair, a sure indication of an abundant sexual appetite. Also like Aphrodite, she holds a mirror. This was a symbol of vanity, but it was also possible to see the future by looking into a mirror: The gift of prophecy was an important attribute of the mermaid, as it was of the siren. In addition to the mirror in one hand, the mermaid invariably has a comb in her other hand. The meaning of this is lost on us today, but in classical times it was directly connected with female sexuality because the Greek word for comb, *kteis,* and the Roman *pecten* were also used for the female pudenda. An alternative interpretation was proposed by Robert Graves, the poet and compiler of a comprehensive encyclopedia of mythology: In *The White Goddess,* he suggested that the mermaid's comb was originally the plectrum that the sirens used to pluck the strings of their lyres.

It is often assumed that the mermaid owes her origin to sailors mistaking the dugong or manatee for a fish-tailed woman, but this is too simplistic an explanation. In the first place, the dugong is a bulky, ugly creature with a shiny, bald head and a mustache: It could only be mistaken for a mermaid by a sailor who was either very nearsighted or very drunk. Likewise, a number of mermaid sightings took place in seas that have never been home to either dugongs or manatees. The dugong lives in the shallow waters of countries bordering the Indian Ocean, Indonesia, and Australia. The manatee frequents the rivers and freshwater lakes in Florida, some of the West Indian Islands, Brazil, and the Congo River in Africa. Neither mammal is known to have lived in the Mediterranean, the North Atlantic, or the North Sea, where so many of the mermaid legends first surfaced. It is possible that the dugong, or the much more attractive seal, may account for some mermaid sightings, but it seems more likely that the mermaid was the creation of poets, writers, and artists. She is one of those creatures like the unicorn and the dragon that appeared in early folktales and took a firm hold on people's imaginations.

Whatever her origin, the mermaid appeared increasingly in writings and pictures from medieval times onward. She was used by the Church in the Middle Ages as a symbol of vice: She was a harlot who tempted men with wild, forbidden pleasures. She stood between man and his salvation and must be resisted by the God-fearing. We therefore find the mermaid in churches and cathedrals, where she is carved on the capitals of columns, on roof bosses, and among the homely and irreverent scenes found on the oak misericords that served as seats for praying monks and clergy. The mermaid often appears in the margins of medieval manuscripts and on countless sea charts. She also features in songs, ballads, and stories.

The most popular of all mermaid stories of the Middle Ages was that of Melusina. The various versions of her story were collected by Jean d'Arras and recounted in his *Chronicle*, published in 1387. It was said that Raymond, the adopted son of the Count of Poitou, came upon three lovely maidens beside a fountain in the forest when he was out hunting. He fell in love with Melusina, who was the most beautiful of the three, and asked her to marry him. She agreed to do so on the condition that he must promise to leave her to herself every Saturday and not interrupt her privacy. Raymond willingly agreed to this, and they were married in a great castle at Lusignan that Melusina gave him as a wedding present. Raymond kept his promise for many years, but he was disturbed by strange tales that reached him concerning Melusina's weekly seclusion. He decided he must investigate, and one Saturday he entered her apartment and found that she had locked herself in the bathroom. Peering through the keyhole, he saw Melusina in the bath and was horrified to find that the lower half of her body had turned into the tail of a fish. When Melusina learned that he had discovered her secret, she fled and Raymond never saw her again. According to legend, her ghostly figure would hover over the battlements whenever a lord of the castle was about to die. The demanding of a promise or the laying down of conditions with awful penalties should they be broken was to be a feature of many other mermaid stories in the succeeding centuries.

The Elizabethan poets tended to stress the beauty of the mermaids' song. In his narrative poem *Hero and Leander,* Christopher Marlowe describes how Leander was pulled beneath the waves to the bottom of the sea where the ground was strewn with pearls and

> Sweet singing mermaids sported with their loves,
> On heaps of heavy gold, and took great pleasure,
> To spurn in careless sort the shipwreck treasure.

In Spenser's *Faerie Queene,* the mermaid is a dangerous enchantress who makes false melodies that lure weak travelers, "whom gotten, They did kill." Perhaps the most haunting passage appears in Shakespeare's *A Midsummer Night's Dream,* when Oberon describes how he was once sitting upon a promontory

> And heard a mermaid on a dolphin's back
> Uttering such dulcet and harmonious breath,
> That the rude sea grew civil at her song.

Each succeeding century has produced its stories and poems about mermaids. The most familiar to people today must surely be *The Little Mermaid,* by Denmark's most famous storyteller, Hans Christian Andersen. First published in 1873, it is one of those children's stories, like *Alice in Wonderland, The Swiss Family Robinson,* and Louisa May Alcott's *Little Women,* that transcend national boundaries. The little mermaid saves the life of a prince in a shipwreck, falls in love with him, and asks the sea witch how she can gain his love. The sea witch makes a cruel bargain with her. She will give the little mermaid human legs in place of her fish's tail, but she must lose her tongue and her lovely singing voice. She must also suffer further, because when she walks, it will feel like walking on knives. She meets the prince but is unable to win his love. When he marries another woman, the mermaid is distraught with grief and dies.

Alongside the stories and myths were factual reports in journals and ships' logbooks by sailors who had sighted mermaids while at sea. There was a spate of mermaid sightings during the age of exploration, as European seafarers ventured across unknown oceans. Many of these sailors would have expected to see monsters and strange creatures during their travels and would have been less likely to cast doubts on a mermaid sighting than sailors in later ages. It has been suggested that sea captains educated in the classics might hope to encounter some of the fabulous creatures of classical mythology, because this would set their voyages in the heroic tradition of Odysseus, Jason and the Argonauts, and the other explorers of antiquity. This is an interesting theory and may provide a more convincing explanation for some of the sightings than the dugong theory. It would certainly help to explain the conviction with which Columbus reported the sighting of three mermaids off the coast of Haiti. He noted that they came quite high out of the water, but he was disappointed because they "were not as pretty as they are depicted, for somehow in the face they look like men."

But what is one to make of the matter-of-fact description that appears among the daily weather observations in the logbook of the explorer Henry Hudson? In April 1608, he set out from London to look for a northwest passage to India. Two months into the voyage, his ship was far out in the Atlantic at latitude 75° north. On June 15, he noted that the wind was in the east and there was clear sunshine, and then he made the following note:

> This morning, one of our companie looking over boord saw a Mermaid, and calling up some of the companie to see her, one more came up, and by that time shee was come close to the ship's side, looking earnestly on the men: a little after, a Sea came and overturned her: from the navel upward, her backe and breasts were like a womans (as they say that saw her) her body as big as one of us; her skin very white; and long haire hanging down behinde, of colour blacke; in her going downe they saw her tayle which was like the tayle of a Porpoise and speckled like a Macrell. Their names that saw her were Thomas Hilles and Robert Rayner.[15]

Two years later, another British seaman saw a mermaidlike creature on the northwest coast of the Atlantic. Captain Richard Whitbourne, who was later knighted and published a book entitled *Discourse and Discovery of New-found-land,* was standing by the waterside in the harbor of St. Johns, Newfoundland, when he saw something swimming toward him that looked very like a woman. It seemed to be beautiful with a well-proportioned face and blue streaks resembling hair down to its neck. It came close enough for him to see that it had white, smooth shoulders and back but that the lower part of its body was shaped like a broad hooked arrow. One of his companions also observed the creature, and it later attempted to board some of the boats in the harbor but was beaten off by one of the sailors, who dealt it a full blow on the head so that it fell back into the water. Whitbourne observed that because much had been written about mermaids, he felt he must relate what he had seen but concluded "whether it were a Mermaide or no, I know not. I leave it for others to judge."[16]

Captain John Smith was so entranced by the sight of the lovely creature that he saw off a West Indian island in 1614 that he began to experience the first effects of love, until she made an unguarded movement and he discovered that from below the waist she had the body of a fish. When he first spotted her she was swimming gracefully near the shore. She had large eyes, a finely shaped nose, well-formed ears, "and her long green hair imparted to her an original character by no means unattractive."[17]

Occasionally, there were reports of mermaids being captured. When the dikes of Holland were flooded during a storm in 1403, a mermaid was washed ashore and was stranded in the mud near the town of Edam. She was found by some women who were on their way to milk their cows. They took her home, and after they had cleaned off the sea moss that stuck to her body, they clothed her and fed her with bread and milk. She was taught to spin and undertake other womanly tasks but had to be watched carefully because she kept trying to sneak back to the sea. She apparently lived fifteen years, but in all that time she remained dumb and never spoke a word.

The most famous mermaid to be caught alive was the mermaid of Amboina, caught off the coast of Borneo in the early eighteenth century. A chaplain working in the Dutch colonies described how the creature survived for four days and seven hours in a jar of water. It refused to eat the fish offered it and uttered plaintive sounds like those of a mouse. The creature was illustrated in the 1754 edition of Louis

Renard's book on fish and is shown with an oval face, brown curly hair, slim arms with webbed fingers, small breasts, and a very long, blue tail more like that of an eel than a fish.

Sightings of mermaids continued at regular intervals over the centuries, and these, together with the poems and the fairy tales, have provided a rich harvest for painters and illustrators. Their images range from the charming and decorative to the wildly sensual. Among the most charming are the woodcuts of mermaids that appear in the fourteenth- and fifteenth-century bestiaries, books filled with descriptions of strange and fabulous creatures that were compiled by monks as a warning against various temptations and sins. In contrast, Victorian artists such as Herbert Draper and John Waterhouse painted a number of highly finished and realistic pictures of the most enticing sirens and mermaids imaginable. Some of the finest pictures of mermaids appear in books illustrated by gifted artists such as Arthur Rackham and Norman Rockwell. But the most extraordinary pictures are those of the German Symbolists and, in particular, Arnold Bocklin, who, seemingly fixated on mermaids, painted a series of pictures in which the most voluptuous mermaids and mermen writhe and frolic in an abandoned manner among the rocks and waves.[18]

Mermaids have been the subject of so many stories, legends, ballads, poems, songs, paintings, drawings, bronze sculptures, and carvings in wood and stone that it is little wonder that to some people they have seemed as real as fairies and witches, and that occasionally sailors have seen them during the course of their ocean voyages. Even today, they continue to inspire writers and artists and have even been the subject of several films, notably the 1984 film *Splash*, in which Tom Hanks falls in love with Daryl Hannah—perfectly cast as everyone's vision of a golden-haired mermaid from the depths of the ocean.

II

A Wife in Every Port

AUGUSTUS HERVEY WAS A WOMANIZER ON AN EPIC SCALE. AS A NAVAL captain in the 1740s and 1750s, he used his aristocratic connections, his charm, and his money to seduce an astonishing number of desirable women. His cruises around the coasts of Europe in command of a British warship were punctuated by a succession of lavish parties, tortuous love affairs, and one-night stands. Society beauties and opera stars, nuns and country girls all fell victim to his insatiable sexual appetite. In his later years, he found himself at the center of a scandal as notorious in its day as the liaison of Nelson and Lady Hamilton. His wife, whose love life was almost as colorful as his own, engaged in a bigamous marriage with the Duke of Kingston and became the first and only woman to be tried on a charge of bigamy before the House of Lords. Hervey was then in his fifties. He had inherited an earldom, was a rear admiral and a Lord of the Admiralty, and was living a relatively quiet life in London with his mistress. After a lifetime of dalliances with other men's wives, he had to endure a torrent of gossip, in which he appeared as the cuckolded party.[1]

Augustus Hervey was born in London on May 19, 1724. His father was Baron Hervey of Ickworth, and his mother was Mary Lepell, daughter of a brigadier general and so famed for her beauty that she inspired eulogies from poets and writers as diverse as Pope, Gray, and Voltaire. His grandfather was the Earl of Bristol, a title to which Augustus would succeed many years later but which first passed to his elder brother, George, on the first earl's death in 1751. Augustus was the second son, and in the usual tradition of aristocratic families, he was expected to go into the navy while his younger brother, Frederick, went into the Church. After spending a few years at Westminster School, he joined HMS *Pembroke*. He was eleven years old, and the captain of the ship was his uncle, the Honorable William Hervey, a man so notorious for his cruelty that he was eventually court-martialed and dismissed from the service. In 1736, Augustus was rated midshipman and moved to the frigate *Greyhound*, which sailed to Gibraltar and the Mediterranean. By 1740, he was back again on a ship commanded by his uncle William, this time HMS *Superbe*. In May of that year, he passed his lieutenant's exam at the unusually young age of sixteen. In the same year, his ship put in to Lisbon after riding out a storm, and it was there that he had what appears to be his first sexual encounter. The woman was Ellena Paghetti, whom he later described as "a very famous Italian singer, and not less so for her beauty."

Postings to other ships followed, and he saw action in the West Indies and then commanded a Navy Board tender on the coast of East Anglia with instructions to impress seamen. It was while on leave during the summer of 1744 that he met Elizabeth Chudleigh at the Winchester races. She was twenty-four and had recently been appointed a maid of honor to the Princess of Wales at Leicester House. Her vivacious beauty had already attracted the nineteen-year-old Duke of Hamilton, who had courted her and promised to marry her when he returned from the Grand Tour on the Continent. In his absence she allowed herself to fall for the charms of Lieutenant Hervey. Both of them were impetuous and rash by nature, and within weeks they were married.

The marriage was conducted in secret and was to remain a secret from English society until the details of the curious ceremony were revealed during the bigamy scandal twenty years later. The principal reason for secrecy was that if Miss Chudleigh were known to be married she would have to relinquish her post as maid of honor and the £400 that went with it. There was also the fact that Hervey's illustrious family would be unlikely to give their approval to the match.

The ceremony took place at eleven o'clock at night in the tiny church at Lainston near Winchester. Apart from the vicar and the bride and groom, there were only four other people present, one of them being Miss Chudleigh's aunt, and another, her maid. Precautions were taken to ensure that the domestic staff of all concerned had no idea what was being planned, and the brief ceremony took place in semi-darkness, the only illumination being a lighted taper stuck in the hat of Mr. Mountenay, one of the witnesses. Afterward the newly married couple returned to the house where they were staying, and Elizabeth Chudleigh's maid helped them to enter by a backdoor unseen so they could creep up to a bedroom and spend their wedding night together. A few days later, Hervey had to rejoin his ship at Portsmouth, and they did not see each other again before he sailed for the West Indies.

Apart from a brief reunion when Hervey returned from Jamaica in 1746, they drifted apart and both sought lovers elsewhere. Miss Chudleigh, as she continued to be known, acquired an increasingly scandalous reputation that was typified by her startling appearance at the Venetian Ambassador's Ball at Somerset House in May 1749. She arrived wearing a costume so transparent and flimsy that most of her lovely figure was revealed. The King and the other men present seem to have been delighted, but the women were not. The Princess of Wales draped her wrap over the bare shoulders and breasts of her maid of honor, and afterward Mrs. Elizabeth Montagu noted, "Miss Chudleigh's dress, or rather undress, was remarkable; she was Iphigenia for the sacrifice, but so naked the high priest might easily inspect the entrails of the victim. The Maids of Honour (not of maids the strictest) were so offended they would not speak to her."[2]

Meanwhile Hervey had embarked on a pattern of life that he was to pursue for as long as he was on active service in the navy. We know the most intimate details of this because he kept a private journal that he later used as a basis for his racy memoir. If this had ever been intended for publication, one would be tempted to think that he had invented the more extraordinary episodes in order to establish his reputation as a great lover, but it was written between 1767 and 1770 (several years before the bigamy scandal) and according to his own words, "I write this over purely for my own satisfaction of recalling to my memory most of the events of all kinds of my life, I pursue the threads of it, just as I had set it down every day of my life as it happened, only not quite all the very particular circumstances attending it."[3]

Hervey had made the crucial step to post-captain in 1747, and his contacts in high places had ensured that after the briefest of spells in command of small warships he was given command of the 70-gun *Princessa*. In this splendid ship of the line, he sailed with Admiral Byng's squadron to the Mediterranean. At this time, the hostilities with France had ended, and the squadron's purpose was to show the flag in various ports and to be ready should hostilities be resumed. The period of peace provided an ideal opportunity for senior naval officers to organize entertainments in foreign seaports and to become acquainted with local society, particularly the ladies. Every ship had musicians, and a prolonged stay in a civilized port like Lisbon or Genoa was marked by a succession of gracious dinners and musical evenings. Hervey reveled in this way of life. In January 1748, at the little port of Vado, near Genoa, he held a masquerade on board and arranged for the whole ship to be so illuminated that "she was as pretty a sight to those on shore as those within her." All the officers of the fleet arrived in fancy dress, and the entire ship's company were persuaded to put on party masks.

A few weeks later he organized an entertainment on a grander scale. At the Italian port of Leghorn, he invited the governor of the province, his mistress, and twenty-eight members of the nobility who were visiting the city from Florence and Pisa. The evening began with a concert on board his ship, and as darkness fell, the guests were rowed in boats along the city's canals. Hervey had arranged for all the bridges to be illuminated, and at intervals along the canals he had boats with musicians playing and boats with food and drink for his guests. Thousands turned out to see the spectacle, some watching from windows and others lining the banks of the canals.

In return, Hervey received numerous invitations to dinners and concerts. He found the ladies of Florence to be the most gallant in Italy and their husbands the least jealous, so that he was able to enjoy the favors of, among others, the Marchesa de Pecori and the Marchesa Acciaiola. Back in Leghorn, he spent his time with the wives of two merchants: "The first I had every enjoyment with I could wish, and she was very pretty as well as entertaining." To show her appreciation, she presented him with her picture and a ring set with diamonds.

By September 1748, the squadron was in Lisbon, which enabled Hervey to renew his acquaintance with Signora Paghetti, the Italian singer who had taken him to her bed when he was a sixteen-year-old lieutenant. He found her still to be very handsome, but he also looked for pleasures elsewhere. He paid several visits to the convent at Odivellas, which had an unusually liberal regime. The previous king had maintained two mistresses there and had a child by each of them. Hervey noted that many of the nuns were ladies of quality and were most beautiful. Of a later visit to the convent he wrote, "We stayed late, making love in the *frereatica* way (as they call it)." By way of contrast he also visited the local prostitutes. He described one morning's work in company with the Duke of Bagnos and Charles Gravier, later Comte de Vergennes and foreign minister under Louis XVI: "We went in cloaks to upwards of, I verily believe, thirty ladies houses—ladies of pleasure, I mean."[4]

Hervey's aristocratic background and social contacts opened doors at the highest level. Leaving his ship at Lisbon, he spent a few weeks in Paris during the summer of 1749. He was presented to the Queen of France, visited Madame de Pompadour and went hunting regularly with the Duke de Penthieve, the grandson of Louis XIV and admiral of France. At this time, it was his custom to get up very early and to keep in good shape by dancing for half an hour each morning and by riding three times a week. If he dined at home, he would spend two hours after dinner playing the harpsichord. The nights were spent with two dancers from the Paris Opéra.

This round of social engagements and casual sexual encounters was somewhat disrupted in November 1749 when he met Susanne-Félix Lescarmot, whom he described as the most beautiful woman in France. She had been groomed to become the mistress of the King, but the Duc de Richelieu had ensured that Madame de Pompadour gained that position, so she had been married off to Monsieur Caze, a *fermier-général* who later became *secrétaire du cabinet*. Hervey was introduced to Madame Caze at a masquerade and fell madly in love with her. He abandoned his opera girls and all other distractions in order to pursue her. Madame Caze was evidently attracted to him, but it was some time before they had an opportunity to meet in private and reveal how they felt about each other. They continued to steal meetings together, and the relationship blossomed to the point where she gave Hervey a ring with the motto *L'Union en la passe* and told him that she was no longer mistress of herself but was all his. Unfortunately, their attempts to consummate their love were frustrated by the presence of others, in particular her husband and her mother. However, one day, several weeks after their first meeting, Madame Caze sent for Hervey when the coast was clear, and they were able to spend one entire afternoon and evening together, "giving and receiving the last charming proofs of an unbounded love, and I never tasted such most exquisite delight, nor was I ever more fit for the scene."[5]

They now arranged to meet every day, and somehow avoided causing a scandal or arousing her husband's jealousy. On one occasion, the lovers were engaged in a tender farewell when Monsieur Caze entered the room. Hervey was able to conceal his aroused state with a large muff that he had slung from his girdle, and although Monsieur Caze observed their guilty confusion, he assumed they were merely kissing. He stomped off to his library, and any suspicions he might have entertained about the true nature of their friendship he kept to himself. Life was simplified for the lovers when Monsieur Caze was appointed *secrétaire du cabinet* and had to spend much of his time at Versailles. This enabled Hervey to spend every night with Madame Caze. He would arrive at her house late in the evening, enter through the stables, and stay with her until two or three o'clock in the morning. Although Hervey seems to have been given considerable latitude by his fellow officers, the time came when he had to return to his ship.

By December 1750, he was back in England, and on half-pay. He used all his contacts to try to get another command and was eventually appointed captain of the *Phoenix,* a 20-gun ship, the smallest class possible for someone of his rank—Lord Anson informed him that there were no larger ships available. While he was supervising her outfitting at Deptford, he received a letter from Madame Caze informing him that she was determined not to injure her husband again and had decided to give up her life to devotion.

In March 1752, Hervey set sail from Portsmouth on the *Phoenix* and headed for Portugal and the Mediterranean. First he sailed into Lisbon, and during the four months that his ship was anchored there, he amused himself by renewing his acquaintance with the ladies in the convent at Odivellas and by making love to the local Portuguese ladies. In August he sailed on to Marseilles, where he met Mademoiselle Sarrazin, a cheerful and spirited Frenchwoman who was the mistress of a French colonel. She insisted that he take her to sea with him. He agreed, and she came aboard with her maid and sailed with him to Mi-

One of the many popular prints devoted to the theme "the sailor's farewell" made in the late eighteenth century. The young sailor's gesture toward the gun and the flag suggests that he is torn between his love for his sweetheart and his patriotic duty to fight for his country.

An engraving by Thomas Rowlandson, entitled *Sea Stores*, shows a naval officer negotiating with prostitutes on the waterfront at Plymouth. The officer has just come ashore from a ship in the harbor and is eager to get down to business.

A sailor enjoys his last moments ashore in this engraving by Thomas Rowlandson, *Dispatch, or Jack preparing for sea.*

Thomas Rowlandson depicts a typical scene in a seaman's tavern in the 1790s. The location is Wapping, the sailors' district on the north bank of the Thames near London Bridge and the Port of London.

This is a detail from a well-known engraving by Thomas Rowlandson, *Portsmouth Point*. The fleet is about to sail, and sailors of all ranks are saying fond farewells to their loved ones before being rowed out to the anchored warships.

An engraving of a cabin boy by Thomas Rowlandson. There were many boys aged from nine or ten and up on warships. They wore loose, baggy clothes and often wore their hair long, which helps explain why young women were sometimes able to pass themselves off as adolescent boys without being discovered.

Richard Parker, the leader of the Mutiny at the Nore, hands a list of the sailors' grievances to Vice-Admiral Buckner on board HMS *Sandwich*. The mutiny began on May 12, 1797, and spread to most of the warships anchored off Sheerness at the mouth of the Thames.

A portrait of Richard Parker, who was condemned to death for his part in the Mutiny at the Nore. Parker's wife, Ann, failed to get a reprieve for him and arrived at the fleet anchorage at the Nore too late to speak to him but not too late to see him hanged.

Mary Anne Talbot, who, according to her biographer, served in the British army and the Royal Navy under the name John Taylor in the 1790s. Engraving by G. Scott, after the portrait by James Green.

Mrs. Hannah Snell, who joined the British army in the 1740s, served as a marine at the siege of Pondicherry in India and then joined the navy as a seaman. Her shipmates were astonished when she eventually revealed that she was a woman.

A painting by Gordon Jackson showing the nineteen-year-old Mary Patten on the deck of the clipper ship *Neptune's Car* in 1856. When her husband, Captain Patten, fell seriously ill during the voyage from New York, Mary took command of the vessel and sailed around Cape Horn to San Francisco.

Ulysses and the Sirens, painted by Herbert Draper in 1909. According to Greek mythology, the beautiful voices of the Sirens always lured sailors to their death, but Homer had Odysseus (in Latin, Ulysses) resist their fatal attraction by getting his crew to block their ears with wax, while he had himself bound to the mast so he could safely hear the Sirens' song, which foretold the future.

A carved and gilded mermaid, the figurehead on the late-eighteenth-century barge of Marie Antoinette of France.

A Mermaid, painted by John William Waterhouse in 1900. In Western art and literature, the mermaid was invariably portrayed as a beautiful creature with long, flowing hair, but, like the Sirens who preceded her, she was a temptress and associated with death.

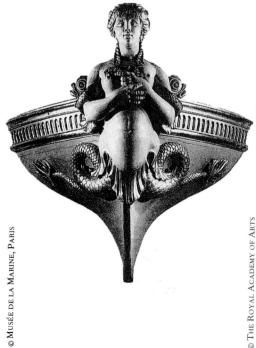

Portrait of Mrs. Mary Nesbitt, painted by Sir Joshua Reynolds. She was the last great love of Captain Hervey's life and became his mistress around 1770. She remained with him until his death in 1779.

Portrait of Kitty Fisher as Cleopatra, painted by Sir Joshua Reynolds in 1759. Kitty Fisher was one of the many society beauties who had a love affair with Captain Hervey when he was on leave in England during the 1760s.

Miss Elizabeth Chudleigh, who secretly married Augustus Hervey in 1744, when he was a young naval lieutenant. She was as unfaithful to him as he was to her, and many years later she bigamously married the Duke of Kensington.

Hervey's wife at a London ball in 1749. Said an observer, "Miss Chudleigh's dress, or rather undress, was remarkable; she was Iphigenia for the sacrifice, but so naked that the high priest might easily inspect the entrails of the victim."

Captain Augustus Hervey in 1768, painted by Thomas Gainsborough. The second son of an English baron, he joined the Royal Navy at the age of eleven and was a captain by the age of twenty-three. During visits to foreign seaports, he slept with a succession of aristocratic beauties, dancers, and servant girls.

Emma, Lady Hamilton as a bacchante, painted by Louise-Elizabeth Vigeé-LeBrun in Naples around 1790. Emma was the young wife of Sir William Hamilton, the British ambassador to Naples. She was famous for her beauty and for her love affair with Lord Nelson.

Horatio, Viscount Nelson, Vice-Admiral of the White, painted by Lemuel Francis Abbot in 1797. Nelson became infatuated with Emma Hamilton during his prolonged stay in Naples after his victory at the Battle of the Nile.

Nelson met and married the young widow Fanny Nisbet on the island of Nevis when he was a naval captain stationed in the West Indies. She is shown here with a bust of her famous husband.

Commodore John Paul Jones, the son of a Scottish gardener, became one of America's greatest naval heroes. His most famous action was the Battle of Flamborough Head, in 1779, in which he captured two British warships after a hard-fought battle that lasted more than three hours.

Portrait of William Darling, keeper of the Longstone Lighthouse on the Farne Islands and father of Grace Darling. After the rescue that made them both famous, William Darling complained that they were so besieged by journalists and artists that he was unable to carry out his lighthouse duties.

Grace Darling, the twenty-two-year-old heroine who rowed through a storm with her father to rescue the passengers and crew of a ship wrecked in a gale in September 1838. The artist Henry Perlee Parker traveled to Northumberland and made this sketch a few weeks after the rescue had taken place.

Ida Lewis rescued two soldiers in the Newport, Rhode Island, harbor in March 1869. The two men were returning to Fort Adams when their boat overturned in a gale. They were almost paralyzed with cold by the time Ida got to them, and it took several hours to revive them.

HARPER'S WEEKLY.

A JOURNAL OF CIVILIZATION

VOL. XIII.—No. 657.]   NEW YORK, SATURDAY, JULY 31, 1869.   [SINGLE COPIES, TEN CENTS. $4.00 PER YEAR IN ADVANCE.

MISS IDA LEWIS, THE HEROINE OF NEWPORT.—Phot. by MANCHESTER BROTHERS, PROVIDENCE, R. I.—[See Page 484.]

Ida Lewis acted as assistant to her father, keeper of the Lime Rock Lighthouse, which was situated on an island in the harbor of Newport. She became so famous for her rescues that she was pictured on the cover of *Harper's Weekly*.

Mending the Nets, by Winslow Homer, 1882. Homer spent several months in the Yorkshire fishing village of Cullercoats and painted many pictures of the local women carrying fish baskets, mending nets, knitting socks, and waiting anxiously on the beach for their menfolk to return from the fishing grounds.

Home from the Sea, by Arthur Hughes, 1862. A sailor boy lies on the grave of his mother, watched by his sister, who is dressed in mourning black.

A Hopeless Dawn, by Frank Bramley, 1888. A fisherman's wife is comforted by her mother as she mourns her husband, who has been lost at sea. Bramley lived for ten years in the Cornish fishing village of Newlyn and observed firsthand the working lives of the fishing families.

The Sailor's Return

Just on the Beach arriv'd, with great Surprize,
Jack sees his Molly; Him too Molly Spies:
What! is it Thou? with open Arms She cries,
Then drops the brittle Goods She sells, for Bread,
While all aghast beside stands Messmate Ned,
And points where flows the Bowl, & Gen'rous Red.

But Molly's Mother, more sagacious, opes
The wealthy Chest, on which She plac'd her hopes,
And for the richest Prizes careful gropes.
The settled Crew gay Mirth and Love proclaim;
One leads aloft the mercenary Dame,
Who drunk, returns her Load from whence it came.

Contemning Wealth, which they with Risk obtain;
Thus Sailors live, and then to Sea again?

Printed for Carington Bowles   in S.t Pauls Church Yard London

Dated 1744, this is an early version of the many popular prints devoted to the subject "the sailor's return." A sailor's wife is surprised by the sudden return of her husband, while her mother dips into his sea chest, which is filled with his prize money.

norca, Gibraltar, and Lisbon, where he set her up in a house that he rented so they could spend time together whenever he was free. This convenient arrangement did not prevent him from enjoying affairs with other women. In October 1752, he was intercepted by a man on horseback. At first Hervey thought the man had orders to assassinate him, but he had been sent to bring him to a lady who wished to make his acquaintance. He was taken to the garden entrance of an estate and led up to a finely furnished apartment in a large house. There he found a lady waiting for him: "She told me our time was short, and we must go to bed, which I did not hesitate as she had fired me all over. I put my pocket-pistols under my pillow, and passed a most joyous night." After several more secret rendezvous with this mysterious woman, he discovered that she was the Duchesse de Cadaval and a princess of the House of Lorraine.

During the next four years, Hervey continued to have affairs with aristocratic ladies whenever his ship was in port long enough. When the *Phoenix* put in to Genoa in August 1754, for instance, he embarked on an affair with Madame Pellinetta Brignole, a good-looking and intelligent woman of thirty from a distinguished Genoese family. She was an accomplished musician and so captivated Hervey that she remained the principal object of his affections during the remaining time he spent in the Mediterranean. She was, of course, married, a fact that had never deterred him in the past but which, in this case, required them to use some ingenuity. In the first instance, Madame Brignole feigned an inflammation of the eye as an excuse for her to go to bed in a darkened room. Hervey crept into her bedroom and lay down next to her under the thick down quilt. When her husband came to say goodnight to her after supper, Hervey remained hidden under the quilt. After a few anxious moments, the husband went out, "leaving me in the arms of one of the loveliest women that ever was. I lay till near daylight and performed wonders." At dawn he managed to creep out of the house and return to his lodgings without being seen. On a later occasion, he was compelled to hide under his mistress's bed for two hours before it was safe for him to emerge and embark on another night of lovemaking.

In addition to his affairs with high-society women, Hervey also made a practice of seducing pretty girls in their teens. In May 1752, he attended mass in Lisbon while his ship lay at anchor in the harbor. Spotting a good-looking country girl in the congregation, he had her

followed and brought to him. She proved to be "a most lovely piece."
In the same city a year later, he laid siege to Donna Felliciana de
Sylvera, a tall and well-built girl of fifteen. He had frequently chatted
with her as she sat at her window and at length persuaded her to go to
bed with him. According to his diary, she gave him as much joy as ever
he could remember. In January 1756, he sailed the *Phoenix* into Port
Mahon. He ordered the ship to be prepared for sea because a declaration of war was imminent, but this did not prevent him from flirting
with the daughter of the tavernkeeper of the inn where he was staying: "She and I agreed very well, and I kept her all the while, and a
sweet pretty creature she was, so that she engrossed my whole time
here, and as I lay at the house we had no interruption."[6]

This life of sensual indulgence was somewhat curtailed in 1756
when war was declared, and for the next seven years he spent much of
his time on active service. He proved a bold and active commander. He
served under Hawke in the English Channel, though he missed taking
part in the Battle of Quiberon Bay. He was with Admiral Keppel at
Belle Isle in 1760 and played a major part in the West Indian campaign
in the capture of Martinique, St. Lucia, and Havana. He did find time
during his periods of leave in England to have several affairs, most notably with Kitty Fisher, a society beauty and courtesan who was a favorite model for Sir Joshua Reynolds, for whom she sat as Cleopatra.
On his return from the West Indies in 1763, he struck up a liaison with
Kitty Hunter, the daughter of one of the Lords of the Admiralty. She
subsequently bore him a son named Augustus, the only child Hervey
ever acknowledged. He grew up to be a charming and impetuous
young man like his father. He joined the navy as a midshipman, but at
the age of eighteen, he was tragically killed in action during the relief
of Gibraltar.

The last great love of Hervey's life was Mrs. Mary Nesbitt. According to an unkind commentator, her origins could be traced to a
wheelbarrow, but her exceptional beauty and bright personality gained
her entrée into society.[7] She married a City banker and, like Kitty
Fisher, was painted by Joshua Reynolds. She was consistently unfaithful to her husband and took up with Hervey around 1770. She was to
remain with him until his death.

Meanwhile, Hervey's wife, the notorious Miss Chudleigh, had become the mistress of the Duke of Kingston. He was a wealthy and

generous man, and she was determined to marry him. It suited her to regard the marriage ceremony she had gone through with Hervey as "such a scrambling shabby business and so much incomplete" that it did not count.[8] In spite of a great deal of society gossip about the true state of affairs, she managed to convince the Ecclesiastical Court that she was a spinster, and in March 1769, she married the duke and became the Duchess of Kingston. Hervey had been contemplating divorcing her anyway and kept his own counsel, but when the Duke of Kingston died four years later, the eldest of his heirs, who had been disinherited, decided to contest his will and challenge the legality of his marriage. The lawyers had a field day, and the former Miss Chudleigh found herself having to face a charge of bigamy.

Hervey had now succeeded to the family title as Earl of Bristol, so the trial had to take place before the House of Lords, because if Miss Chudleigh's marriage to Hervey was legal, she was the Countess of Bristol and if not, she was the Duchess of Kingston. Either way, she was a peeress and must be tried by peers. There was so much interest in the case that the trial had to be moved from the House of Lords to Westminster Hall to accommodate all the spectators. The Queen, the Prince of Wales, and most of London society were present to listen to the arguments for the defense and the prosecution. In the end, the Lords ruled that Miss Chudleigh's marriage to Hervey was legal and that she was therefore guilty of bigamy. However, no action was taken against her. She left for the Continent and died in Paris in 1788.

Hervey had wisely left the country and retreated to Nice during the proceedings. At the time of the trial in 1776, he was fifty-one and a man of wealth and property. He died three years later on December 22, 1779, at the family's London house in St. James's Square.

Hervey's amorous adventures make a fascinating case study, but to what extent was he typical of the naval officers of his day? The evidence suggests that he was unusual in terms of the sheer number of women he slept with, but that in other respects his life was not so different from those of other officers with aristocratic connections and wealth derived from prize money or private incomes. On foreign postings, particularly during periods of peace, many officers enjoyed a glamorous social life. Concerts, dances, and parties on board ship and ashore were a common occurrence. Every ship's crew included one or two men who could play the fiddle, and in the eighteenth century, it was common practice for British warships to have a fife and drum band. Some captains ensured that there were enough musicians on board to make up a small orchestra. This practice was not confined to naval vessels. The larger merchant ships, particularly those carrying passengers, often provided musical entertainment for those on board. William Hickey gives us a vivid glimpse of this in his memoirs, as he describes his experiences aboard the East Indiaman *Plassey* in 1769:

> Each of the ships 5 English, 4 Swedish, 6 French, 4 Danish, 3 Dutch had an excellent band, consisting of every description of wind and martial instruments, the whole striking up the moment the sun appeared above the horizon and continuing to play for an hour. The same thing was done in the evening one hour previous to sunset. I never heard anything that pleased me more.[9]

The lavish parties ashore that Hervey attended were not uncommon, as the wealthier naval officers sometimes entertained on a spectacular scale. In the *Portsmouth Telegraph* of April 7, 1800, there is a description of a party hosted by Admiral Edward Russell on the grounds of a nobleman's house near Lisbon. More than 6,000 guests were entertained, and the focal point of the evening was a large marble fountain in the gardens. Russell had arranged for the fountain to be filled with a traditional punch made from 4 large barrels of brandy, 8 of water, 25,000 lemons, 20 gallons of lime juice, 1,300 pounds of fine white sugar, 5 pounds of grated nutmeg, 300 toasted biscuits, and a cask of Málaga mountain wine. A large canopy was erected over the fountain, and a small boat with a young sailor boy floated among the lemons and grated nutmeg on the surface of the punch. During the evening, the boy rowed around the fountain filling up the cups of the delighted guests.

And as for affairs with local women, Captain Hervey may have been more promiscuous than most, but there were plenty of other sailors who had flings when they went ashore. Apart from the gossip contained in newspapers and in the letters and diaries of contemporaries, there is revealing evidence of naval officers' extramarital affairs in some of their wills. When Admiral Lord Colvill drew up his will in 1767, he made special provisions for his three illegitimate children, Charles, James Alexander, and Sophia. The two boys had been born in England, but Sophia was born in Halifax, Nova Scotia.[10]

An interesting source for the amorous activities of naval officers below the rank of admiral is a volume in the Public Record Office that details the deliberations of a body in charge of providing pensions for naval widows.[11] The full title of this body was "The Court of the Commissioners for Managing the Charity for the Relief of Poor Widows of Commission and Warrant Officers of the Royal Navy." It was set up in 1732 and distributed money that had been deducted from the pay of naval officers. The commissioners met several times a year, and their decisions were duly recorded by a clerk. Usually they were routine, but occasionally, their lordships were faced with a dilemma when two wives applied for the pension of the same man. At the meeting on January 3, 1750, for instance, we find, "Two separate applications of Meliora and Elizabeth Warren claiming each the pension as widow of Thos. Warren late master of the *Invincible*. . . ." At the same meeting, Francis Picton claimed to be the lawful widow of John Picton, late second master of the sloop *Mortar,* but an application was also received from Sarah Picton, who provided proof that she too was his lawful widow. The commissioners also received a petition from Mary Squire and another woman, both claiming they had been married to Captain Matthew Squire, who had been lost on board HMS *Saphire's Prize.*

An examination of the records shows that between 1750 and 1800, there were twenty-two cases in which two wives applied for the pension of the same man. The dead men included three captains, five lieutenants, four masters, two pursers, six boatswains, one surgeon, and one carpenter. The charity commissioners' method of deciding between the claims of two wives was to find out which woman had been the first to marry the sailor in question. As long as she could provide sufficient proof of the date of her marriage, she was awarded the pension, and the second wife went without. The records do not provide enough detail to indicate whether the sailors had married their second wife in a foreign port. The names of all the women concerned are common British names such as Mary, Margaret, Ann, Sarah, and Elizabeth, suggesting no more than that the sailors might have had a second bigamous marriage in Britain or in any overseas port with a British population or British descendants.

The sailors' reputation for casual flings in foreign seaports was well established by the eighteenth century, and there are frequent references to this in pictures and poems. During the wars against Revolutionary France, when the activities of the Royal Navy were constantly in the headlines, there was a spate of caricatures in which sailors were featured. A favorite subject was a picture of a cheery young sailor picking up a pretty girl as he came ashore. The caption invariably made use of a nautical phrase along the lines of "A man-of-war towing a frigate into a harbour." The theme continued to be popular in Victorian times. A charming hand-colored engraving is entitled "The Signal for an Engagement" and consists of two pictures side by side. One shows a sailor in a British seaport with his arm around the waist of a pretty girl, a bonnet tied on her head with ribbons and bows. His other arm holds aloft a purse with his wages as his signal for engagement. The second picture shows a sailor in a tropical setting who is flirting with a dusky maiden adorned with feathers and what appears to be a lion skin. This sailor's signal for engagement is a watch that he dangles before her eyes.[12]

Sea chanties and ballads made much of the sailors' amorous activities in foreign seaports, and some specifically warned young women against falling in love with a sailor. Typical of the genre is one entitled "Advice to Young Maidens in Chusing of Husbands." This began,

> You pretty maids of Greenwich, of high and low degree,
>   Pray never fix your fancys on men that go to sea;

and it went on to remind maidens that being married to a sailor was fraught with problems:

> Besides the many dangers that are upon the seas,
>   When they are on the shore, they will ramble where they please;
> For up and down in sea-port town they court both old and young:
>   They will deceive; do not believe the sailor's flattering tongue.

The poem ended by advising the maiden to fix her fancy on an honest tradesman who would always be around "to take a share in all the care."[13]

Since the majority of sailors were young and unmarried, it was inevitable that they should look for female company whenever they stepped ashore. Jack Cremer, who spent many years as a common seaman in the navy in the mid-eighteenth century, described a lively encounter when his ship sailed into Port Mahon. He went ashore with the ship's carpenter, and they headed for a Spanish brothel situated by an old church. They had plenty to drink and were soon chatting with "two fine, black, swarthy, good-looking girls."[14] The girls had already been booked by two English officers, but Jack and his shipmate did not know this. The girls promised them an hour or two in bed, so they took them back to their ship. Their lovemaking was interrupted by the appearance of the two officers, who demanded the women. The officers drew their swords and a fight ensued, during which Jack grabbed hold of one of the officers around his neck and threatened to kill him. The women promptly disarmed the officers, and Jack and his mate won the day.

On a more peaceable note, we find the naval surgeon Leonard Gillespie recording his liaison with a native woman in his journal. During his stay at the Naval Hospital in Martinique, he fathered two children by a local mulatto girl, whom he refers to simply as Caroline in his journal. It seems likely that she was his servant or housekeeper. The first child he described as "a quadroon boy," whom he baptized and named Leonard. Then on January 2, 1800, he noted, "On this day at eight o'clock A.M. Caroline was delivered of a female child said to be fathered by me."[15] When his time came to leave the island, he left the girl with Caroline and took the boy back to Ireland with him.

WHEN A WARSHIP RETURNED TO HER HOME PORT AT THE END OF A voyage, many captains anchored offshore, and instead of allowing the sailors ashore and risk their deserting, let wives and other women come out to the ship. The same pragmatic approach was often adopted when a ship arrived in a port overseas. Edward Thompson recorded the occasion when his ship visited English Harbor at Antigua in October 1756. In a letter to a friend, he said that every Sunday they had a general visit from the Negro women of the different parts of the island. Although the smells of unwashed seamen, the ship's animals, and foul bilge water should have inured him to most odors, he particularly noted the distinctive scent of the black population of the island:

> But bad smells don't hurt the sailor's appetite, each man possessing a temporary lady, whose pride is her constancy to the man she chooses, and in this particular they strictly so. I have known three

hundred and fifty women sup and sleep on board on a Sunday evening, and return at daybreak to their different plantations.[16]

His impressions of the women on the remote Atlantic island of St. Helena were more favorable. The island itself he thought was romantic beyond description, with the serenest climate he had ever inhaled. He compared it to the island where Circe cast her magic spells over Odysseus and his companions, but it was the women of St. Helena he found even more spellbinding. He described them as delicately fair, with hair like Venus and the Graces. They were so amiable and endearing that he felt no man ever visited St. Helena without leaving his heart with a nymph of the island. He left his heart with one woman whose beauty surpassed all description, "a very Calypso to detain young Telemachus; and so entangle him in the web of love."

Sailors felt much the same way about the young women of the South Sea islands, and in particular Tahiti, which gained a reputation among seamen as an earthly paradise. The British ship *Dolphin*, under the command of Captain Samuel Wallis, had first come across the island in June 1767. Wallis had left England ten months earlier with orders to search for the great southern continent that was believed to lie somewhere in the South Pacific. He had sailed across the Atlantic to South America, where his men had gone ashore and found that the stories of giants in Patagonia were greatly exaggerated (the tallest of the Patagonians proved to be six foot seven, and most were between five foot ten and six feet tall). From Patagonia he sailed through the Straits of Magellan and then headed westward across the Pacific. After six weeks, there was still no sign of land, and some of the sailors were suffering from scurvy.

On the afternoon of June 19, they were running before a strong easterly wind. The sky was clear, but there was a haze obscuring the horizon. At three o'clock that afternoon, they sighted the peaks of several high mountains rising above the haze and altered course toward them. They sailed on through the night, and the next morning they could clearly see the shape of a green and mountainous land before them. As they drew closer, they saw the white surf of the breakers on the reef and counted more than a hundred canoes being paddled toward them. The men in the canoes seemed astonished at the sight of the three-masted sailing ship, but they cheerfully acknowledged the sailors' friendly gestures and one of them threw a plantain branch in the sea as a gesture of peace. After some inconclusive negotiations, the *Dolphin* bore away to the west, her officers looking for a gap in the reef and a safe place to anchor. As they sailed along the coast, they could see hundreds of men, women, and children lining the shore beneath the coconut palms. George Robertson, the thirty-five-year-old master of the *Dolphin*, wrote in his journal that "the country had the most beautiful appearance it is possible to imagine."[17] He noted that there was a coastal strip two or three miles deep that was laid out in plantations, among which were houses resembling long barns, all very neatly thatched. Beyond the houses and the pastures, the mountains soared up into the clouds, their slopes thickly covered with a dense foliage of tall trees.

For several days, the *Dolphin* proceeded cautiously along the coast, pausing every now and again to trade with the hundreds of canoes that accompanied their progress. Robertson reckoned that one morning there were nearly 4,000 men in the canoes lying around their ship. In several canoes there were young women whose beauty and provocative gestures attracted the open admiration of the young sailors. The men in the canoes were quick to spot this and endeavored to use the women as decoys to enable them to board the ship or entice the sailors ashore. The British were desperate to stock up on food and water, but attempts to go ashore in boats were hampered by the jostling and jeering men in the canoes. There were several ugly incidents, in one of which the Tahitians began pelting the ship with stones, and it was not until the British had demonstrated the firepower of their muskets and cannon and had killed and wounded several Tahitian men that an uneasy truce was called.

On June 25, the *Dolphin* dropped anchor in five fathoms of water in a great curving bay that was sheltered by the outlying reef. This was Matavai Bay, which Robertson thought was "as fine a bay as any in the world" and was later to be one of the favorite anchorages of Captain Cook. There was a river at the head of the bay, and the water there was as calm as a millpond, so the sailors could beach their boats and keep their firearms dry as they jumped ashore. At night, the air was filled with the sweet smells of tropical flowers and vegetation.

With the ship safely anchored, relations with the islanders rapidly improved. This was due in large part to the young women of the island, who were encouraged by the older men to fraternize with the sailors. Robertson described the sailors' first encounter with the women when a boat from the *Dolphin* was eventually able to land on the beach.

> But our young men seeing several very handsome young girls, they could not help feasting their eyes with so agreeable a sight. This was observed by some of the elderly men, and several of the young girls was drawn out, some a light copper colour, others a mulatto and some almost white. The old men made them stand in rank, and made signs for our people to take which they like best, and as many as they liked and for fear our men had been ignorant and not known how to use the poor young girls, the old men made signs how we should behave to the young women. This all the boats crew seemed to understand perfectly and begged the officer would receive a few of the young women on board.[18]

The sailors made signs to the girls that they were not so ignorant as the old men supposed, which pleased the old men, "but the poor young girls seemed a little afraid, but soon after turned better acquainted."

The officer in charge of the landing party had no orders to bring any of the natives aboard, so he indicated to the women that they would return soon and ordered his men back into the boat. Back on the *Dolphin*, all the sailors swore that they had never seen handsomer women in their lives and declared they would rather take a two-thirds cut in their daily allowance than lose the opportunity of having a girl apiece. Wallis bowed to the inevitable, and soon the sailors were exchanging presents with the young women and getting acquainted. The Tahitians, like most of the South Sea islanders, particularly valued the iron nails, hatchets, and other metal objects that the British had on their ship and used every opportunity to steal them. They were now able to get as much iron as they wanted by bartering their women. The sailors found that one nail was generally the price exacted by the women for their sexual favors. The trade became so brisk that one of the carpenters reported to Robertson that every iron cleat on the ship was gone and that most of the men had abandoned their hammocks and were sleeping on the deck because their hammock nails had been removed.

By the time the *Dolphin* set sail on July 27, six weeks after first sighting Tahiti, the initial hostilities between the islanders and the

British had been replaced by the warmest friendships on both sides. When the *Dolphin* returned to England in May 1768, Captain Wallis reported that Tahiti was an ideal base in the Pacific for provisioning ships. It had plentiful supplies of food, wood, and fresh water, it had sheltered bays and safe anchorages, and it had friendly inhabitants. The Admiralty and the Royal Society, which were preparing a scientific expedition to the South Seas, decided that Tahiti would make an ideal location for observing the transit of Venus across the sun—an exercise that would help to determine the distance of the Sun from the Earth.

On April 5, 1769, two years after the *Dolphin*'s visit, the converted collier *Endeavour*, under the command of Captain James Cook, dropped anchor in Matavai Bay. The activities of the *Endeavour*'s artists, astronomers, and naturalists on this, the first of Cook's great voyages of exploration, established the reputation of Tahiti as a paradise on earth.[19] The drawings of Sydney Parkinson and the observations of the sailors confirmed the handsome appearance of the inhabitants. Joseph Banks, the wealthy young scientist who accompanied Cook, had needed little persuasion to take one of the Tahitian women as his mistress during the three months of the *Endeavour*'s visit, and he later wrote:

> In the island of Otaheiti where Love is the chief occupation, the favourite, nay almost the sole luxury of the inhabitants; both the bodies and souls of the women are modelled into the utmost perfection for that soft science; idleness the father of Love reigns here in almost unmolested ease. . . .[20]

The reputation of the Tahitian women was confirmed by the visits of French explorers, most notably that by Louis de Bougainville, who dropped anchor some miles to the east of Matavai Bay on April 2, 1768, less than a year after the departure of HMS *Dolphin*. Bougainville was a former soldier and diplomat who was later to achieve international renown when he published his book *Voyage autour du monde*, a detailed description of the discoveries made during his circumnavigation. He was accompanied on his voyage by an astronomer and by Philibert Commerson, a naturalist and distinguished member of the Académie des Sciences, who unwittingly added another female sailor to the list of those that have been recorded. Commerson

had a youth traveling with him as his valet, and it was not until they
reached Tahiti that he discovered his valet was a woman. Her name
was Jeanne Bare, and she had managed to deceive all the men on
board; but when they landed at Tahiti, the islanders saw through her
disguise at once.[21]

Bougainville spent no more than ten days in Tahiti, but it was long
enough for him to be entirely beguiled by the place. He named it New
Cythera after the Greek island where Venus, the goddess of love, first
arose from the waves. He thought the climate was the most perfect in
the world: "Nature herself dictated the laws. The inhabitants follow
them in peace and constitute perhaps the happiest society which the
world knows." As for the men and women, they were like Greek gods
and goddesses. "I never saw men better made, and whose limbs were
more proportionate," he wrote, "in order to paint Hercules or a Mars,
one could nowhere find such beautiful models." On one occasion, a
young Tahitian woman was standing on the deck of his ship next to the
capstan. She negligently let fall her robe, "and stood for all to see, as
Venus stood forth before the Phrygian shepherd; and she had the ce-
lestial shape of Venus. The sailors rushed to get at the hatchway, and
never was a capstan turned with such eagerness."[22]

Twenty years after the visits of Cook and Bougainville, Captain
Bligh arrived at Tahiti in HMS *Bounty*. He had first seen the island in
1777 when he was master of the *Resolution* on Cook's third voyage,
and this time he fell completely under its spell. A strict and demanding
captain when at sea, he fatally allowed himself and his crew to relax
under the benevolent influence of the island's climate and her carefree
people. The purpose of the *Bounty*'s voyage was to take the seedlings
of the breadfruit tree that grew in such profusion in Tahiti and transport them to the British colonies in the West Indies, where it was believed they would provide food for the slaves working on the
plantations. The *Bounty* was equipped with special racks to accommodate several hundred flowerpots, and as soon as she was safely anchored in Matavai Bay, and greetings and gifts had been exchanged
with the islanders, Bligh set his botanists to cultivating a nursery garden on Point Venus. During the five months it took to cultivate the
seedlings and transfer them to the flowerpots, the *Bounty*'s crew enjoyed the delights of the island, and in particular the young women,
whom they found to be every bit as attractive and willing as they had

been led to believe. While Bligh remained faithful to his wife, Fletcher Christian and several other members of the crew took up permanent residence ashore and formed liaisons with Tahitian women that were to last beyond the mutiny. Christian, the master's mate, was twenty-five years old and was the son of a Cumberland lawyer. He had a cheerful, handsome face, a lively manner, and considerable charm. A former shipmate remarked that he was "a great man for the women." He was renowned for his physical strength, but he was also subject to black moods of depression on occasion. After making love to several of the Tahitian girls, he settled on an outstandingly beautiful young woman named Mauatua, who was the daughter of a chief. He renamed her Isabella, and she remained his partner until his violent death several months later.

The *Bounty* sailed from Tahiti on April 4, 1789, loaded with more than a thousand breadfruit plants and a crew that had become soft and lazy. Three of the men had attempted to desert some weeks earlier, and nearly half the crew were suffering from venereal disease. Bligh made strenuous efforts to restore discipline, but he lacked the natural authority that had enabled Cook to take his crews through thick and thin with scarcely a murmur of discontent. Bligh was a small man with a quick temper, a sarcastic tongue, and a habit of humiliating his officers in front of the men. Within three weeks of leaving Tahiti, he had provoked Christian beyond endurance, and at daybreak on April 28 a mutiny broke out that led to Bligh being cast adrift in an open launch with eighteen of the crew.

While Bligh made his way across 4,000 miles of ocean to Batavia, the mutineers led by Christian sailed the *Bounty* to the island of Tubai. There they experienced a situation similar to Wallis's first encounter with the Tahitians. The islanders came out in canoes and swarmed over the ship stealing any loose items they could lay their hands on. They were driven off the ship by the mutineers, but the next morning a canoe came alongside with eighteen young women escorted by five men. The women had been deliberately chosen for their beauty, and like the Tahitian girls, they had dark, lustrous eyes and manes of fine black hair that fell to their waists. While the women occupied the attention of the *Bounty*'s crew, the Tubaians launched their attack. Fifty canoes manned by armed warriors converged on the ship. Christian ordered the guns to be loaded with grapeshot and fired into the canoes at point-blank range. In the resulting carnage, a dozen islanders were killed, many more were wounded, and the rest fled back to the shore. It was an ominous beginning for the mutineers in their search for a place of refuge. They named the spot Bloody Bay, and although they landed and began work on building a fort, they decided after a few weeks that they should return to Tahiti. According to mutineer John Adams, "We lacked women and remembering Tahiti, where all of us had made intimate friendships, we decided to return there, so that we could each obtain one."[23] So they sailed back to Tahiti and dropped anchor in Matavai Bay on June 6, 1789. They dared not stay too long, because they knew that the navy would send a warship to track them down and Tahiti would be the first place they would look, so they loaded the *Bounty* with goats, hogs, and chickens and persuaded four of the Tahitian women and seventeen men and boys to accompany them. They also tricked seven more women into coming with them by luring them aboard and then weighing anchor before they could get ashore.

For the next six months, the mutineers roved the Pacific seeking a suitable island paradise where they could settle with their women. In the end, Christian decided to head for Pitcairn Island. He had found a description of it in a volume of Hawkesworth's *Voyages,* and its remote location some 3,000 miles east of Tahiti seemed promising. It took them two months to find it, but at last its rocky profile was spotted on the horizon. On January 18, 1790, they dropped anchor in an exposed bay, later to be called Bounty Bay, and sent an armed party ashore in the cutter. The island seemed ideal for their purpose. It had rich soil, abundant fruit and water, numerous fish in the surrounding seas, and a pleasant climate. It was uninhabited, so they did not have to contend with attacks from hostile natives. And it was unlikely the navy would find them there because it had been incorrectly charted.

They unloaded the ship, built themselves simple houses on a small plateau above the bay, and set about planting crops. For the first few months all seemed to be well, but problems were brewing. There were rivalries and resentments among the mutineers, and Christian, who was racked with guilt at provoking the mutiny, proved to be a moody and ineffective leader. The Tahitian women were strong and capable but were homesick for their friends and families. More serious was the resentment felt by the men from Tahiti and Tubai, who were treated as servants and laborers, and had to share three women among five of them. When one mutineer's woman died, he insisted on taking one of the three women, which infuriated her husband. Plottings and killings followed, culminating in a bloody massacre one hot afternoon in which five of the mutineers were shot or battered to death by the Polynesians. Christian was shot in the back of the head while he was digging in his garden, and his face was smashed in with an axe. The bloodshed did not end there. The Tahitian women were distraught and angry at the murder of their white husbands and took revenge on their fellow islanders. The Tahitian woman named Jenny later described how two of the Tahitian men were lying in the sun outside one of the houses at noon, when "one of the women took a hatchet and cleft the skull of the latter; at the same instance calling out to Young to fire which he did, and shot the other native dead."[24] Within the space of a few days, no fewer than eleven of the fifteen men who had arrived on Pitcairn had met a violent end. The population of the island was reduced to two white men, eleven grieving Polynesian women, and several children.

The mutineers' dream of ending their days on an island paradise with their women ended in carnage and disillusion. But thanks to the subsequent reporting of the mutiny and the various films that have been based on the story, it is the confrontation between Captain Bligh and Fletcher Christian that has fascinated subsequent generations—this, and the exotic images of Tahiti and those lovely young women with hibiscus flowers in their hair, which made such an impression on all the sailors whose ships dropped anchor in Matavai Bay.

12

Two Naval Heroes and Their Women

IT IS HARD TO FIND ANOTHER BRITISH SAILOR WITH A WOMANIZING record equal to that of Augustus Hervey, but the American navy's most famous sailor also acquired a considerable reputation as a ladies' man. Like Hervey's, his later life was overshadowed by scandal. John Paul Jones never married, but he clearly adored women and they in turn found him attractive, particularly after he became a naval hero. He has often been compared to Nelson, and there were indeed many similarities. They were both slight in build and small in stature but were fiercely ambitious and recklessly brave. They both went to sea at an early age (Nelson at twelve and Jones at thirteen) and assumed command of ships while in their early twenties. They both had an instinctive grasp of battle tactics and a killer instinct when confronting the enemy. They were inspirational leaders in action, refusing to accept defeat when all seemed lost, and encouraging their men to fight until the enemy was annihilated or forced to surrender. They both achieved spectacular victories that made them famous across Europe, though the British never acknowledged Jones's achievements. Smarting from the military defeats they had suffered during the American Revolution, the British were outraged by his audacious attacks on their shipping and persisted in regarding him as a rebel and a pirate. Jones's misfortune as a commander was that he never had the opportunity to lead a fleet into battle and had to content himself with small-scale actions involving three or four ships. Nevertheless, for the generations of American seamen who followed him, his words and deeds continued to be an inspiration.

Like many of America's most famous sons, John Paul Jones was an immigrant. He was born in Scotland on July 6, 1747, the fourth of five children.[1] His father was a gardener on an estate at Arbigland on the shores of the Solway Firth. His mother was Jean Macduff, the daughter of a local farmer. In 1761, John Paul was apprenticed as a mariner and went to sea as a ship's boy on the brig *Friendship*. The brig sailed from Whitehaven and crossed the Atlantic to Barbados. There she took on a cargo of rum and sugar and headed north to Hampton, Virginia, where she arrived in May 1761. From Hampton, the *Friendship* sailed up Chesapeake Bay to Fredericksburg, where John Paul was reunited with his eldest brother, William, who had set himself up as a tailor there.

For the next seven years, John Paul continued to sail to and fro across the Atlantic on merchant ships trading between Whitehaven, the West Indies, and the American east coast. He completed his apprenticeship, and in 1768, at the age of twenty-one, he was appointed master of the 60-ton brig *John* of Liverpool. His first voyage as a ship's captain was from the Scottish port of Kirkcudbright to Kingston, Jamaica. His second voyage was to the Windward Islands. In 1772, he took command of a larger ship, the *Betsy*, and his voyages in her took him from London to Ireland, Madeira, and Tobago and back. On his second voyage he ran into major trouble. At Tobago, his crew became mutinous when he refused to advance them their wages. The ringleader, a powerful man who had proved insolent on the outward voyage, attacked John Paul with a blunt instrument and drove him into his cabin. John Paul picked up his sword and in the ensuing scuffle ran the man through and killed him. He went ashore at once and offered to give himself up to the local justice of the peace. Although he would undoubtedly have been cleared by an Admiralty court, John Paul was advised by his friends to flee the island before the local people decided to avenge the death of the man he had killed. He took passage in a local vessel, and nothing is known of his movements for the next year and

a half. When he reappeared on the scene, he had changed his name
from John Paul to John Paul Jones.

In December 1775, he joined the American navy. The country was
on the verge of the war with Britain that would culminate in American independence. Congress had appointed George Washington commander in chief of the newly created Continental Army and had
issued orders for the creation of a navy. At this stage in its existence,
the entire American navy, then called the Continental Navy, consisted
of two ships, two brigs, three sloops, and a schooner. They were all
converted merchant vessels. The British navy at this date had 400 ships
of the line and 800 frigates, brigs, and sloops.

John Paul Jones was appointed first lieutenant of the 20-gun ship
Alfred. At 350 tons, and with a crew of 220 men, she was the largest
vessel in the hastily convened fleet. The *Alfred*'s first operation was to
sail in company with three other American ships to the Bahamas. The
aim was to capture gunpowder and weapons for Washington's army
from the British base at Nassau. There were no troops or warships to
defend the island of New Providence, and so the American ships were
able to take Nassau without a fight and come away with eighty-eight
guns and a useful supply of powder and ammunition. A month later,
on April 6, 1776, the American squadron encountered the British warship *Glasgow,* 20 guns, near Block Island and went into action. After a
two-hour battle that was notable for the energetic but inaccurate gunfire on both sides, the *Glasgow* was forced to break off the fight and
retreat to Newport. The first naval action of the American Revolution
was declared a glorious victory by the American press and by Congress. Soon afterward, John Paul Jones was given command of the
sloop *Providence* with the temporary rank of captain. In August 1776,
he headed out from the Delaware Capes and in less than five weeks
had captured seven merchant ships belonging to Britain or her
colonies.

In October 1776, Jones was back on the *Alfred,* this time as her
commander. His orders were to raid Cape Breton and capture British
ships. Again he showed a ferocious appetite for action. He captured
three merchant ships and an armed transport ship and sent boats into
the port of Canso, where his men set fire to a British supply ship and
captured a small schooner. He went on to capture three colliers off
Louisbourg, and a British privateer. Heading back south with his string

of prizes, he encountered the frigate HMS *Milford* off Cape Cod. In the ensuing action, the British ship managed to recapture the privateer, but Jones escaped with his remaining prizes and returned to Massachusetts Bay.

Jones spent the winter of 1776 in Boston, staying in a tavern. On June 14, 1777, Congress appointed him commander of the *Ranger*, 18 guns. She was one of the new ships built for what was now called the United States Navy. Compared with the ships in which Nelson made his reputation she was tiny, but she was sufficient for Jones's purpose. He sailed her across the Atlantic to France, where Britain's old enemy helped him outfit the ship for an ambitious raid on shipping in British waters. While the *Ranger*'s rig and armament were being overhauled in a French dockyard at Paimboef, Jones embarked on a love affair with Madame Thérèse de Chaumont, the wife of a French entrepreneur who had made a fortune in the East India trade and bought a château on the Loire and a magnificent town house in Passy. Monsieur de Chaumont owned a fleet of merchant ships, and in addition to procuring supplies for the French navy, he had negotiated with Benjamin Franklin, the American commissioner in Paris, to supply the American navy. He invited Jones to stay in his town house, and when he went away on a business trip, Jones took the opportunity to make love to Madame de Chaumont. This was by no means Jones's first affair, but it was the first of a number of relationships he was to have with rich or well-born ladies in France.

In February 1778, he set off from Brest, captured two ships in the Irish Sea, and then led a raid on his old port of Whitehaven in Scotland. Anchoring off the harbor, he took two boat parties of armed men ashore. They spiked the guns of the battery that protected the entrance to the port and then set fire to a collier in the harbor before heading back to the ship. He then sailed across the Solway Firth to St. Mary's Isle with the aim of taking hostage the Earl of Selkirk. Unfortunately, the earl was away and Jones's men were faced by a resolute Lady Selkirk. Rather than come away empty-handed, they ordered her to hand over the family silver, and she reluctantly agreed to do so.

News of the raid spread like wildfire and caused panic along the coast. Although there had been no loss of life and the damage inflicted was minimal, it was the audacity of the raid that upset the British, who had not experienced an enemy attack on their coast since the Dutch raid on the Medway in 1667. The Admiralty ordered warships in the Irish Sea to hunt down the *Ranger,* and on April 24, Jones encountered HMS *Drake,* 16 guns, in the seas off Belfast. A fierce battle took place. After an hour of heated exchanges, the captain of the British ship was killed, his first lieutenant mortally wounded, and the ship surrendered. She was so badly damaged that Jones took her in tow until his men could repair her rig. On May 8, the *Ranger* entered the French port of Brest together with the captured British warship flying the British colors inverted under the American Stars and Stripes. Jones's brief cruise of twenty-eight days was a major propaganda coup for the Americans, and although his achievements attracted little attention in France, he became a notorious figure in England, where he was the subject of much alarmist gossip and wicked caricatures.

In February 1779, Jones was given command of the *Bonhomme Richard,* a former French East Indiaman of 40 guns that was being outfitted at Lorient. He was also put in charge of six other vessels and was able to style himself "the Honorable Captain John P. Jones, Commander in Chief of the American Squadron in Europe." In August he set sail with his squadron, and the subsequent raids in the British Isles were to be the most spectacular exploits of his career. During the course of his cruise around Ireland and Scotland, he captured half a dozen merchant ships. He sailed up the Firth of Forth and was only prevented from attacking Leith by a westerly gale that forced him to bear away. He headed south looking for more prizes, and on September 23, he sighted a fleet of ships off Flamborough Head. It proved to be a convoy of some forty merchant ships from the Baltic escorted by two British warships: the *Serapis,* 44 guns, and the *Countess of Scarborough,* a sloop of 20 guns.

The subsequent Battle of Flamborough Head centered around a heroic duel between the *Bonhomme Richard* and the *Serapis,* commanded by Captain Pearson. It was a duel that lasted three hours and cost the lives of more than 150 men. The action began about 7:20 P.M., and the booming explosions attracted a crowd of spectators to the nearby cliffs. By eight o'clock, the sun had set and most of the battle took place by the cold light of a full moon. Apart from the *Pallas,* which engaged the *Countess of Scarborough* and after a sporadic action forced her to surrender, the other ships in Jones's squadron took little part in the action. Indeed, the *Alliance,* commanded by Captain Pierre

Landais, a mad and malevolent Frenchman, fired on Jones's ship a number of times and killed several of his men.

Jones's aim was to engage the *Serapis* at close quarters and board her, because he soon realized that she was faster and better armed and would pound him to pieces if he let her fire broadsides into the elderly hull of the *Bonhomme Richard*. After an hour of ferocious gunfire in which each captain tried to gain the most advantageous position, the two ships became locked together. Captain Pearson, observing the damage that his broadsides had inflicted, shouted across, "Has your ship struck?" to which John Paul Jones made the famous reply, "I have not yet begun to fight."

By the end of the second hour, the *Bonhomme Richard* was so battered that she seemed in danger of sinking. One of Jones's men approached him and pleaded, "For God's sake, Captain, strike!" to which Jones answered, "No, I will sink, I will never strike." At half past ten, Captain Pearson tore down his red ensign and surrendered. A few minutes later, the mainmast of his ship came crashing to the deck. Both ships were devastated by the battle, but the *Bonhomme Richard* was leaking so badly that she had to be abandoned and later sank. Jones transferred his flag to the *Serapis*. When news of the battle reached the Admiralty in London, a squadron of five warships was dispatched from Spithead to pursue Jones, but he eluded them and sailed the two captured British ships and the rest of his squadron to Holland, where they dropped anchor in the roadstead of the Texel.

The victory of John Paul Jones was warmly received in America, caused an outcry in Britain, and made him a hero in France. Benjamin Franklin wrote to him from Paris saying that "scarce anything was talked of at Paris and Versailles but your cool conduct and persevering bravery during the terrible conflict."[2]

During May, Jones found himself lionized in the French capital. He stayed there six weeks as the guest of Benjamin Franklin's secretary, Dr. Edward Bancroft. He had become a celebrity, cheered by people in the streets and acclaimed on his visits to the opera. He was taken to Versailles and met the King, who presented him with a gold-hilted sword engraved with a Latin motto that translated read, "Louis XVI rewards the stout vindicator of the freedom of the seas." The King also promised to invest him as a Chevalier of the Order of Military Merit, which Jones later received after the American Congress had agreed to his accepting a foreign order. Jean-Antoine Houdon, the leading sculptor of France, was commissioned to make a portrait bust, which was exhibited in the Paris Salon and remains the finest of the many likenesses that were subsequently made of him.

What made his stay in France most enjoyable was his reception by so many beautiful women. We learn from Caroline Edes, an English journalist, that "He is greatly admired here, especially by the ladies, who are all wild for love of him, as he for them, but he adores Lady —— who has honored him with every mark of politeness and attention."[3] The lady in question was Madame la Comtesse de Lowendahl, the twenty-six-year-old daughter of a prince of the royal blood. According to Edes, she was blessed with "youth, beauty and wit, and every other female accomplishment." She was also married to a brigadier general, and though she was happy to be courted by the dashing naval hero, she was not prepared to go to bed with him. He wrote flattering and elegant letters to her, and she painted a most accomplished portrait miniature of him but eventually tired of his pursuit of her and ended their relationship.

He fared very differently with Delia, Comtesse de Nicolson. She came from a Scottish family and had married Count William Murray, also a Scot. They had a château near Pontoise and a house in a fashionable part of Paris. Jones met her in May 1780 and spent five passionate days with her at Hennebont, a few miles from the port of Lorient. Several of her letters to Jones have been preserved, and indicate the strength of her love for him:

> My angel, my adorable Jones! When shall we meet never to be separated? . . . I feel that I never lived except those five days which passed, alas, like a dream . . . I have little thought of my fortune. I cannot render you happy with it, nor live with you in an opulent manner; for me a cabin and my lover, and I would be too happy![4]

When she learned that Jones was having difficulty raising the money to pay his crew, she offered to help: "In the name of all the love with which I am consumed, command me if I can be useful. I have diamonds and effects of various kinds; I could easily find a sum: command your mistress, it would make her happy." And in another letter, she said that rather than lose him she would willingly be the lowest member of his crew. While Jones returned her love with affection, he was still besotted by the beautiful Madame de Lowendahl, and his affair with the Comtesse de Nicolson ended when he put to sea in September. These two love affairs did not prevent him from dallying with other women. While his new command, the *Ariel*, was being outfitted at Lorient, he spent a night with the pretty seventeen-year-old wife of James Moylan, an elderly Irish merchant. On another occasion, he took a prostitute to the theater and then went back to her lodgings. He also kept up the naval tradition of generous hospitality by organizing a "Grand Entertainment" on board his ship, which was attended by a prince, three admirals, and numerous ladies of quality.

The pleasant interlude in France came to an abrupt end on September 5, 1780, when Jones sailed from Lorient in the *Ariel*. Fierce gales forced him to spend a month anchored in Groix Roads, and when he finally put to sea on October 7, his ship was dismasted in a gale and nearly wrecked on the Penmarch Rocks. He put back in to Lorient for repairs and then sailed across the Atlantic to the West Indies, where he had an abortive encounter with a British privateer. From the Caribbean, he sailed north and arrived in Philadelphia on February 18, 1781. However successful Jones was as a man of action, he lacked the diplomatic skill necessary to win influential friends and secure the promotion he felt he deserved. He also failed to gain command of the newly built ship *America*, which he dearly wanted. After much lobbying, he did persuade his masters to send him back to Europe to recover the prize money due to the officers of the *Bonhomme Richard, Alliance,* and *Ranger.* Congress agreed to his request, and he sailed from Philadelphia on November 10, 1783.

Back in Paris, he found a place to stay in Montmartre and renewed his political and social contacts. He met the French minister of marine and the French foreign minister. He was presented to the King again, and he saw a great deal of Benjamin Franklin, who was minister plenipotentiary. He was still regarded as a hero in French society, and while carrying out the lengthy negotiations for the prize money, he was entertained by a wide circle of people. Marie-Louise-Elisabeth Vigée-Lebrun, the painter, often dined with him and thought she had never met a more modest man: "It was impossible to make him talk about his great deeds; but on any other subject he conversed freely with great wit and without affection."[5] He also had an affair with a lady he refers to in his memoirs as Madame T——, who claimed to be the daughter of King Louis XV but is now known to have been a Mrs. Townsend, the widow of an Englishman. She was to be his mistress for the next few years and gave birth to a son during this period, probably his although he never publicly acknowledged this.

Unlike Nelson, whose life ended in a blaze of glory at Trafalgar, the life of John Paul Jones went steadily downhill following his first triumphant visit to Paris after the heroic action off Flamborough Head. His second visit to Paris lasted three years, but however pleasant his social life, his naval career was effectively at an end. All his efforts to achieve the rank of admiral in the American navy and the French navy came to nothing, and he was never given command of another ship in the navies he had served so well. He was eventually recommended to Catherine the Great of Russia, who appointed him rear admiral of the Imperial Russian Navy in 1788. He traveled to St. Petersburg to meet the Empress and then on to the Black Sea, where he raised his flag on the Russian ship *Vladimir* and took charge of the squadron there. He was then forty-one, and in spite of the disappointments of the preceding five years, he made a good impression on the Russian seamen. One sailor said, "He was dressed like all of us, but his weapons were excellent. He was of brave appearance; his hair was a little gray but he was still strong, fit for work and full of keen understanding of our task."[6]

In June 1788, he led the Russian fleet into action against a Turkish fleet at Liman at the mouth of the Dnieper River. The first battle of Liman was indecisive. Two weeks later, the second battle took place. In a confused and bloody mêlée in which many of the Turkish vessels ran aground, the Russian fleet gained a decisive victory. The Turks lost fifteen vessels, with 3,000 men killed and 1,673 taken prisoner. The Russians lost only one frigate, with 18 killed and 67 wounded. The victory owed much to the strategy of John Paul Jones, but it was a Russian admiral who got the credit. It was Jones's last action. He was awarded a minor order and shortly afterward retired to St. Petersburg. There he lived in some style. He took an apartment in a house near the Admiralty building and made social calls and went to parties. His household consisted of an interpreter, a manservant, a Russian seaman orderly, and a peasant coachman. Then in April 1789, his world fell apart when the police reported that he had attempted to rape a ten-year-old girl, Katerina Goltzwart. She was the daughter of a German immigrant who ran a dairy nearby, and she delivered milk to Jones's apartment and other houses in the neighborhood. The numerous versions of the story have been meticulously examined by Jones's most distinguished biographer, Samuel Eliot Morison. His conclusions are that Jones did have sexual contact with her but not full sexual intercourse, and that Jones's protestations that he would not use force on a woman and did not take her virginity are likely to be the truth. In a remarkably frank statement to the chief of police, Jones admitted that she had come to his house several times before, and he had always given her money: "I thought her to be several years older than Your Excellency says she is, and each time that she came to my house she lent herself very amiably to do all that a man would want of her." Whatever the truth of the matter, Jones found himself spurned by most of his friends and acquaintances in St. Petersburg.

He had a final audience with the Empress in June 1789, and in August he left Russia and traveled via Warsaw, Vienna, Amsterdam, and London to Paris, where he took an apartment at 52 rue de Tournon, near the Palais de Luxembourg. Many of his aristocratic friends had fled the country, which was in the grip of revolution. The King and Queen had been ejected from Versailles by the Paris mob and were confined to the Tuileries. John Paul Jones spent his time writing letters, almost alone in the city that a few years earlier had fêted him as a hero. He suffered from jaundice, contracted bronchial pneumonia, and on July 18, 1792, died at the age of forty-five. A quiet funeral took place two days later in a nearby cemetery. The coffin was preceded by a detachment of grenadiers from the gendarmerie. It was perhaps all that could be expected in view of the conditions in Paris at the time, but it was in stark contrast to the magnificent funeral that was staged for Nelson after his death at the Battle of Trafalgar.

THE MOST FAMOUS OF ALL SAILORS' WOMEN MUST SURELY BE LADY Hamilton. Her very public affair with Admiral Nelson delighted the gossipmongers of the day and provided a rich subject for the cartoonists. It has continued to be a source of fascination and has been the inspiration for numerous books, a distinguished play, and several films, notably *That Hamilton Woman,* in which the part of Nelson was played by Laurence Olivier and that of Lady Hamilton by Vivien Leigh. In the process, the love affair has been romanticized and has taken on a mythic quality that it never had at the time. The fact is that when Nelson and Lady Hamilton met in Naples after the Battle of the Nile, they could scarcely have been more different from the attractive figures portrayed in *That Hamilton Woman*.[7] Nelson was only thirty-nine years old, but he was exhausted by pain and the responsibilities of command. His hair was gray, his cheeks were sunken, and he rarely smiled. His right arm had been amputated, and he had the empty sleeve of his coat pinned across his chest. "He looks very old," wrote Lord Elgin, "has lost his upper teeth, sees ill of one eye, and has a film coming over both of them."[8] A German observer thought he was one of the most insignificant figures he had ever seen, "a more miserable collection of bones and wizened frame I have yet to come across."

Lady Hamilton was no longer the young woman whose face and figure had attracted the attention of princes and aristocrats and had inspired painters and poets. She was thirty-three and had put on a great deal of weight. A Swedish diplomat remarked that she was the fattest woman he had ever laid eyes on but thought she had the most beautiful head. James Harris, a young English aristocrat who saw her when her affair with Nelson had become common knowledge, considered her to be "without exception the most coarse, ill-mannered, disagreeable woman I ever met with."

So what did these two people see in each other? Nelson's outward appearance may have been unimpressive, but he had a simple directness in his speech, a boldness in his manner, and a lively animation of countenance that charmed both men and women. The son of a Norfolk parson, he had gone to sea at the age of twelve and had seen active service in the West Indies. While a young captain stationed in the Leeward Isles, he had met and married Fanny Nisbet on the island of Nevis. She was a twenty-seven-year-old widow with a young son. The daughter of a judge, she would have made an ideal wife for a lawyer, a doctor, or a parson (indeed she was to get on famously with Nelson's father). She was poised and ladylike with refined good looks and a genteel air, but she was not the most suitable wife for a sailor, particularly one with a genius for battle and a thirst for glory. She was lonely and unhappy when Nelson was away at sea and frequently urged him not to put his life in danger: "I sincerely hope, dear husband, that all these wonderful and desperate actions such as boarding ships you will leave to others."[9] This was a reference to Nelson's actions at the Battle of Cape St. Vincent in 1797, when he made his name in spectacular fashion by his unorthodox tactics. As commodore of the 74-gun ship *Captain*, he had pulled his ship out of the line of battle to prevent the escape of the Spanish ships. He ranged his ship alongside the 80-gun ship *San Nicolas*, led a boarding party that succeeded in capturing her, and then took his men across her decks to the huge Spanish ship *San Josef*, which had become locked alongside. At the fierceness of his attack, her officers surrendered, and the action became immortalized as "Nelson's patent bridge for boarding first-rates." His daring exploits were rewarded with a knighthood and promotion to rear admiral in command of the British fleet in the Mediterranean.

The following year, he tracked down the French fleet that was anchored in a strong defensive position in Aboukir Bay near the mouth of the Nile. In the late afternoon of August 1, 1798, he sighted the French masts. Instead of conducting a reconnaissance and preparing to attack the next morning, he sailed headlong into the bay and caught the French off guard. The battle began around 6:30 P.M., and within two hours five of the French ships had surrendered. At ten o'clock, the French flagship *L'Orient* blew up, and the battle continued until the early hours of the next morning. Nine French ships of the line were captured, and only two escaped. It was one of the most complete and devastating naval victories of all time. Nelson was wounded above his blind eye and thought his hour had come. "I am killed. Remember me to my wife," he said as he was led below to the surgeon.[10] But the wound proved to be relatively minor, and he was able to dictate a report of the action to his superiors.

News of the victory resounded across Europe and was received with relief and joy in Naples. Lady Hamilton, who had met Nelson briefly some years before when he was an unknown captain, was so overcome with emotion that she fell to the ground. When she recovered, she dashed off a letter to the admiral. Her eccentric spelling betrayed her lack of formal education but her sentiments shine through:

> My dear, dear Sir,
> 　　How shall I begin, what shall I say to you. 'tis impossible I can write, for since last Monday I am delirious with joy,

and assur you I have a fervour caused by agitation and pleasure. God, what a victory! Never, never has there been anything half so glorious, so compleat. I fainted when I heard
the joyful news, and fell on my side and am hurt, but well of
that, I shou'd feil it a glory to die in such a cause. No, I wou'd
not like to die till I see and embrace the Victor of the
Nile. . . .[11]

And embrace him she did. Nelson's flagship, the *Agamemnon*, arrived in Naples three weeks after the battle, and Lady Hamilton and
her husband were among the first to greet him. They were taken out
to the anchored flagship in a boat. As soon as they were alongside,
Lady Hamilton hurried aboard and fell into Nelson's arms exclaiming,
"Oh, God, is it possible." She was dazzled by his fame and wanted
nothing more than to share in his glory. And the welcome Nelson received that day was like the victorious homecoming of a Roman general. The whole town turned out to greet the conquering hero. The
local people let loose flocks of birds from wicker cages as a traditional
celebration of victory, and the bay echoed with the stirring sounds of
bands playing their own versions of "Rule, Britannia!" and "God Save
the King." The King of Naples came out to greet Nelson in his royal
yacht, which was decorated with colorful awnings and emblems.
Dozens of local craft filled the bay, with people on board cheering and
hailing Nelson as their liberator.

Sir William Hamilton invited Nelson to stay at his house, and
gratefully Nelson retired to a room in the ambassador's residence
overlooking the bay. In addition to the pain of his head wound, he was
suffering from a recurrence of the malaria that he had contracted in the
West Indies. Lady Hamilton took charge of nursing him, a role she delighted in and was to be a feature of their future relationship. When he
was able to get up and about, she continued to fuss over him, and later
when they toured Europe together, she would lead him by the hand,
cut up his food for him at meals, and treat him as if he were still an invalid.

At his previous meeting with Lady Hamilton, Nelson had described her as "a young woman of amiable manners, and who does
honour to the station to which she is raised." He now wrote to his wife
and told her, "She is one of the very best women in the world. How
few could have made the turn she has. She is an honour to her sex and

proof that even reputation may be regained but I own it requires a great soul." It is clear that he was aware of her past and had nothing but admiration for the way she had transformed herself.

Emma, Lady Hamilton, had come a long way from her humble beginnings on the Wirral Peninsula, near Liverpool. Her father, a blacksmith who worked for the local colliery, had died two months after her birth, and she owed her early advancement to her mother, who brought her to London and found her employment as a maidservant in various households. Numerous stories have gathered around her activities at this time. It is unlikely that she ever posed for the life classes at the Royal Academy, but she may have worked as a prostitute in a high-class brothel run by Mrs. Kelly on Arlington Street. She certainly stayed with Mrs. Kelly for a while. It was around this time that her exceptional beauty brought her to the attention of Sir Harry Fetherstonhaugh, a young baronet. In 1781, at the age of sixteen, she became his mistress and was installed in a cottage on his estate at Uppark in Sussex. It was said that she danced naked on the dining-room table for the entertainment of Sir Harry and his friends, and she later wrote of this time in her life, "Oh, my dear friend, for a time I own through distress my virtue was vanquished, but my sense of virtue not overcome."

Sir Harry soon tired of Emma and brought her back to London, where she persuaded Charles Greville, one of his friends, to take her under his protection. He set her up in a house on Edgware Road with her mother and paid her living expenses on the condition that she abandon her promiscuous life and remain faithful to him. Emma, who had fallen in love with Greville, was very happy with this arrangement. She lived a relatively quiet life, of which the highlights were her visits to the studio of George Romney, who was commissioned by Greville to paint her portrait. Romney was so entranced by her appearance and by her ability as an actress to take on many different roles that she became his favorite model and the inspiration for a series of pictures in which she appeared as Ariadne, Circe, Juno, Medea, and a host of other women from the stories of classical Greece.

The quiet life in London's West End did not last long. Greville was fond of Emma and liked showing her off, but he had many other interests, and he also had financial problems. His solution was to marry an heiress and persuade his uncle, Sir William Hamilton, to take Emma off his hands. Sir William was fifty-three years old and recently wid-

owed. He had met Emma several times and later admitted that her exquisite beauty had much affected him during his visits to England, but
he had reservations about taking her back to Naples with him. After
lengthy negotiations between uncle and nephew, it was agreed that
Emma and her mother should travel to Italy in the spring of 1786 while
Greville was traveling in Scotland.

It was not until Emma had been ensconced for several weeks in Sir
William's delightful villa overlooking the bay of Naples that she
learned that Greville had no intention of coming back to collect her.
For a while she was inconsolable. "I find life is unsupportable without
you," she wrote to Greville. "Oh my heart is intirely broke." But soon
her cheerful, outgoing nature and Sir William's flattering attentions
lifted her spirits. Within a few months, she was enjoying the delights
of life in Naples. She attended the theater, went sailing on the bay,
toured the surrounding countryside. She was painted by many of the
artists who were living in the city, and she became a favored guest at
the court of the King and Queen of Naples. Sir William provided her
with a language master, a singing master, and a music teacher and encouraged her to sing in front of invited audiences. In March 1787, a
year after her arrival, Goethe paid a visit to the city and recorded his
impressions of Emma acting out a series of sketches based on the attitudes and gestures of Greek and Roman statues:

> Sir William Hamilton has now, after many years of devotion to
> the arts and the study of nature, found the acme of these delights
> in the person of an English girl of twenty with a beautiful face
> and a perfect figure. He has had a Greek costume made for her
> which becomes her extremely. Dressed in this, she lets down her
> hair and, with a few shawls, gives so much variety to her poses,
> gestures, expressions, etc., that the spectator can scarcely believe
> his eyes. He sees what thousands of artists would have liked to
> express realized before him in movements and surprising trans-
> formations—standing, kneeling, sitting, reclining, serious, sad,
> playful, ecstatic, contrite, alluring, threatening, anxious, one
> pose follows another without a break.

Toward the end of 1786, Emma succumbed to Sir William's advances and became his mistress, and five years later, during a visit to
London in September 1791, they were married. Sir William was sixty,
and Emma was twenty-six. She had become an accomplished hostess
and was renowned for her extraordinary beauty, her singing, and her

unusual theatrical performances, which had become known as Lady Hamilton's Attitudes.

This was the woman with whom Nelson now found himself spending every hour of the day. He admired her and felt at ease with her. He may have been a much-fêted admiral, but with his provincial background, he was without grand connections. He no doubt felt more in common with her than with most of the aristocratic ladies he met. And he certainly reveled in her flattery. He had always felt himself a man of destiny: He had thirsted for recognition and for glory, and she constantly reminded him of his fame and his achievements. For his fortieth-birthday party in September 1798, a few weeks after his arrival in Naples, she arranged the most extravagant celebration. Eighty guests dined at Sir William's house, and nearly 2,000 people attended a ball. Patriotic songs were sung in Nelson's honor, and the people danced in a salon dominated by a triumphal column inscribed with the names of the heroes of the Nile.

Emma and Nelson were drawn closer together by dramatic events that took place at the end of the year. In December, the French army invaded the Kingdom of Naples and advanced on the city. Nelson supervised the escape of King Ferdinand and his Queen from their palace through a subterranean passage to the water's edge. On an overcast, blustery night, they were rowed out to HMS *Vanguard*. The Hamiltons were already on board, and two days before Christmas, they weighed anchor and headed for Palermo, the capital of Ferdinand's other kingdom, Sicily. On Christmas Eve, they ran into the fiercest storm Nelson had ever encountered. The *Vanguard*'s topsails were torn to shreds, and the sailors stood by with axes ready to cut away the rigging if the masts were brought down by the hurricane-force winds. Most of the passengers were prostrate with fear and seasickness, but Emma proved herself a heroine. While Sir William wedged himself into a chair with loaded pistols in each hand ready to shoot himself if the ship went down, Emma never once retreated to her bed but looked after the children of the royal family. The youngest one became critically ill and died in her arms. The *Vanguard* reached the safety of the harbor at Palermo on December 26, Boxing Day.

Thanks in large measure to Nelson's resolute but brutal behavior during the next few months, the French withdrew from Naples, the Italian rebels were hanged by the mob, and King Ferdinand was restored to his throne. Returning to Sicily after the restoration of the

monarchy in Naples, Nelson was once again at the center of celebrations and parties in his honor. Admiral Lord Keith, commander in chief
in the Mediterranean, called to see him and could scarcely conceal his
disapproval: "The whole was a scene of fulsome Vanity and Absurdity
all the long eight days I was at Palermo." It was during February 1800
that Nelson's relationship with Emma developed from one of mutual
admiration into physical intimacy and a full-blown affair. It had become the habit of Sir William to retire after supper to bed, leaving
Emma and Nelson alone in the private apartments of the Palazzo
Palagonia. They spent many evenings gambling at the card tables, and
their behavior caused Troubridge, one of Nelson's most loyal captains, to send him a note of warning: "If you knew what your friends
feel for you, I am sure you would cut out all the nocturnal parties; the
gambling of the people at Palermo is talked of everywhere. I beseech
your Lordship, leave off. Lady Hamilton's character will suffer; nothing can prevent people from talking."[12] Troubridge only mentioned
the gambling, but of course people were also talking about a love affair that had become obvious to all.

Nelson ignored the warning, and in April 1800, he offered to take
the Hamiltons on a cruise in the *Foudroyant*. They sailed to Syracuse,
where they went ashore and viewed the antiquities. From there they
sailed to Malta and arrived in the harbor of St. Pauls Bay on May 4. It
was during this cruise that Emma conceived her twins.

This hedonistic life of parties, card games, and cruises under the
Mediterranean sun could not last forever. Sir William learned that he
was to be replaced as British minister in Naples, and Nelson received
a brisk letter from Lord Spencer, the First Lord of the Admiralty. The
gossip had reached London, and Nelson's superiors were losing patience with him. He had pleaded his ill health as a reason for staying in
Italy, but Lord Spencer told him he was more likely to recover his
strength in England than in an inactive situation in a foreign court,
"however pleasing the respect and gratitude shown to you for your
services may be." Nelson's request to sail home in his flagship was refused, so he made plans to return overland with the Hamiltons. The
Queen of Naples decided to join them for part of the journey, because
she wanted to visit Vienna to see her daughter, who was now Empress
of Austria.

So began an extraordinary triumphal journey across Europe. On
July 12, 1800, a cavalcade of fourteen coaches and four baggage wag-

ons set off from Leghorn, heading for Florence. The party included Nelson, Sir William Hamilton, Lady Hamilton and her elderly mother, the Queen of Naples, three of the Queen's daughters, and a retinue of royal servants. They arrived at Trieste on August 1 to find the town celebrating the second anniversary of the Battle of the Nile. With much of Europe crumbling under the advance of Napoleon's armies, Nelson was fêted as the man who had inflicted a crushing defeat on the French fleet and thwarted Napoleon's plans in Egypt. From Trieste they traveled on to Baden. Wherever they went, there were banquets and receptions in honor of Nelson, and everywhere his devotion to Emma was noted. One of the highlights of the tour was a visit to Eisenstadt, where Joseph Haydn was the court musician. To Sir William's delight, the composer accompanied Emma when she sang, and in one concert she performed Haydn's *Arianna a Naxos* to considerable acclaim. A newspaper review described her as "a thirty-five-year-old, tall Englishwoman with a very handsome face, who knows well how to demean herself. One of her many rare qualities is her clear, strong voice with which, accompanied by the famous Haydn, she filled the audience with such enthusiasm that they almost became ecstatic."[13]

There was a tearful parting from Queen Maria Carolina and her retinue in Vienna, and the Hamilton party headed for Hamburg, where they boarded a ship bound for England. They arrived at Great Yarmouth on November 6 to a noisy welcome. A cheering crowd assembled on the beach and then hauled the carriage of the homecoming hero through the streets. This cheerful reception was followed by an icy welcome from Nelson's wife when they finally reached London. Fanny was well aware of the rumors of Nelson's affair and had been dreading the meeting. There followed several weeks of miserable public occasions, as she was expected to accompany her husband to a series of parties, dinners, and visits to the theater. Nelson treated her with cold detachment and reduced her to tears at a dinner given by the First Lord of the Admiralty. Emma, who was now seven months pregnant, found the situation equally difficult. She was jealous of Fanny's elegant manners and was chilled by her hostility. Fortunately, they were all rescued by the Admiralty, which promoted Nelson to vice admiral and ordered him to join his flagship in Portsmouth. He told Fanny, who had gone to stay in Brighton, that on no account was she to visit him.

On January 29, 1801, Emma gave birth to twin daughters at a house in Piccadilly. She decided that under the circumstances, one child was more than enough to handle. She arranged for the second baby to be looked after by a nurse and then sent to the Foundling Hospital in Holborn.[14] Nelson was told that only one baby had survived, and as soon as he could arrange for a few days' leave, he hurried to London to be reunited with his mistress and their daughter, who was to be called Horatia. "A finer child was never produced by any two persons," he wrote. "In truth, a love-begotten child!"

Poor Fanny was now frozen out of Nelson's life. Following his victory over the Danish fleet at the Battle of Copenhagen in April 1801, she wrote him a letter to congratulate him and added, "Let me beg, nay, intreat you to believe no wife ever felt greater affection for her husband than I do. And, to the best of my knowledge, I have invariably done everything you desired. If I have omitted anything I am sorry for it."[15] Pathetically, she concluded, "What more can I do to convince you that I am truly your affectionate wife?"

Nelson never replied to her letter; their relationship was effectively finished. Meanwhile, he wrote daily, sometimes several times a day, to Emma. When he returned from the campaign in the Baltic, he and Emma took up residence at Merton Place, a small but pretty country house in a village near Wimbledon in Surrey. Sir William Hamilton, who had remained a staunch friend to Nelson since their first meeting in Naples and had been prepared to turn a blind eye to his wife's infatuation with the naval hero, at last began to complain about Emma's way of life, particularly her lavish dinner parties. "I by no means wish to live in solitary retreat," he told her, "but to have seldom less than twelve to fourteen at table, and those varying continually, is coming back to what was becoming so irksome to me in Italy during the latter years of our residence in that country."[16] He wanted to keep their expenses down, but he also wanted a quiet life. In the spring of 1803, he moved to London, and there he died in Emma's arms with Nelson holding his hand.

Following the Peace of Amiens, signed in March 1802, Nelson could have expected to have time to enjoy the pleasures of Merton Place, but it soon became apparent that the peace between Britain and France was only a temporary interlude. Napoleon was determined to resume his plans for the conquest of Europe, and in particular the invasion of England. The Admiralty decided that the man to prevent the realization of Napoleon's plans was Nelson. He was given command of the British fleet in the Mediterranean, and in May 1803, he hoisted his flag on HMS *Victory*. For the next two years, he was almost continuously at sea. When the French fleet under Admiral Villeneuve succeeded in eluding the British blockade of Toulon, Nelson with a fleet of twelve ships chased him across the Atlantic to the West Indies. Villeneuve eluded him there and sailed back to Cádiz to join forces with the main body of the Spanish fleet, where the combined fleet was penned in by twenty-five British ships under the command of Collingwood. Nelson now returned to Portsmouth and hired a post chaise to take him to Merton, where he enjoyed an ecstatic welcome from Emma.

Nelson spent twenty-five days in England before being recalled to his ship and setting off to meet the French fleet off Cape Trafalgar. They were happy days. There were numerous official meetings in London, but there was also time to be with his beloved Emma. The extensive gardens at Merton were flourishing in the late-summer sun, and the house, laden with pictures and trophies of past battles, was full of children. Lord Minto visited one Saturday and found Nelson just sitting down to dinner with a family party consisting of his brother William Nelson, William's wife and their children, and the children of a sister. Emma was seated at the head of the table, and her mother, old Mrs. Cadogan, at the other end. Nelson was unusually relaxed: "He looks remarkably well and in spirits. His conversation is cordial in these low times. . . ." As for the relations between Nelson and Emma, Lord Minto noted that "the passion is as hot as ever."[17]

At five o'clock on the morning of September 2, a carriage swept up the gravel drive. Captain Blackwood had driven straight from Portsmouth with urgent dispatches from the fleet off Cádiz. Nelson hurried to London, where he was asked to resume his command. Within two weeks he was back on board HMS *Victory* and heading down the English Channel. On September 28, the day before his forty-seventh birthday, he rejoined the fleet, where he was greeted with enthusiasm by Collingwood and his fellow officers. Everyone was aware that a great battle was imminent. On October 19, Nelson wrote to Emma from the great cabin of his flagship:

> My dearest, beloved Emma, the dear friend of my bosom. The signal has been made that the enemy's combined fleet are coming out of port. We have very little wind, so that I have

no hopes of seeing them before tomorrow. May the God of Battles crown my endeavours with success; at all events, I shall take care that my name shall ever be most dear to you and Horatia, both of whom I love as much as my own life. And as my last writing before the Battle will be to you, so I hope in God that I shall live to finish my letter after the battle.[18]

On October 20, Admiral Villeneuve slipped out of Cádiz with the combined fleet of thirty-three French and Spanish ships of the line. At dawn the next day, the waiting British fleet saw their topsails on the eastern horizon. Nelson had twenty-seven ships of the line under his command and was so confident of the spirit of his men and the firepower of his ships that he planned to approach the enemy's line of battle in two long columns. This would expose his leading ships to the full broadsides of the enemy but would enable the British to cut the enemy's line in two places, and then outnumber and overwhelm the ships in the center and rear before the van could turn and rescue them. A storm was brewing out in the Atlantic, and the ships rolled in a long ocean swell; but that morning there was only a light westerly breeze, so it took six hours for the fleets to cover the ten miles separating them. Shortly before noon, the guns of the French ship *Fougueux* opened fire on Admiral Collingwood's flagship *Royal Sovereign*, which was leading one of the British columns. Soon the sound of the bands playing martial music was drowned out by the booming roar of great guns and the crackle of shot from the sharpshooters in the fighting tops.

Back in England, Nelson's women anxiously awaited news, and it was Fanny who was the first to hear the outcome of the battle. She was staying in Bath, and on November 6, she received a letter from the First Lord of the Admiralty, which began:

> Dear Madame, it is with the utmost concern that, in the midst of victory, I have to inform your Ladyship of the death of your illustrious partner, Lord Viscount Nelson. After leading the British fleet into close action with the enemy and seeing their defeat, he fell by a musket ball entering his chest.[19]

Lady Hamilton was in bed at Merton, feeling rather unwell on account of a rash, when a carriage drew up, and Captain Whitby of the Royal Navy was shown to her room.

"We have gained a great victory," he said in a faint voice.

"Never mind your victory," said Emma. "My letters—give me my letters." She then became aware that his face was deathly pale and that there were tears in his eyes. Realizing what this meant, she screamed and fell back on the pillows. According to her own account, she could neither speak nor shed a tear for ten hours.[20] When a friend called to see her a week later, she was still in bed and seemed unable to understand the full extent of her loss. "What shall I do? How can I exist?" was all she could say.[21]

The entire country mourned with an outpouring of grief that has been matched in our own day only by the assassination of President John F. Kennedy and the untimely death of Princess Diana. Nelson's death overshadowed a victory that was so complete that it ensured British maritime supremacy for the next hundred years and put an end to any French plans for an invasion. After lying in state in the Painted Hall at Greenwich Hospital, the coffin bearing Nelson's body was brought up the Thames, accompanied by a vast flotilla of barges and small craft. It was then paraded through the streets on a magnificent funeral carriage drawn by six black horses to St. Paul's Cathedral and buried in the crypt. Neither Lady Hamilton nor Lady Nelson was present at the funeral service.

During that long morning before the ships were joined in battle, Nelson had drawn up a document in which he left Lady Hamilton as a bequest to the nation and asked that she and his daughter, Horatia, be provided for by his country. While Fanny received an annual pension of £2,000 and Nelson's brother, William, received an earldom and a pension of £5,000 a year (as well as £99,000 for the purchase of an estate), Lady Hamilton was not granted a pension and was deserted by all but a few faithful friends. Nelson had left her Merton Place with its seventy acres of land, and she had an inheritance from Sir William Hamilton. She should have been able to live in reasonable comfort, but she was quite incapable of altering her extravagant lifestyle. Soon she was so deep in debt that she was forced to sell Merton Place, and by the spring of 1808, she owed more than £8,000. In 1813, she was arrested for debt and spent time in the King's Bench Prison in Southwark before friends came to her rescue. She was by now drinking heavily and subject to the blackest of moods. By the summer of 1814, she decided that the only way to escape her creditors was to go abroad. She and her daughter, Horatia, who was now thirteen, boarded a packet boat in the Pool of London and sailed to Calais. They took lodgings in the town, and there Emma died in January 1815. The British consul and his wife arranged for Horatia's return to England, where she was welcomed and looked after by Nelson's family. In 1822, she married Philip Ward, the vicar of Tenterden, Kent. They had nine children, and Horatia lived to the age of eighty. A photograph taken of her in 1859 shows how strongly her features resembled those of Nelson. Although she knew who her father was, she never knew that her biological mother was Lady Hamilton and believed to her dying day that she had been adopted by her.

13

The Lighthouse Women

IN BRITAIN IN THE NINETEENTH CENTURY, AS IN PREVIOUS CENTURIES, the newspapers frequently recorded the bleak details of ships lost at sea or ships driven onto rocky shores. There was one shipwreck in particular that captured the public imagination. It took place in the darkness on a remote stretch of the northeast coast of England during a September gale. The ship was a paddle steamer, the *Forfarshire*, and the event would have received no more than a short notice in the local paper had it not been for the circumstances surrounding the rescue of nine lives.

What made the rescue unusual was that it was carried out by a lighthouse keeper and his daughter. For a woman to row out to a shipwreck in a storm was unheard of, and the story received even more attention for the fact that the woman was twenty-two years old, had a pleasant face and modest manner, and had a name that might have come straight from the pages of a Victorian novel. Within the space of a few weeks, Grace Darling became a national heroine. Artists were dispatched to paint her picture, poems were written about her exploits, Staffordshire figures were made in her likeness, and hundreds of engravings were produced to commemorate the rescue. In households throughout Britain, mementos of the lighthouse keeper's daughter could be found on the mantelpiece or sideboard.

Although Grace Darling was undoubtedly brave and played a crucial part in rescuing some of the survivors of the shipwrecked vessel, her exploits scarcely bear comparison with some of the American lighthouse women, notably Ida Lewis, who single-handedly saved the lives of at least eighteen people over a period of twenty-five years. But there was a peculiar drama associated with the wreck of the *Forfarshire* that made it into a story, and though some key features of the story were entirely fictitious, it is not difficult to see why it should have taken such a hold on the public imagination.

The Farne Islands, where the drama took place, lie off the coast of Northumberland opposite the small town of Bamburgh. Unlike Holy Island, which lies ten miles to the north and is large enough to support a small community, the Farne Islands are little more than a collection of rocky outcrops. At high tide, many of the rocks and islets are partially or wholly submerged and consequently have always presented a dangerous hazard for ships passing up and down the coast. A lighthouse was built on one of the inner islands of the group but failed to prevent frequent shipwrecks, and so a new lighthouse was built on Longstone, the outermost island, and went into operation in 1826.

The Longstone lighthouse consisted of a round tower eighty-five feet high. There were seven circular rooms in the tower, and alongside were some low outbuildings, including an oil store and a boathouse. Grace Darling's grandfather had looked after the earlier lighthouse. His youngest son, William, succeeded him as keeper in 1815 and in due course moved into the new lighthouse with his wife, Thomasina. They had nine children, who seem to have spent more of their time on the mainland than on the barren island. By 1838, when the wreck of the *Forfarshire* took place, the children had grown up, and all except two of them were living in Bamburgh or further afield. Only Grace and her younger brother were living with their parents in the light tower.[1]

William Darling, who was fifty-two at the time of the rescue, appears to have been a stolid, resolute character. There is a fine portrait of him by Thomas Musgrave Joy, which depicts a handsome man with a strong, lean face, dark eyebrows, and a watchful expression. He had acted as boatman to the lighthouse for several years before being appointed keeper. He was therefore extremely experienced in handling a rowboat in all conditions and knew intimately all the currents and overfalls in and among the islands. His journal is a model of brevity and is similar in tone to the logbooks of many naval captains. His entry for December 27, 1834, is typical. In a few terse sentences, he describes a heroic rescue during a winter storm in which he and his sons nearly lost their lives:

> Wind S. by E., fresh gale. 11pm, the sloop "Autumn" of and to Peterhead, with coals from Newcastle, struck east point of Knavestone, and immediately sank. Crew of three men: two lost, one saved by the Lightkeeper and three sons, viz, William, Robert, and George, after a struggle of three hours. Having lost two oars on the rock, had very narrow escape.[2]

William Darling's wife scarcely features in any of the accounts of the drama and remains a shadowy figure. She was sixty-four years old at the time, and having borne and reared nine children, she was probably feeling her age. It is worth remembering that being married to a lighthouse keeper on an offshore tower was a lonely and demanding life that was very much dependent on the weather, particularly during the winter months.

As for Grace Darling herself, we have a multitude of portraits to choose from. As far as one can tell, the best likeness was captured by the little-known artist Henry Perlee Parker, who produced a fine watercolor sketch and a sensitive portrait in oils. They confirm the view of a journalist who interviewed her and said she had "a comely countenance—rather fair for an islander—and with an expression of benevolence and softness most truly feminine in every point of view."[3] The journalist had evidently expected to find a big, strapping country girl and was surprised that she was in no way masculine in her appearance. In fact, at five feet three inches, she was somewhat below average height. Everyone commented on her quiet and reserved manner and her modesty, which remained unchanged by the adulation she received.

At the center of the drama was the steamboat *Forfarshire*. She too was painted by several artists, notably by John Ward, a talented marine artist from Hull who specialized in ship portraits. He painted her soon after she was launched in 1834, and his picture shows that she was typical of the early steamers used for coastal trade and passenger traffic.

She had large paddle wheels on either side of the hull, a tall, slender smokestack, and two masts with sails in case she suffered from engine failure. She was commanded by Captain Humble, who was later described by John Tulloch, the ship's carpenter, as "a steady, trustworthy man and always attentive to his duty both on sea and land and a good seaman."[4]

The *Forfarshire* sailed from Hull on September 5, 1838, bound for Dundee with a mixed cargo of hardware, fine cloth, soap, boilerplate, and spinning gear. In addition to Captain Humble and his wife, she had on board fifty-five passengers and crew. As the ship headed north up the coast, the wind increased steadily, and by the time they were off Flamborough Head, there was a heavy sea running and the starboard boiler was leaking boiling water into the bilges. The pumps were having difficulty clearing the water, but the captain decided to keep going rather than seek shelter at Whitby or the mouth of the River Tyne. The boiler was repaired, and at six o'clock in the evening of September 6, they passed the Farne Islands, steaming through the Fairway or Inner Sound between the mainland and the offshore islands. The wind was behind them from the south-southeast and swept them northward at a steady pace.

As night fell, the situation deteriorated rapidly. When they were off Berwick, the wind backed from the south to north-northeast and rose to gale force. The defective boiler began leaking so badly that the pumps were unable to clear the boiling water, and the captain had no choice but to shut down the engines. He turned the ship south, set the fore-and-aft sails, and ran before the gale, intending to make for the shelter of the Tyne. With her unwieldy paddle boxes, the steamer would have been difficult to control under sail in storm conditions, and things were made worse by driving rain and flying spray that cut down the visibility. It seems that Captain Humble was planning to retrace the route he had taken and pass between the Farne Islands and the coast. When he saw a light ahead of him, he assumed it was the Inner Farne light and that he was on course to pass through the Fairway. In fact, it was the Longstone light, and he was headed straight for the rocky island in the center of the outer island group. By the time anyone on board had seen or heard the waves breaking ahead of them, it would have been too late, and the 400-ton vessel drove hard onto the western end of Harker's Rock. With the full force of the gale behind her and the sea pounding on the rocks, she began to break up. In less than fifteen minutes, the deck opened up and the ship split in two just aft of the paddle boxes. The stern section was swept away into the darkness and sank, drowning Captain Humble and his wife, and forty-one passengers and crew.

The forward section of the ship was left stranded on the rocks with twelve people, including a woman, two children, a clergyman (Reverend Rob), fireman Daniel Donovan, and John Tulloch, the ship's carpenter. Tulloch took charge, and when daylight came and the tide began to fall, he managed to get them to leave the wreck and take shelter among the rocks. Their situation was bleak. They were stranded on an offshore island. They were bitterly cold and soaking wet from the rain and spray. Their only hope was that they might be seen by the people manning the distant lighthouse before they died of exposure and hypothermia. But the lighthouse was on another island nearly a mile away across a gray expanse of heaving water.

High tide was at 4:13 A.M. on the day the *Forfarshire* struck. Anticipating an exceptionally high tide, William Darling woke his daughter in the early hours. They went down to the yard at the base of the light tower, carried all the movable gear indoors, and made sure the boat was secured to the stanchions. When everything was secure, Grace took over the watch beside the lantern at the top of the tower while her father went to get some sleep. At 4:45, there was just enough light for her to make out the outline of a ship on Harker's Rock. She woke her father, and they used a telescope to see if they could discern any sign of life; but the overcast sky, the rain, and the clouds of spray thrown up around the wreck made it difficult to make out any detail. They took turns observing the wreck, but it was not until seven o'clock when the tide had fallen further that they observed three or four men on the rock.

William Darling now had a difficult decision to make. The lighthouse boat was a heavily built coble, a local type of craft with a high bow and curving sheer designed to be launched and landed through the surf. The cobles were famously seaworthy, but they were open and could therefore be swamped in heavy seas. The Longstone boat was twenty-one feet in length overall, with a five-and-a-half-foot beam. She could easily be rowed by four men and in normal conditions could be rowed by two. Unfortunately, the lighthouse keeper's twenty-year-old son, William, had gone ashore some days previously, which meant that Darling had only his elderly wife and his daughter to assist him. He presumed there was no possibility of a lifeboat being launched from the mainland in an onshore gale, so he must either leave the people on Harker's Rock to die or attempt to reach them in the coble. He could not row to the rock and bring off the survivors on his own, but it might be possible with the help of his daughter. According to the legend, Grace had to persuade her father to launch the boat and insisted that she come with him to the wreck. The truth seems to be that it was a joint decision. In a letter that he wrote to Trinity House (the institution responsible for the lights and lighthouses around the coast of England and Wales) later, William Darling described how they spotted the men on the rock, and "we agreed that if we could get to them some of them would be able to assist us back, without which we could not return; and having no idea of a possibility of a boat coming from North Sunderland, we immediately launched our boat. . . ."[5]

If they took the direct route from the lighthouse to the wreck, they would be overwhelmed by the violence of the waves or swept onto the northern edge of Harker's Rock, which was a lee shore, so they headed through Crayford's Gut toward the more sheltered waters on the south side of the rocky island. The passage through the Gut was exposed to the full force of the gale and would have been extremely turbulent. The reason William Darling needed additional help on the way back was that he would have to negotiate the Gut against the combined effect of the wind and tide. With Grace heaving on one oar and William on the other, they rowed away from the landing place on Longstone Island while Mrs. Darling watched their progress from the lantern. At one point the boat disappeared from her sight, and thinking it had been swamped and she had lost her husband and daughter, she blacked out and collapsed. When she recovered and took another look through the telescope, she caught sight of them rowing steadily toward Harker's Rock.

They succeeded in reaching the relative safety of the lee of the island and headed toward the western end, where the survivors were gathered. The cold had proved too much for three of them. The clergyman had died during the early hours of the morning, and the two children had died in their mother's arms some time later. That left nine people to be rescued, which William Darling reckoned was too many to take in the boat at one time in the prevailing conditions. He jumped onto the rock to prevent them all from crowding aboard and persuaded four of them to wait for him to make a second trip. Meanwhile, Grace was left to manage the heavy coble on her own and to hold it off the rocks. She later recalled her horror at the sight of the wreck and said, "At the time I believe I had very little thought of anything but to exert myself to the utmost, my spirit was worked up by the sight of the dreadful affair that I can imagine I still see the sea flying over the vessel."[6]

The woman and four of the men clambered aboard the coble, and they set off on the mile-long haul back to the lighthouse. This time they were able to use four oars, but with seven people the boat was heavily laden, which must have been particularly alarming as they moved out from the shelter of Harker's Rock and plowed into the broken water of Crayford's Gut. They reached Longstone Island safely, however, and William Darling set off on the second journey to the wreck assisted by two of the men he had rescued. It was now approaching low tide, which meant that there was additional shelter in the lee of Harker's Rock. The four remaining survivors were picked up and brought back to the lighthouse. It was now around nine o'clock. The entire rescue attempt had taken just under two hours.

As it happened, the wreck of the *Forfarshire* had been spotted by someone on the battlements of Bamburgh Castle. A gun was fired to let any survivors know they had been seen, and a fishing coble was launched from North Sunderland. It was manned by seven men, one of whom was William Brooks Darling, the lighthouse keeper's son. They had an arduous and dangerous journey of seven miles out to the Farne Islands and reached the wreck at ten o'clock, only to find that they had been forestalled and their rescue mission was in vain. However, they carried the bodies of the dead clergyman and the children to the highest part of the rock and then headed for Longstone Island. They had great difficulty in landing in the stormy conditions but eventually found a place to beach their boat and clambered ashore. The gale continued to blow strongly from the north, and it was two days before the seas calmed down sufficiently for them to be able to leave the island and row back to the mainland.

It was several days before the story of the rescue became public knowledge. On September 15, the local paper, the *Berwick & Kelso*

Warder, carried a brief mention. Shortly after this, Mr. Scafe, a local citizen of Bamburgh, wrote to the Duke of Northumberland to draw his attention to the brave actions of William Darling and his daughter and enclosed a short report of the rescue, which was signed by two of the survivors, John Tulloch and Daniel Donovan. The duke sent his secretary to investigate, and the Darlings were interviewed. Evidently much impressed by his secretary's report, the duke wrote to the Royal Humane Society (of which he was president) and to the master of Trinity House. Things now began to gather pace. *The Times* published an account of the rescue that elevated Grace Darling to the level of a national heroine:

> It is impossible to speak in adequate terms of the unparalleled bravery and disinterestedness shown by Mr. Darling and his truly heroic daughter, especially so with regard to the latter. . . . Is there in the whole field of history, or fiction, even one instance of female heroism to compare with this?

The editor of the *Berwick & Kelso Warder* realized that there was a bigger story than he had first thought and sent a group of reporters to the Longstone lighthouse to get a firsthand interview with the Darling family. The reporters noted, "When we spoke of her noble and heroic conduct, she slightly blushed and appeared anxious to avoid the notice to which it exposed her; she smiled at our praise but said nothing in reply."

During the next four years, Grace Darling had to face the sort of adulation that in more recent times is experienced by film stars and royalty. The Longstone lighthouse became a tourist attraction, and during the summer of 1839, steamboat excursions from nearby harbors brought a continual stream of curious visitors. So many portrait painters were dispatched to capture likenesses of Grace and her father that William Darling complained that they were preventing them from carrying out their lighthouse duties. Letters and gifts (mostly Bibles and religious tracts) poured in, and Grace was asked for locks of her hair. She and her mother were constantly having to tidy up the lighthouse and entertain visitors. So demanding was the pressure that the Duke and Duchess of Northumberland stepped in to protect her from the demands of the public. Grace and her father were invited to visit them at Alnwick Castle in December 1838, and following the visit, it was agreed that the duke would become her guardian.

However, the momentum continued. Panoramas based on the story of the rescue were shown at the Theatre Royal in Newcastle and at the Sunderland Theatre. A play called *The Wreck at Sea* was specially written and performed at the Adelphi Theatre in London. Wordsworth was one of several poets who were inspired to write poems in praise of Grace Darling's feat. There was also recognition from official sources. The Royal Humane Society agreed unanimously that Grace and her father should be awarded the highest honor they could bestow, the Honorary Gold Medallion. The citation for Grace referred to her "singular intrepidity, presence of mind and Humanity," which urged her "to expose her life in a small Boat to the impending danger of a heavy Gale of wind and tremendous Sea, in her intense desire to save nine of the sufferers who were wrecked. . . ."[7] She also received silver medals from the Humane Societies of Glasgow, Edinburgh, and Leith.

But it gradually became apparent that Grace was not well. She was suffering from a persistent cough, and her family was so concerned that they took her ashore. She spent the summer of 1842 staying with her sister Thomasin in Bamburgh. The Duke of Northumberland sent his doctor to see her, and the duchess paid her a visit. Her father then moved her to the cottage under the walls of Bamburgh Castle where her grandparents had lived and where she had spent her earliest years. There she died on October 20, 1842, at the age of twenty-six in the bed in which she had been born.

Her death only fueled the interest in her, because she now had attained that special attraction reserved for celebrities who die young. As the story circulated, it concentrated increasingly on the role of Grace at the expense of her father. One version of the story (which helped to create the legend and will still be found today in many children's books and encyclopedias) told how Grace woke her father when she heard cries of help coming from the wreck and in vain implored the assembled boatmen to make one effort to rescue the drowning people. (As we know, the boatmen did not arrive until after the survivors had been rescued.) According to this story, her father was so moved by her tears of pity that he exclaimed that the girl must have her way and agreed to launch the boat. The two of them rowed out into the storm and rescued all the people gathered on the rock. This version did not mention the second trip made by William Darling.

The Darling family did their best to set the record straight. Grace herself pointed out in a letter, "I was very anxious, and did render every assistance that lay in my power, but my father was equally so and needed not to be urged by me, being experienced in such things and knowing what could be done."[8] And her sister Thomasin, who published an account based on family papers and also edited William Darling's journal, made it clear that "portions of the popular romancing story of William Darling's deferring to his daughter's entreaties, and so forth, are pure invention."

One reason for the extraordinary popularity of the Grace Darling story was that it was so unusual. Just as women were not expected to become sailors or fishermen, so they were not expected to play an active part in the lighthouse service. Only men were permitted to become official keepers of lighthouses in Britain. Wives and children were able to live in shore-based lights, but offshore lights on rocks or small islands were generally all-male preserves. In America, things were rather different. Male keepers were always in the majority, but a surprising number of women received official appointments to lighthouses and were in many cases in sole charge of the operation of the lights. The women who were appointed were usually related to men who had been keepers, and their salaries were invariably lower than what the men received for the same duties. When Betty Humphrey retired in 1880 after serving as keeper of Monhegan Island light in Maine for eighteen years, her annual salary was $700, $100 less than her husband had earned at his death.[9] But at least the U.S. Lighthouse Service recognized that women were capable of carrying out the job.

In some respects the running of a lighthouse required the sorts of skills traditionally carried out by men: the painting and upkeep of the exterior of the light tower, the repairs to the building and its machinery, the trips to and fro in a heavy boat, and the loading and unloading of supplies. But the most essential job, which was tending the light itself, could be carried out by a woman just as well as by a man, and indeed there was a historical precedent going back to biblical times for the care of lamps to be a female task.

The oil-burning lights that were common in the nineteenth century needed constant attention. Many of them required filling with oil at sundown and again at midnight. In very cold weather, the whale oil that was used tended to congeal, and it was necessary to warm it up on the kitchen stove to enable it to function properly. After lighting the lamp or lamps at sunset, the keeper must trim the wicks at regular intervals: In summer this might need doing only once, around midnight, but in the long winter nights, it was necessary to trim the wicks around ten o'clock at night and again around two in the morning. The light must then be extinguished at sunrise. Women keepers tended to be particularly conscientious about ensuring that the light was functioning properly. Ida Lewis had her bed positioned so she could see the light and trained herself to wake every half hour to check that the lamp was burning.

During the day, the keeper was kept busy on a continuous round of cleaning and polishing. The prism lens must be kept spotlessly clean and polished, and carbon from the burning lamp must be cleaned off the reflectors. And any moving parts must be kept oiled and polished. Whenever sea fog or mist appeared in the vicinity of the lighthouse, the keeper must sound the necessary fog signals until it cleared away. Few of the nineteenth-century lighthouses had any form of automatic fog signal, and in many cases, the keeper was required to ring a bell. Clara Maddocks, keeper of the Owl's Head light in Maine, reported that in any one year she might spend some 2,000 hours ringing the bell. Juliet Nichols at the Angel Island lighthouse in San Francisco noted in her log that once she struck the bell by hand for twenty hours and thirty-five minutes, until the fog lifted.

The first woman on record to have an official appointment as a lightkeeper in America was Hannah Thomas. She and her husband were responsible for looking after the twin lights that were built on their property at Plymouth, Massachusetts, in 1769. At first Mrs. Thomas assisted her husband, but when he died, she took over sole responsibility. In addition to looking after the lights, she raised a family, and when she retired around 1790, her younger son took over for her. This was a fairly typical arrangement, because the running of a lighthouse was often regarded as a family concern and in some respects was rather like running a farm or a family store. Everyone took a turn at domestic duties, as well as ensuring that the lights were lit and in good order and that a regular lookout was kept. The government, which was responsible for the Lighthouse Service, evidently recognized the benefits of this system, because it continued to appoint wives, provided they had sufficient experience. By 1851, no fewer than thirty wives had taken over as keepers on the death of their husbands.

Abbie Burgess, who was one of America's first lighthouse heroines, was born into a lighthouse family. Her father, Samuel Burgess, was appointed keeper of the twin lights at Matinicus Rock in Maine in 1853. His wife suffered from a long-standing illness that required constant medical attention, so Samuel took on additional work as a lobster fisherman to pay for medicine and doctor's fees. When she was fourteen, Abbie began assisting her father with the lights, which left him free to spend more time with his lobster pots. She soon proved to be as capable at looking after the light as she was at tending her younger sisters and her pet chickens.

In January 1856, a vicious winter gale howled across Penobscot Bay with such force that it shook the foundations of the old keeper's house on Matinicus Rock. Samuel Burgess was twenty miles away on the mainland, where he had gone to stock up on supplies, and was unable to return to the lighthouse due to the violence of the storm. Abbie, who was then sixteen, found herself having to keep the lamps burning in both towers while looking after her sick mother and her frightened sisters. As the tide rose, the sea began to break over the rocky island and to wash every movable thing away. The old keeper's house began to break up and to show every sign that it might collapse. Abbie moved her mother and sisters into the north tower, which was more sheltered from the wind, and then ran out to the chicken coop to rescue her pet hens. She later described why it was so important to her to save them:

> You know the hens were our only companions. Becoming convinced, as the gale increased, that unless they were brought into the house they would be lost, I said to my mother, "I must try to save them." She advised me not to attempt it. The thought, however, of parting with them without an effort was not to be endured, so seizing a basket, I ran out a few yards after the rollers had passed and the sea fell a little, with the water knee deep, to the coop, and rescued all but one.[10]

The waves were now breaking over the lower section of the keeper's house, and as the storm reached its height, the house crumpled and fell into the sea. For the next four weeks, the rough weather prevented any boat from coming out and landing on the island. During that time, Abbie continued to tend the lights and look after her family. Supplies were so low that they were largely dependent on the eggs from the chickens she had saved. "Though at times greatly exhausted by my labours, not once did the lights fail. Under God I was able to perform all my accustomed duties as well as my father's."

When the Republicans were elected to power under Lincoln in 1860, Abbie's father lost his job. Many lighthouse appointments were dependent on political contacts, and because Samuel Burgess did not have connections in the right places, he was replaced by John Grant, a staunch Republican. However, Abbie was allowed to stay on for a while to show the new keeper the workings of the lighthouse and explain the necessary routines. Grant brought with him his son, Isaac, who had been appointed assistant keeper. Abbie was now twenty-two and so impressed Isaac that within a few weeks of working alongside her, he proposed marriage. They were married the following year, and Abbie was appointed second assistant keeper. Since she had admirably performed all the duties of official keeper for many years, she must have felt the injustice of this, but at least she did not have to abandon lighthouse life. She brought up four children on the rock, and they continued to live there, as she and her sisters had done, until her husband was transferred to White Head lighthouse near Spruce Head, Maine, in 1872. When her husband died in 1875, she took over as official keeper, and according to the records, she continued as keeper until a year or so before her death in 1892 at the age of fifty-two. In her last letter, she looked back on her thirty-odd years of tending the lights and wrote, "I wonder if the care of the lighthouse will follow my soul after it has left this worn out body! If I ever have a gravestone, I would like it in the form of a lighthouse or beacon."[11] She was buried in Spruce Head Cemetery, and fifty years after her death her wish was granted—a small lighthouse was placed on her grave.

Katie Walker did not come from a lighthouse family and was horrified by the bleak situation of the lighthouse she ended up in, yet, like so many other lighthouse women, she showed an extraordinary devotion to looking after the light. She was a German immigrant and met Jacob Walker while she was waiting tables at the boardinghouse where he dined. Jacob was keeper of Sandy Hook light in New Jersey. He taught her English, fell in love with her, and persuaded her to marry him. The Sandy Hook light was situated on a promontory in a picturesque setting with a good road into town so that contact with friends and neighbors was easy. Unfortunately, in the 1870s Jacob was appointed to another lighthouse in a very different location. This was Robbins Reef light, a squat tower on a concrete platform on the west side of New York Bay's main channel. The accommodations were cramped in the extreme. The kitchen and dining room were squashed into a circular extension built at the base of the tower, and there were two bedrooms above in the tower itself. The views of Staten Island and Brooklyn were no compensation for the rural life that Katie had begun to enjoy at Sandy Hook. She was so unhappy when they first arrived she thought she would be unable to stay; she later recalled, "When I first came to Robbins Reef, the sight of water, whichever way I looked, made me lonesome. I refused to unpack my trunks at first, but gradually, a little at a time, I unpacked. After a while they were all unpacked and I stayed on."[12]

As so many women have done in similar situations, she decided she would have to make the best of it. She set about making the place as comfortable as possible. She helped her husband with his lighthouse duties, and she brought up their two children. When the children reached school age, she rowed them across to Staten Island every morning and collected them in the afternoon. In 1886, when the children had grown up and left home, Jacob fell ill and died of pneumonia. He was buried in a Staten Island cemetery. His last words to his wife were "Mind the light, Katie." For several weeks, she debated whether to leave Robbins Reef, but she continued to look after the light and after a while decided to apply for the keeper's post. She was under five feet tall, and the Lighthouse Board had doubts about her fitness for the job. However, she was obviously capable of handling the lighthouse boat and had shown herself able to manage the light and its machinery on her own, so they agreed to her appointment. They were well rewarded for their faith in her, because she continued to manage the light for the next thirty-five years, during which time she was responsible for more than fifty rescues in New York Harbor.

It is curious how many of the American lighthouse women seemed to become strangely attached to the lonely but demanding pattern of life on their seabound rocks and islands. Instead of gratefully heading for the mainland and a cottage in the country on the death of their fathers or husbands, they often made a deliberate choice to continue tending the lights, keeping a watch on passing ships, and rescuing people who got into trouble. None showed more dedication to the task than Ida Lewis, the most famous of all of America's female lighthouse keepers.[13] Like Grace Darling, she became a heroine while still in her twenties, but unlike Grace Darling, Ida Lewis lived on to the age of sixty-nine and carried out a succession of rescues over a period of more than fifty years. Born in Newport, Rhode Island, in 1842, she was the daughter of Captain Hosea Lewis, a coast pilot. In 1853, he was appointed keeper of Lime Rock light, which was on a small island in Newport Harbor less than half a mile from the shore. For several years, Captain Lewis and his family continued to live in Newport because the first light on Lime Rock was no more than a beacon with a shed alongside to provide some temporary shelter. In 1857, however, a solid four-square building with a low pitched roof was built on the island, and the family moved in.

The traditional lighthouses of New England have inspired some memorable paintings by Edward Hopper and have been the subject of thousands of photographs. They come in a variety of shapes, sizes, and materials, and tend to be considerably more picturesque than most British lighthouses. Unhappily, Lime Rock light looked nothing like the usual picture most of us have of a lighthouse. There was no tower, and the light was simply incorporated into one side of the keeper's house. On the seaward-facing side there was a narrow, square-sectioned column projecting slightly from the building with a three-sided window at the top containing the lamp.

The interior of the lighthouse was as plain as the white-painted exterior. A Newport journalist visited the place when Ida Lewis had become famous and described the interior in some detail. On the ground floor there was a parlor, a hall, a dining room, and a kitchen. On the floor above were three bedrooms with a passageway leading to the lantern. The walls were bare, and "Ida's own particular sanctum is fitted with a cheaply finished cottage set, only remarkable as exhibiting a rude painting of a sinking wreck upon the headboard of her couch."[14] He noted that a sewing machine "and some little feminine nick-nacks complete the interior." The best aspect of the house was the view from the upstairs windows. Ida's room commanded a fine vista of the harbor looking toward the town.

Within a few months of the family's moving into the house on Lime Rock, Captain Lewis had a stroke that left him so paralyzed he was no longer able to carry out his duties. His wife took over as the official keeper, but in addition to her disabled husband, she had four children to look after. She increasingly relied on Ida, the eldest child, to maintain the light. Ida was fifteen at this time, and during the next few years she also took responsibility for rowing her younger sister and two brothers to school. Although the island was only half a mile from the shore, a strong or gale-force wind would rapidly turn the peaceful waters of the harbor into a mass of short, steep waves. Captain Lewis would keep a lookout from his window when his children were due to return in the boat and frequently feared for their lives when they rowed back in heavy weather. He told a newspaper reporter:

> I have watched them till I could not bear to look any longer, expecting any moment to see them swamped, and the crew at the mercy of the waves, and then I have turned away and said to my wife, let me know if they get safe in, for I could not endure to see them perish and realize that we were powerless to save them.[15]

Ida's early experience with the lighthouse boat stood her in good stead over the years. Her first recorded rescue took place in September 1859, when she was eighteen. Four college students were sailing a catboat across the harbor after dark. They were larking about and one of them climbed up the mast and began rocking the boat so violently that it capsized. None of them could swim, but they managed to cling to the upturned hull. Ida heard their shouts, and she immediately launched the boat and set off toward them. She later said that by the time she reached them they were "two-thirds dead—awfully weak and white-faced, and almost inanimate." She managed to haul them into her boat over the stern and took them back to the lighthouse, where the family helped to revive them.

The next rescue took place on a freezing day in February 1866. Three soldiers rashly decided to return to Fort Adams in a decrepit old skiff. They managed to get some way out into the harbor when one of them put his foot through a rotten plank in the bottom of the boat, which rapidly filled and sank to the gunwales. Ida Lewis spotted the men in trouble and rowed to their assistance. Two of the men abandoned their grip on the old skiff and attempted to swim toward her, but the cold overcame them and before they could reach her they sank and drowned. When Ida reached the skiff, she found the third man was so numb with cold he could scarcely move, and she had to heave his body unaided into her boat to save his life.

The following year she rescued three shepherds who got into trouble, and in November of the same year, she saved two sailors. But the rescue that captured the headlines took place on March 29, 1869. The wind had risen to gale force during the night, and when Ida's mother woke in the morning, she was horrified to see a capsized boat drifting among the foaming waves. There were two men clinging to the upturned hull. According to one report, Ida did not even stop to put on shoes or an overcoat but hurried outside in a thin brown poplin dress and stockings with a white shawl around her shoulders. The weather was atrocious, with a fierce wind, snow, and sleet sweeping across the gray waters of the harbor. With an angry surf breaking on the island, it took Ida fifteen minutes to launch the boat and get clear of the shore. As she approached the stricken boat, the story goes, one of the men cried in despair, "It's only a girl," and letting go of his hold, he sank beneath the waves. He reappeared moments later, and Ida grabbed his hair, managed to drag him to the stern of her boat, and hauled him aboard over the transom. The second man was almost paralyzed with cold, and he too had to be heaved aboard. With both men lying almost unconscious on the floorboards, Ida headed back through the breaking waves toward Lime Rock. Back in the lighthouse, she and her mother spent hours reviving the two men, who proved to be soldiers from Fort Adams, as well. They had apparently been in a hurry to get back to the fort before their leave expired and had engaged a local boy to row them across to the promontory. The boy was drowned when the boat capsized.

What is curious about the whole episode is that most of the accounts indicate that Ida Lewis carried out the rescue single-handedly, but a painting that was later commissioned by the U.S. Coast Guard shows her younger brother, Rudolf, with her in the boat. The artist received instructions about the clothes Ida wore and how she handled the boat and must presumably have been told whether Ida was assisted in the rescue. While the presence of her brother in no way diminishes the courage and determination she showed on that winter morning, it does help to explain how a young woman was able to haul into her boat two men who were helpless with cold and weighed down by soaking-wet clothes.

The news of this rescue provoked a public reaction similar to the adulation experienced by Grace Darling thirty-two years earlier. The local people honored Ida Lewis with a special parade on Independence Day, 1869, and presented her with a new boat built of mahogany with red velvet cushions and gold-plated rowlocks. The Life Saving Benevolent Association of New York awarded her their silver medal, as well as a check for $100. Articles devoted to the rescue appeared in the *New York Tribune* and other major newspapers, and her picture was featured on the cover of *Harper's Weekly* with the caption "The heroine of Newport."

The Lime Rock lighthouse suffered the same fate as the Longstone lighthouse, becoming a place of pilgrimage. Captain Lewis sat in his wheelchair counting visitors and reckoned that in one summer alone 9,000 people came out to the island hoping to catch a glimpse of Ida Lewis. The most famous of the visitors in 1869 was the President of the United States, General Ulysses S. Grant. He arrived with Vice President Colefax and was rowed out to the lighthouse. According to the local legend, the President got his feet wet as he stepped ashore. "I have come to see Ida Lewis," he said, "and to see her I'd get wet up to my armpits if necessary."

Among the numerous letters and gifts that followed the news of the rescue were many offers of marriage. Ida Lewis was persuaded to accept one of these, and in 1870, she married Captain William Wilson of Black Rock, Connecticut. Whether Captain Wilson was unable to accommodate himself to Ida's fame and way of life, or whether Ida was reluctant to change her island routine—or whether they were simply incompatible—is not altogether clear, but in less than two years, they separated. She kept the name Mrs. Lewis-Wilson but reverted to her single status and never remarried. In any case, she had more than enough to keep her busy. In 1872, her father died and her mother was officially appointed keeper in his place, but she fell ill and was soon a helpless invalid. Ida found herself not only having to carry out the daily lighthouse duties but also having to look after her mother. Eventually, Ida's years of service as unofficial keeper were recognized, and in 1879 she was herself appointed keeper and received the annual salary of $750.

In 1881, she carried out another rescue that was almost as hazardous as that in the storm of March 1869. Once again, it took place in freezing winter weather, and again it was men from the garrison at Fort Adams who were involved. Much of the harbor had frozen over, and in the late afternoon of February 4, two soldiers who were walking across the ice when it gave way beneath them found themselves up to their necks in icy water. Ida heard their frantic cries and ran across the ice toward them, bringing a rope with her. She flung the rope to them, and by the time she had helped one of the men out of the water, her brother had come to her aid and together they got the second man to safety. The U.S. Life Saving Service was so impressed by her bravery on this occasion that it presented her with its highest award for her "unquestionable nerve, presence of mind, and dashing courage." It pointed out that the ice was in a very dangerous condition and noted that shortly afterward two other men fell through the ice and were drowned in the immediate neighborhood of the rescue.

Ida Lewis's position as a national heroine was consolidated. She was awarded the Congressional Gold Medal "for rescuing from drowning at various times at least thirteen persons," and received a silver medal from the Massachusetts Humane Society. From the great mansions of Newport came a stream of society ladies to shake her hand, including Mrs. Astor, Mrs. Belmont, and Mrs. Vanderbilt. She was also visited by General Sherman. According to Ida, the general "sat out on the rock for nearly an hour, asking me questions about my life, and saying he was glad to get to such a peaceful place."[16]

She seems to have taken the adulation and fame in stride. She made no changes in her way of life but continued to live a monastic existence, keeping watch during the day and waking through the night to mind the light. Her brother continued to help her, particularly with the upkeep of the lighthouse, but as she entered her sixties, the stream of visitors diminished and there was even a rumor that Lime Rock light was to be replaced with a small beacon on the neighboring Goat Island. Before this happened, Ida Lewis was dead. Her brother arrived one morning in 1911 and found her unconscious on the floor of the lantern room. She died later that day. The news was passed along the waterfront, and that evening, all the vessels in Newport Harbor rang their bells in her honor. She was buried in a local cemetery. The lighthouse she had made famous eventually became a yacht club, but the name of her small island was changed from Lime Rock to Ida Lewis Rock.

14

The Sailors' Return

A LARGE WARSHIP ENTERING HARBOR UNDER THE COMMAND OF A CONfident captain with a well-trained crew was a magnificent sight. She would surge toward the anchorage under full sail, with a hissing bow wave, and flags and pennants billowing in the breeze. When she drew level with the fort guarding the entrance of the harbor, her guns fired a salute to the port admiral. As the clouds of gunsmoke drifted across the harbor, she rounded up into the wind and let go the anchor, and the men high up on her yardarms heaved up her sails. Within minutes she was lying quietly to her anchor, and her boats were being lowered into the water.

This disciplined and orderly procedure was followed by the most disorderly scene imaginable. A small armada of rowboats and barges pushed off from various points along the waterfront and headed for the anchored ship. Most of these were bumboats, the name given to small boats used to sell provisions to ships lying at a distance from the shore. The bumboats were often owned by local women and were loaded like floating market stalls with piles of fruit and vegetables, baskets of bread and meat, dairy produce, tobacco, liquor, and anything else the sailors might buy. The other vessels were rowboats filled to the gunwales with cargoes of women. A few of the women were sailors' wives, who had probably traveled many miles in order to meet the incoming ship. Most of them were prostitutes who hoped to earn a few shillings by selling their favors to the men on board. The boatmen who rowed these women out to the ship treated the exercise as a speculative venture. No money changed hands until the boats jostled alongside the massive wooden hull of the ship; then, depending on the attitude of the ship's officers, the men could either climb into the boats or lean over the ship's side to choose a woman. The sailor then paid her fare, and she was allowed to clamber up the ship's side. The noise and confusion resulting from the various transactions may be imagined with the bumboat women bartering their produce, prostitutes clamoring to attract the sailors' attention, and the sailors themselves shouting and swearing ribald comments.

Within an hour or so, the ship was heaving with humanity. It was not uncommon for as many women to come aboard as there were men on the ship, so a 74-gun ship with a crew of 500 or 600 would find her 170-foot length crammed with more than a thousand men, women, and children. Most of these went belowdecks to the sailors' quarters. The officers had makeshift cabins constructed of canvas screens that allowed them some privacy, but the ordinary seamen hoisted their hammocks in a low-ceilinged, cavernous space with no privacy whatsoever. Here, among the guns and the seamen's chests, wives were reunited with their husbands, and prostitutes went about their business with the men who had paid for their services. Soon the confined space was teeming with people chattering, laughing, crying, shrieking, and swearing. As the liquor smuggled on board by some of the women took effect, the noise increased and scuffles broke out. Here and there a sailor struck up a tune on a fiddle or flute, and couples began dancing. Others gambled away their pay. Pervading all was the reek of unwashed humanity, mingling with the stench of bilge water and the more wholesome smells of tar, hemp, damp wood, and any livestock that had survived the voyage home without being eaten.

Old seamen writing their memoirs recalled with shame some of the scenes that took place. Samuel Leech, who had been on HMS *Macedonian* as a boy, seen action in the War of 1812, and later joined the crew of the U.S. brig *Swan*, thought there were few worse places for the moral development of young boys than a man-of-war, where there was: "Profanity in its most revolting aspect; licentiousness in its most shameful and beastly garb; vice in the worst Proteus-like shapes."[1] He recalled the boatloads of women who came on board at Portsmouth and Plymouth: "Many of these lost unfortunate creatures are in the springtime of life, some of them not without pretensions of beauty." Samuel Stokes, who had been an able seaman on the *Dreadnought* in 1809, thought: "The sins of this ship was equal to the sins of Sodom, especially on the day we was paid, for we had on board thirteen women more than the number of our ship's company, and not fifty of them married women."[2]

Admiral Hawkins was so concerned about the effects of allowing women on board ships at anchor that he published a pamphlet in 1822 entitled *Statement of Certain Immoral Practices in HM Ships*—his descriptions of what went on were so graphic that it was widely circulated and went into a second edition. He thought the women were treated like cattle and was appalled at "the disgusting conversation; the indecent, beastly conduct and horrible scenes; the blasphemy and swearing."[3] He described how men and women squeezed into hammocks a few inches away from each other so that they were witnesses of each other's actions. According to his account, they indulged in "every excess of debauchery that the grossest passions of human nature can lead them to." Captain Griffiths, who had been in the Royal Navy for thirty-two years, could not recall any such scenes, though he agreed they might take place on hulks where the seamen were not on the same deck as the midshipmen. He did concede that admitting profligate women on board was an evil practice that offended the respectable married women on the ship and had a demoralizing effect on the younger members of the crew.[4]

It was perhaps inevitable that admirals and captains whose first priority was the well-being of their ships and crew should show little sympathy for the women, who had to suffer the public humiliation and degrading treatment. Most of them blamed the women for what went on. Admiral Hawkins described them as "the vilest of women," and Leech referred to them as "defiled and defiling women." The women were certainly blamed for the increase in venereal disease that invariably occurred after a ship had spent time in port.

Alexander Whyte, the surgeon of HMS *Bellerophon*, wrote in his journal on November 19, 1804, at Spithead, "Heavy Rain—Ship very

wet and extremely filthy from so many women being on board."[5] The
visit of these women resulted in four crew members' contracting the
worst cases of venereal disease ever sent to the navy's hospital at
Haslar. While the surgeon's sick list was usually dominated by men
with fevers and fluxes, ulcers and catarrhal complaints, Whyte
recorded that after the time at Spithead, 67 men out of a total of 287
sick were suffering from venereal disease, far more than were suffering from fevers, ulcers, wounds, and other illnesses. The effect of the
loose women on the younger members of the crew is starkly illustrated
by an entry in the journal of James Farquehar, surgeon of HMS *Captain*. On October 1, 1798, he treated William Farley, who was officially
described as a third-class boy aged fifteen, but the surgeon noted that
"Though he says he is fifteen years of age I have reason to believe he
is not near so old as he has not the least appearance of having arrived
at the age of puberty."[6] The boy had slept with one of the seamen's
girls the night before they sailed from Cawsand Bay and had contracted virulent gonorrhea; the swellings around his groin were so bad
that he could hardly walk.

The sailor's return from the sea was usually portrayed in popular
prints as a joyful occasion: the sailor returning to the arms of his
sweetheart, or carousing in a waterfront tavern with the local women.

We'll spend our money merrily,
  When we come home from sea;
With every man
  A glass in his hand
And a pretty girl on his knee.

The more mischievous cartoons showed the innocent Jack-Tar
being fleeced of his wages by a pretty girl and an aged crone, or returning to find that his girl had taken up with another man in his absence. And there were numerous accounts of sailors coming ashore
after a long voyage, cheerfully and noisily squandering their money in
the whorehouses, dance halls, and drinking dens to be found in every
busy port. But the sailor's homecoming was not always an occasion for
drunken revelry. There is a memorable picture in the Ashmolean Museum in Oxford, entitled *Home from the Sea*. It is a meticulously rendered oil painting of a country churchyard. It is summer, and a young
girl dressed in black kneels on the grass beside her brother, who lies

grief-stricken on the spot where their mother has recently been buried. The boy is dressed in a sailor suit, and next to him can be seen his straw sailor hat and a bundle containing his belongings wrapped in a large handkerchief. Beyond the two figures in the foreground are a few ancient gravestones, and beyond them the decaying walls of a small country church surrounded by yew trees. A sheep and a lamb have wandered into the churchyard from the distant fields, and so vivid is the painting that one can almost hear the leaves rustling in the trees overhead and the calls of distant jackdaws.

The picture was painted by Arthur Hughes in 1862. The setting is Old Chingford Church in Essex, and the model for the sister of the sailor boy was Hughes's young wife, but as far as we know, the picture was not based on any particular event or occasion known to the artist. However, many a young sailor came home from the sea to find that one of his family had died. There is a moving passage from the memoirs of William Richardson, who went to sea as a boy on merchant ships. Returning from a voyage to the Baltic, his ship was delayed by wind and weather but eventually reached the port of Shields and was moored alongside a quay to unload her cargo of tar barrels. Richardson recalled the occasion many years later:

> I never remember being so anxious in getting on shore to see my mother again, as at this time. I never met with a greater shock. When I entered the house I perceived the family were in mourning, and inquiring the cause, was told that my poor mother had departed this life six weeks ago. I thought it impossible, and went up to her bedroom; but she was not there. I came down again almost distracted, then sat down and wept bitterly, but I could not rest—went out, and then on board, wept in silence, and thought I should never know happiness again.[7]

For sailors' wives who had waited months for news of their husbands, the sailors' return was of critical concern, because all too often the sailors did not return. The great killer of seamen was not enemy action or shipwreck but disease. The figures speak for themselves. During the French Wars from 1793 to 1815, approximately 100,000 British seamen died. Of this number, about 12 percent died from enemy action, shipwreck, or similar disasters; 20 percent died from accidents; and no less than 65 percent died from disease.[8] The diseases that most afflicted seamen were scurvy, typhus, and yellow fever. Scurvy was the result of a lack of vitamin C in the diet, and it decimated crews on lengthy voyages until the recommendations of the naval surgeon Dr. James Lind were finally put into practice toward the end of the eighteenth century. Typhus was often brought aboard ships by press-ganged men who had been confined for weeks in overcrowded and unsanitary conditions. With several hundred men crammed into a ship, it could spread rapidly, and men died horribly within two or three weeks of going down with the disease.

Even more feared by seamen and soldiers alike were the tropical fevers that made a posting to the West Indies or the tropical coast of Africa appear like a sentence of death. In 1726, an expedition to the Caribbean under Admiral Hosier lost more than 4,000 dead out of a squadron of 4,750. This was an unusually high proportion, but malignant yellow fever continued to wreak havoc among the crews of ships stationed in West Indian harbors. In 1806, William Turnbull published *The Naval Surgeon,* a massive volume based on his practical experience as a surgeon in the navy. He warned that the West Indies was the most unhealthy of all stations and advised captains of ships to anchor as far from land as possible. Of yellow fever, he wrote that "the first symptoms are sudden giddiness and loss of sight, to such a degree as to make the person fall down insensible." During the final stages, "the foam issues from the mouth; the eyes roll dreadfully; and the extremities are convulsed, being thrown out and pulled back in violent and quick alternate succession."[9]

Many of the sailors who survived disease returned home with crippling injuries from shipboard accidents or wounds sustained in action. Nelson, who lost his sight in one eye during the siege of Calvi in 1794, and had his right arm amputated following a disastrous attack on Tenerife, was only the most famous of many. Disabled sailors with begging bowls were a familiar sight on the streets of London, Portsmouth, and other ports, and the naval hospitals were filled with men suffering from appalling injuries.

There is a passage in the memoirs of William Spavens that describes the state of the men in the queue for the Chatham Chest, the pension board for disabled seamen. After long service in the navy and on East Indiamen, Spavens suffered a major injury to his right leg while handling casks in a longboat alongside his ship and had to have the limb amputated. He was in good company at Chatham. There were men swinging on crutches with a wooden leg below the knee, or above the knee, or with both legs missing. There were men with their noses shot off, or pieces torn from their cheeks, or missing their jawbones or chins. One man had his skull fractured and trepanned and a silver plate substituted for the missing bone. There were many who had lost a hand, an arm, or both arms. Some had their limbs permanently contracted by their injuries; "some with a hand off and an eye out; another with an eye out and his face perforated with grains of battle-powder, which leaves as lasting impression as though they were injected by an Italian artist."[10] These were the victims of the shipboard accidents and the naval wars of the Napoleonic period. At the Battle of Camperdown in 1797, for instance, there were 244 men killed and 796 wounded in the British fleet alone. At Trafalgar, 1,700 men were killed and wounded in the British ships, and three times that number among the French and Spanish ships.

The navy had arrangements in place during the eighteenth century that in theory provided some support for seamen's widows. In practice the systems were haphazard and in some cases entirely unsatisfactory. When a ship's company was paid off after a voyage, a seaman's widow was entitled to her husband's back pay, but this was not as simple as it might appear. The woman would first have to make her way to the port where the ship was being paid off (it could be several hundred miles from where she lived and involve an expensive journey). She then had to provide written proof that she was the widow of the deceased man. And having arrived at Spithead or Plymouth or the Nore and tracked down her husband's ship, she could find that payment was delayed because the men's wages were in arrears since paying off could take months or even years. However, things were improved by an Act of Parliament of 1792, which decreed that seamen, marines, and warrant officers could collect all of their accumulated pay upon their arrival in Britain or Ireland, even if their ships had not yet been paid off. The same act allowed them to send pay to their families while abroad, and if they died, the pay could be remitted to their families via a local office or agent. From 1797, seamen received their full pay while injured until they either recovered, were discharged to Greenwich Hospital, or were given a pension from the Chatham Chest.

For seamen killed at sea in a shipboard accident or during battle there was an established tradition that the clothes and belongings of the dead man should be auctioned off to the members of the crew

and the proceeds passed on to his widow. Seamen were usually generous in their bids, but this could only provide temporary relief. The
most ingenious system devised by the navy was the practice of listing
"widow's men" on the muster book of every vessel in commission. It
was a system that dated back to the reign of Henry VIII and was originally intended for the widows of commissioned and warrant officers;
from 1733, it was applied to all seamen who died on board. Two
widow's men were listed on the books for every hundred men in the
crew: They were rated as able seamen but were entirely nonexistent.
The pay of these fictitious men became a pension fund for widows of
seamen who died during the course of the voyage. The irony of the
system, as Suzanne Stark has pointed out, was that the navy paid out
for the invisible widow's men listed in the muster book, but it was not
prepared to list on the muster book and pay or provide victuals for the
warrant officers' wives who were very much alive and present on large
numbers of ships in the fleet.

The most satisfactory system was that introduced in August 1732,
"for the relief of Poor Widows of Commission and Warrant Officers
of the Royal Navy."[11] Three pence of every pound was deducted from
the pay and half-pay of officers, and this, together with any benefac-
tions from well-disposed persons, was put into a fund administered by
a Court of Commissioners, who distributed the money to naval officers' wives who could provide satisfactory certificates in support of
their claims. The governors of the court were extremely grand (in
1750, Lord Sandwich was president of the court and with him were
Lord Anson, Lord Barrington, and Admiral Townsend), but the
records indicate that they dealt fairly and sympathetically with all the
petitions presented to them. In July 1733, an advertisement was published in the *Gazette and Daily Courant* setting out the rules of the system and how the widows might apply. At one of the first meetings of
the court, on July 3, 1733, the sum of £542 was divided up and distributed to the widows of six boatswains, two gunners, two carpenters,
two pursers, two surgeons, three masters, "and one Susan Perry,
widow of a Master of a Vessel appointed by the Navy Board."

Naval widows fared best if their husbands died during one of
those sea battles that captured the popular imagination and were hailed
at home as glorious victories. Such battles would invariably be followed by a public outpouring of thanks and generosity. After Lord

Howe's victory over the French at the battle of the Glorious First of June in 1794, Dr. Thomas Trotter, physician to the fleet, reckoned that gifts from the people of London for the widows and orphans of those killed amounted to between £20,000 and £30,000.[12] The company of the Theatre Royal, on Drury Lane, gave a performance that raised £1,800, and Lord Howe himself gave his own share of the prize money for the wounded. After the Battle of Camperdown in 1797, Lloyds of London opened a Patriotic Fund, which collected £52,609 from all parts of the kingdom for the benefit of the wounded seamen and the widows of those killed.[13]

For the seaman's wife whose husband survived tropical fevers, scurvy, shipboard accidents, sea battles, or shipwreck, and who returned home without serious injuries, life could still be very hard. The wage of an ordinary seaman in the mid-eighteenth century was 19 shillings a lunar month (20 shillings and 7 pence a calendar month), an amount that had not changed since Cromwell's day. From this sum was deducted 1 shilling for the Chatham Chest, and 6 pence for Greenwich Hospital. Most seamen also owed money to the purser for clothing and tobacco. The remaining sum did not compare badly with wages for unskilled laboring jobs on land, but the problem was the very long intervals between payments. Payment was not made until a ship ended her commission, which could be anything from six months to three years from the moment the seaman signed on. To discourage the men from deserting, the payments were usually made shortly before the ship sailed on her next commission, and with the ship anchored in the outer reaches of the harbor well away from the shore. If a seaman's wife wanted to be certain that she got a share of her husband's wages, she would have to be on board when the commissioner of the dockyard and his clerks came out with the wages in cash to pay the ship's company. If she was not present at the time, many seamen would have been tempted to squander the cash at the first opportunity they had to go ashore.

The scandal of the long delays in payment was acknowledged by the Navy Act of 1758, which required ships in home waters to be paid a year's wages every eighteen months, a gesture toward the seamen's problems. The difficulties experienced by seamen's families were also recognized by the 1758 act, which provided the mechanism to enable seamen to send money to their relations free, via government channels.

However, very few seamen seem to have taken advantage of this piece of legislation. This may have been because the bureaucracy of the system was too daunting, or it may simply reflect the fact that a relatively small proportion of ordinary seamen were married. The majority of the married men in the British Navy were commissioned officers or warrant officers, and most of these would have made their own financial arrangements through lawyers or dockyard agents.

Although naval officers were better paid than their men, they were paid no more frequently and had many more expenses than an ordinary seaman. The principal expense for a young naval officer was his uniform: The full-dress uniform for a commander cost 16 to 20 guineas; his undress coat and epaulette were 8 guineas; his gold lace hat cost 5 guineas; and a sword and knot cost 6 guineas. In total, this was likely to cost him considerably more than his first quarter's pay.[14] On top of this, he had to pay for his navigational instruments and books. A young lieutenant even had to pay 11 shillings and 6 pence for the piece of parchment confirming his commission. It was not until 1795 that officers could have all their half-pay and an advance of three months' full pay on appointment to cover expenses, and could receive part of their pay while abroad. Officers who were living on their pay, which was quite normal, could suffer considerable hardship even while employed—and this meant that their wives and children suffered, too.

Admirals, who received the lion's share of prize money from the capture of enemy ships in wartime, could earn very large sums, and a few were able to buy themselves splendid houses and country estates. However, this in itself could be a burden for the admiral's wife, especially if her husband was away on active service for any length of time. During the long months that Admiral Boscawen was at sea, his wife, Fanny, was responsible not only for bringing up their five children but also for running their country house near Guildford and overseeing the acres of farmland that came with it. In a letter written to her husband on June 9, 1755, she described a typical day.

She rose at half past six, and her first task was to feed the forty ducks and chickens that she kept under the laundry window. She then paid a visit to Mrs. Farr, the housekeeper, and ordered dinner and discussed household affairs: "By the way, beef is 4 pence a pound, and they threatened me with 4½ pence when first I came, and made me pay that price for one sirloin."[15] Along with her two daughters, who had been woken at six o'clock by Nanny Humphreys, she proceeded to the farmyard, where she inquired about the horses and had a discussion with Woodrose, the estate manager. They then walked into the village and back, and at nine they sat down to breakfast in the admiral's dressing room. After breakfast, the girls spent the morning working while she wrote letters. At around one o'clock, they walked to the grove, and at exactly two o'clock, the bell rang for dinner, "for Mrs. Farr is very exact, but I think, not much of a cook."

In the afternoon, they fed the chickens again, went for another walk, and then settled down in the dressing room where Fanny worked while Miss Pitt read aloud. This continued until almost eight o'clock, when the girls went to bed. An evening walk in the park was followed by another conference with Woodrose. Supper was at nine, and it was not until eleven that Fanny went to bed. On the surface, it was a pleasant, untroubled existence, reminiscent of the lives of many of Jane Austen's heroines fifty years later. One suspects, however, that Fanny did not wish to burden her husband with more worries than he already had, and the evidence suggests that she took the running of the estate very seriously and was a first-class manager. Writing a few weeks later, Fanny was able to report that the estate was flourishing under her administration: The hay had been got in and stacked; the turnips were sowed; the two pastures in the park had been rolled; the horses were thriving; and her barley was not only the finest in the parish, but was a fortnight ahead of schedule and entirely free from weeds.

The wives of ordinary seamen in the Royal Navy did not have great estates to manage. Precise details about the plight of these women in the eighteenth and early nineteenth centuries are hard to come by, but from a variety of sources we catch glimpses of women struggling to support themselves and their families, sometimes having to resort to desperate means to do so. From the accounts of the chaplain of Newgate prison, we learn of sailor's wives who were hanged for resorting to theft. Mary Dutton, the widow of a sailor killed at Cartagena, was hanged at Tyburn on January 13, 1742, for stealing a watch in Piccadilly. Elizabeth Fox, a sailor's wife, was hanged on March 18, 1741, for stealing £9 and five Portugal pieces from a dwelling house.[16] She was reputed to have been one of the most notorious pickpockets in London. The drawings and engravings of artists and caricaturists like Rowlandson and Cruikshank frequently drew attention to the poverty-stricken state of naval wives; popular ballads sometimes did the same. There was, for instance, a ballad entitled "The Sea Martyrs; or, the seamen's sad lamentation for their faithful service, bad pay, and cruel usage." This was prompted by the case of a group of sailors from HMS *Suffolk* who had protested over lack of pay and had been executed. The ballad argued their case with passion:

> Their starving families at home
>   Expected their slow pay would come;
> But our proud Court meant no such thing,
>   Not one groat must they have till spring;
> To starve all summer would not do,
>   They must starve all winter too.
>
> Their poor wives with care languished,
>   Their children cried for want of bread,
> Their debts increased, and none would more
>   Lend them, or let them run o' th' score.
> In such a case what could they do
>   But ask those who money did owe?[17]

In Portsmouth, the local churchwardens were forced to appeal to the Admiralty for financial assistance because they could not afford to provide relief for "the great number of Sailors and Soldiers, their Wives and Families, and others, who Daily resort there."[18] The 1821 census listed the town as having 2,881 males to 4,388 females, and in some areas of the town, most of the young women had resorted to prostitution in order to support themselves. No doubt, many sailors' wives took in lodgers, went into domestic service, took in laundry, and did other menial work to earn a livelihood. Some are known to have run taverns and lodging houses. But all this had to be done in addition to having to bring up a large family.

For many women, the worst thing about being married to a sailor or a deep-sea fisherman was the prolonged separation from their husband. They were left to fend for themselves in a predominantly male-oriented society, and they suffered from loneliness and the constant anxiety of wondering whether their husband would be lost at sea. This was the case whether they were married to admirals or able seamen or fishermen. "O my Rodney, what pain and anxiety does your absence cause me," wrote Jenny to her husband, Captain George Rodney, in

1756.[19] Somehow the sailors' women and their families survived, partly through their own efforts, and partly through the help of friends and relations. But always hanging over them was the knowledge that their husbands, sons, or brothers might not return from the sea.

The agony of the parting and the worry about the safe return of loved ones affected sailors' women of every age and every seafaring country. It is nowhere more poignantly expressed than in a letter written by Sarah Atrander of New York to her young brother Henry, who had run off to sea. She was devastated by his departure and was worried not simply for herself but for her older brother John and for their aged parents, who she feared would not be alive when he returned. The letter, dated May 28, 1845, is so evocative that it deserves to be quoted at some length:

> Many hours have I sat by my window watching the passers by and listening to the door thinking to see my dearest Brother. Oh Henry how can I bear to hear little Sis lisp your name when she returns which she will do, who love you so dearly. The same afternoon you left John went up to see you and imagine his feelings when told you had gone he returned home with a heavy heart late at night and said you had gone oh Henry how could you leave us all and John who has done so much for you he would have spent his last breath for you. . . . John is not very well and I think you may never see him again he is about doctoring but he is born down with trouble and you leaving is the greatest.

She gave him news of the family and concluded:

> And remember there is a God who rules all and to whom we must all render an account at the day of judgement and I have no more time but must say that all the Family wishes you well and would like to see you home again and now I must bid you a fond Farewell and dear Henry the tears trickle down my cheeks when I must say Farewell again and I fear forever where the Seas I fear will be your burial place if you are spared write an answer immediately and send to your dear Sister She can have only one lock of your hair as a remembrance do send it me if possible I can't write more your aged and afflicted Father wants to carry this to John.
>
> From your dear and affectionate Sister,
> Sarah

May God see fit to make you one of his followers and
spare you once more to return to the arms of your friend
which will always be open to receive you. Farewell Henry.[20]

The seafarers who tend to be forgotten were the offshore fishermen. Throughout the year, they put to sea in relatively small open
boats. Sometimes they launched their boats through the surf off open
beaches, sometimes they set off from river estuaries with constantly
changing mudbanks and shoals. The more fortunate fishermen sailed
out of fine natural harbors; the less fortunate sailed from tiny harbors
constructed around inlets on rocky coasts, which were difficult and
dangerous to enter in onshore winds. A variety of sizes and shapes of
fishing vessels were developed over many generations to cope with the
local conditions, and most were famously seaworthy in normal conditions. But all fishing boats, particularly those that were open or half-
decked, were vulnerable to capsizing or swamping by the seas in
violent storms. In the days before scientific weather forecasting, even
the most careful fishermen could be caught out at sea by an unexpected
squall or by the rapid buildup of storm-force winds.

In the autumn of 1881, the east coast of Britain from the Orkneys
to the English Channel was hit by a storm that seemed to come out of
nowhere. On Friday, October 14, forty-five fishing boats manned by
279 men and boys put to sea from the various fishing villages along the
coast of Berwickshire. They headed out to the fishing grounds and
shot their lines when they were some eight miles from the shore. The
sea was calm, and conditions were ideal for fishing. Some of those on
shore noted an ominously rapid fall in the barometer, and toward mid-
day, heavy thunderclouds began to gather. The wind rose to hurricane
force and soon whipped up a raging sea. The boats ran for shelter, but
only twenty-six made it back to harbor, many of which lost men who
were washed overboard; several boats were hurled onto the beaches
and wrecked in full view of those on shore; 189 men and boys were
drowned. The fishing village of Eyemouth lost 129 men, Burnmouth
lost 24, and the rest came from other villages on the Berwick and Loth-
ian coast. The figures may seem small compared with the numerous
disasters we constantly hear of today, but the effect on the close-knit
fishing villages was devastating: 263 children were left fatherless.
There was scarcely a household in Eyemouth that had not lost a father,
husband, or son, and formerly prosperous communities were ruined.[21]

The same gale was witnessed by the great American artist Winslow Homer, who had taken residence a few months earlier in the Yorkshire fishing village of Cullercoats. He made several sketchbook studies of the Tynemouth lifeboat being launched off the beach and rowing out to rescue the crew of the bark *Iron Crown,* which had been driven aground while trying to make for the shelter of Tynemouth Harbor. But more memorable than his pictures of the lifeboat and the wreck are his brilliantly executed watercolors of the fisherwomen and girls of Cullercoats. He shows them mending nets, knitting socks, and carrying fish baskets along the beach. Several depict the young women on board the fishing boats alongside the men. But the most evocative are those that show the women waiting. Some of them huddle by the lifeboat station; others stand on the windswept shore staring out to sea, hoping and praying that their men will return safely.

Similar themes were taken up by the English artists of the Newlyn School. A group of some thirty artists took up residence in the Cornish fishing village in the 1880s. Their unofficial leader was Stanhope Forbes, and their principal subject matter was the daily life of the local people. The artists painted their weddings and their funerals, their houses, the harbor, and the fishing boats. Above all, they painted the fishermen's wives and children, and in doing so, they provide us with an extraordinarily vivid picture of what went on indoors and outdoors in a typical late-nineteenth-century fishing community. They are a salutary reminder of the crucial part the women played in keeping the local economy going. Of course, they carried out all the unsung jobs of bringing up the children, shopping, making the meals, and doing the washing. But they also made the seagoing gear for the fishermen. They knitted their jerseys and socks, sewed up their oilskins, and made their flannel shirts. They repaired the nets, helped the men unload the boats, and packed the fish in barrels. They worked hard, but compared to the lives of many women in the industrial towns and cities of their period, they seemed to live an idyllic existence. The paintings of the Newlyn artists show the children playing with toy boats at the water's edge or picking apples in the orchards. The sun sparkles on the water in the harbor. A pretty young mother sits beside a basket of onions tying them in bunches, while her little boy sits beside her showing her with delight the tiny crab he has caught.

But the artists also captured the somber side of Newlyn life. They lived long enough in the village to observe firsthand the tragedies that took place when fishing boats failed to return. One picture in particular sums up the precarious nature of life in such a community. It is entitled *A Hopeless Dawn,* and it was painted by Frank Bramley in 1888. The artist spent nearly ten years in Newlyn, living in a small, two-room fisherman's cottage, and the oil painting established his reputation when it was hung at the Royal Academy. The other Newlyn artists were generous in their praise. Stanhope Forbes later wrote, "Bramley's picture strikes me more than ever. I cannot describe how beautiful it is," and Dame Laura Knight said of it, "Tears came into my eyes, I thought it so wonderful."[22]

The painting shows the interior of a fisherman's cottage at dawn. A table is laid in readiness for his return. Through the window can be glimpsed a cold gray sky and an angry gray sea. Kneeling on the floor with her head in her mother's lap is the young fisherman's wife, who now knows that her husband will never return. There is a large family Bible open beside the fisherman's mother, who has evidently been trying to comfort her daughter with readings from the scriptures. The face of the daughter is hidden, and the mother's face can scarcely be seen. All is revealed in their gestures. More clearly than any words, the picture reminds us of the grief that has been the lot of so many seafarers' women.

GLOSSARY OF SEA TERMS

aft, after—Situated at or toward the back, or stern, part of a vessel.

block and tackle—An arrangement of pulleys and ropes used to raise heavy loads, and to increase the purchase on ropes used for the running rigging.

boatswain (bosun)—The warrant officer in charge of sails, rigging, anchors, and associated gear.

bowsprit—A heavy spar pointing forward from the stem, or front, of the vessel.

brace—A rope used to control the horizontal movement of a square-sailed yard.

brig—A two-masted vessel, the foremast square-rigged and the mainmast rigged with a fore-and-aft sail on the lower part and a square topsail and topgallant.

brigantine—A two-masted vessel with a square-rigged foremast and a fore-and-aft rigged mainmast; until about the middle of the eighteenth century, the mainmast had a square sail on the topmast.

broadside—The simultaneous firing of all the guns on one side of a ship.

bulkhead—A vertical partition inside a ship.

bumboat—A small boat used to bring out and sell fruit, vegetables, and other produce to the sailors on ships anchored some distance from the shore.

caulk—To seal the gaps between the planks with oakum and pitch.

clipper—A very fast square-rigged sailing ship that was used to transport tea, wool, and other valuable bulk cargoes in the second half of the nineteenth century.

colors—The flags worn by a vessel to show her nationality.

cutter—A small one-masted vessel rigged with a fore-and-aft mainsail, foresail, and jib; in the eighteenth century, a cutter usually had a square topsail as well.

deadeye—A round wooden block with three holes for securing the shrouds to the sides of the ship at the chainplates.

fathom—A measure of six feet, used to describe the depth of water, length of rope, etc.

East Indiaman——A large ship engaged in, and usually built for, trade with the East Indies.

flagship——A ship commanded by an admiral and flying his distinguishing flag.

flag captain——The captain in command of a flagship. (Captain Hardy was Nelson's flag captain on board HMS *Victory* at the Battle of Trafalgar.)

fore——Situated in front; the front part of a vessel at the bow.

fore-and-aft——At bow and stern; backward and forward; along the length of the ship, or in the direction of its principal axis.

fore-and-aft rig——Having only fore-and-aft sails, i.e., sails set lengthwise and not across the ship's hull. *Compare* square-rig.

forecastle, fo'c'sle——The short deck built over the fore part of the main deck; the forward part of a ship where the sailors lived.

foremast——The mast at the front of the vessel.

frigate——A fast-cruising warship, less heavily armed than a ship of the line; in the Royal Navy, frigates were Fifth or Sixth Rates with between 40 and 20 guns carried on a continuous single deck and on the quarterdeck.

halyard——A rope for raising and lowering a sail or yard.

galley——The ship's kitchen.

grog——A drink of rum diluted with water.

gunwale——The uppermost planking along the sides of the vessel.

hatch boat——A type of fishing boat used in the Thames Estuary.

heave to (past tense: *hove to*)——To check the course of a vessel and bring her to a standstill by heading her into the wind and backing some of the sails.

helm——The tiller or wheel that controls the rudder and enables a vessel to be steered.

lee——The side or direction away from the wind, or downwind.

lee shore——The shore onto which the wind is blowing; a hazardous shore for a sailing vessel, particularly in strong or gale-force winds.

mainmast——The mast at the center of the ship or vessel, always the largest in square-rigged ships; the name of the first section of the mainmast in a square-rigged ship: the others are the maintopmast, maintopgallant mast, and main royal mast.

man of war——An armed ship belonging to the navy of a country or state.

mizzenmast——The mast toward the stern, or back, of a ship or vessel.

pink——A flat-bottomed merchant vessel with a relatively shallow draught and a narrow stern, variously rigged as a brig, a sloop, or a ship; a type of Dutch fishing boat that was launched off the beaches near Scheveningen.

poop deck——The aftermost and highest deck of a ship, in the largest ships.

port——The left side of a vessel, facing forward.

press gang—A group of men, led by an officer, who rounded up men for service in the Royal Navy.

quarterdeck—A deck above the main deck, which stretched from the stern to about halfway along the length of the ship. It was from this deck that the captain and officers controlled the ship.

rate (as in *First Rate, Second Rate,* etc.)—Warships in the Royal Navy were grouped into six different categories according to the number of guns they carried. In the middle of the eighteenth century, a First Rate ship had 100 guns, a Second Rate ship had 90 guns, a Third Rate had 80 to 70 guns, a Fourth Rate had 64 to 50 guns, a Fifth Rate had 40 to 28 guns, and a Sixth Rate had 24 and 12 guns. As time went on and ships got larger, the number of guns in each rate increased.

reef—To reduce the area of a sail by rolling it up or bundling part of it and securing that part to the yard with short lines called reef-points.

schooner—A two-masted vessel, fore-and-aft rigged on both masts; some schooners had square topsails on the foremast or on both topmasts.

scuppers—Holes in a ship's side for carrying off water from the deck.

sextant—An instrument with a graduated arc of 60 degrees used for navigation.

sheet—A rope leading aft from the lower corner of a sail to control its position.

ship—A vessel with three or more square-rigged articulated masts (articulated masts could have the topgallant and topmast removed for safety in high weather: *see* mainmast); informally, any large seagoing vessel.

ship-of-the-line—A warship large enough to take her place in the line of battle; in the late eighteenth century, this usually ranged from Third Rate ships of 74 to 80 guns up to First Rate ships of 100 guns or more, and their foreign equivalents.

shrouds—The set of ropes forming part of the standing rigging and supporting the mast, topmast, and topgallantmast laterally.

slop seller—A supplier of clothes for sailors.

sloop—A vessel having one fore-and-aft rigged mast with mainsail and a single foresail; in the Royal Navy, any ship or vessel commanded by an officer with the rank of master and commander, usually rigged as a ship or brig and with 16 to 18 guns.

spar—A stout wooden pole used for the mast or yard of a sailing vessel.

square-rig—Having principally sails set to yards across the ship's hull, often with additional fore-and-aft sails, e.g., jibs set on the bowsprit. *Compare* fore-and-aft rig.

starboard—The right side of a vessel, facing forward.

supernumerary—A person borne on the ship's books surplus to the established complement.

tack—To change the direction of a sailing vessel's course by turning her bows into the wind until the wind blows on her other side. *Compare* wear. To be on the port/starboard tack is to sail with the wind coming over the port/starboard quarter.

tender—A vessel attending a larger vessel and used to supply stores or convey passengers.

three-decker—The largest class of warship, with upward of 90 guns on three gundecks, as well as the quarterdeck, forecastle, and often poop deck.

top (as in *foretop, maintop, mizzentop*)—A platform built at the head of the lowest section of the mast, serving to spread the topmast rigging and provide a place for sailors working aloft.

topmen—The sailors who went aloft to raise or lower the sails.

topsail—A sail set on the topmast.

warrant officers—These ranked below the commissioned officers (the captain and lieutenants) and included the master, purser, surgeon, gunner, boatswain, and carpenter.

wear (as in *to wear ship*)—To change the direction of a sailing vessel's course by turning her bows away from the wind until the wind blows on her other side. *Compare* tack.

weigh—To pull up the anchor.

yard—A long spar suspended from the mast of a vessel to extend the sails.

yardarm—Either end of a yard.

NOTES

Key to Abbreviations Within the Notes

ADM   Admiralty and Navy Board records held in the Public Record Office, London
CO   Colonial Office records
HMSO   Her Majesty's Stationery Office
PRO   Public Record Office, London
PROB   Probate: copies of sea officers' wills held in the Public Record Office, London

Introduction

1. ADM 1/5383.
2. Captain's Orders, HMS *Indefatigable*, quoted from *Shipboard Life and Organisation, 1731–1815*, ed. B. Lavery (Navy Records Society, Aldershot, U.K., 1998), 188.
3. *The Annual Report of the U.S. Life Saving Service*, 1881, quoted from M. L. Clifford and J. C. Clifford, *Women Who Kept the Lights* (Williamsburg, Va., 1993), 96.
4. David Spinney, *Rodney* (London, 1969), 115.

1. Women on the Waterfront

1. Bracebridge Hemyng, "Prostitution in London," in Henry Mayhew, *London Labour and the London Poor* (first published 1851; edition cited London, 1967), 233.
2. John Cremer, *Ramblin' Jack: The Journal of Captain John Cremer, 1700–1774*, ed. R. Reynell Bellamy (London, 1936), 32.
3. Ned Ward, *The London Spy* (first published 1703; edition cited Folio Society, London, 1955), 250.
4. Ibid., 251.
5. For much useful information on the role of women in alehouses, see Peter Clark, *The English Alehouse: A Social History, 1200–1830* (London, 1983), 203–6, 225, 235–36, 285.
6. Ibid., 285 and 302.
7. John Stow, *A Survey of London*, quoted by Stephen Inwood, *A History of London* (London, 1998), 185.
8. The details of the life of Damaris Page are taken from E. J. Burford and Joy Wotton, *Private Vices—Public Virtues: Bawdry in London from Elizabethan Times to the Regency* (London, 1995), 70–76.

9. Report by Patrick Colquhoun, quoted by John Pudney, *London's Docks* (London, 1975), 18.

10. Quoted by Lawrence Stone, *The Family, Sex and Marriage* (edition cited paperback, London, 1990), 392.

11. Ibid., 393.

12. John Harris, *Harris's List of Covent-Garden Ladies: Or, Man of Pleasure's Kalender, for the Year 1788* (London, 1788), 25.

13. Ibid., 141.

14. Ibid., 91.

15. Hemyng, 231.

16. Ibid., 229.

17. John Binney, "Thieves and Swindlers," in Mayhew, 365.

18. Hemyng, 230.

19. Timothy Gilfoyle, *City of Eros: New York City, Prostitution, and the Commercialization of Sex, 1790–1920* (New York, 1992), 50.

20. Quoted by Gilfoyle, 49.

21. William Sanger, *The History of Prostitution: Its Extent, Causes and Effects Throughout the World* (first published 1858; edition cited New York, 1939), 562.

22. *National Police Gazette* (New York), March 20, 1847.

23. *National Police Gazette* (New York), March 6, 1847.

24. *National Police Gazette* (New York), May 22, 1847.

25. Gilfoyle, 63.

26. Ibid., 55–56.

27. *National Police Gazette* (New York), January 2, 1847.

28. Gilfoyle, 70.

29. Marilynn Wood Hill, *Their Sisters' Keepers: Prostitution in New York City, 1830–1870* (Berkeley, Los Angeles, and London, 1993), 102–3.

30. Hill, 282–84; Gilfoyle, 71.

31. Gilfoyle, 71.

32. Frank Soule, John H. Gihon, and James Nisbet, *The Annals of San Francisco* (New York, San Francisco, and London, 1855), 176.

33. Soule, 355, 391, 427.

34. Most of the details for the description of life in San Francisco are taken from Herbert Asbury, *The Barbary Coast: An Informal History of the San Francisco Underworld* (London, 1934), and Stan Hugill, *Sailortown* (London, 1967), which contains graphic accounts of San Francisco as well as the more notorious sailors' districts of other ports around the world.

35. See Reverend G. P. Merrick, *Work Among the Fallen, as Seen in the Prison Cell* (London, New York, and Melbourne, 1891).

36. Merrick, 38.

37. Gilfoyle, 64.

38. Sanger, 563.

39. Merrick, 51.

40. Judith R. Walkowitz and Daniel J. Walkowitz, " 'We Are Not Beasts of the Field': Prostitution and the Poor in Plymouth and Southampton under the Contagious Diseases Acts," in *Clio's Consciousness Raised*, ed. Mary S. Hartman and Louis Banner (New York, 1976). See also Judith R. Walkowitz, *Prostitution and Victorian Society: Women, Class and the State* (London and New York, 1980); and Linda M. Maloney, "Doxies at Dockside: Prostitution and American Maritime Society, 1800–1900," in *Ships, Seafaring and Society: Essays in Maritime History*, ed. Timothy J. Runyan (Detroit, Mich., 1987).

2. The Sailors' Farewell

1. See chapter 14, "The Sailors' Return," for a description of the extraordinary scenes that took place on board many naval ships when they returned to harbor.
2. The origins of the naval press gang go back to Tudor times and earlier. Originally, the word was "imprest," which derived from the Latin word *praestare*, to be a surety for something, and the old French word *prest*, meaning a loan or advance. "Imprest" therefore meant money paid in advance to somebody for state or government business. By the late eighteenth century, the word had become "impress," and the groups of men under an officer who carried out impressment were called press gangs.
3. Nicholas Blake and Richard Lawrence, *The Illustrated Companion to Nelson's Navy* (London, 2000), 64.
4. Nicholas A. M. Rodger, "The Naval World of Jack Aubrey," in *Patrick O'Brian: Critical Appreciations and a Bibliography* (London, 1994), 51. For a detailed description of impressment in the Royal Navy during the Seven Years' War of 1756 to 1763, see N. A. M. Rodger, *The Wooden World: An Anatomy of the Georgian Navy* (London, 1986); and for a description of impressment in the wars against France of 1794 to 1815, see Dudley Pope, *Life in Nelson's Navy* (London, 1981, and paperback edition, 1997). For a useful general survey, see J. R. Hutchinson, *The Press-gang Afloat and Ashore* (London, 1913).
5. William Spavens, *The Narrative of William Spavens, a Chatham Pensioner, Written by Himself* (Louth, England, 1796), 38.
6. ADM 1/1490.
7. ADM 1/1534.
8. ADM 1/1537.
9. Ibid.
10. Ibid.
11. Spavens, 36.
12. William Richardson, *A Mariner of England: An Account of the Career of William Richardson from Cabin Boy in the Merchant Service to Warrant Officer in the Royal Navy*, ed. Colonel Spencer Childers (London, 1908), 292.
13. Charles Cunningham, *A Narrative of the Mutiny at the Nore* (Chatham, 1829), 23.
14. ADM 1/920.
15. Jesse Lemisch, "Jack Tar in the Streets: Merchant Seamen in the Politics of Revolutionary America," in *William and Mary Quarterly* 25 (1968) 383–84.
16. Lemisch, 391.
17. William Nevens, *Forty Years at Sea: or a Narrative of the Adventures of William Nevens, Being an Authentic Account of the Vicissitudes, Hardships, Narrow Escapes, Shipwrecks and Sufferings in Forty Years Experience at Sea, Written by Himself* (Portland, Maine, 1850).

3. Ann Parker and the Mutiny at the Nore

1. The details of the Mutiny at the Nore and the story of Ann Parker are taken from *The Whole Trial and Defence of Richard Parker . . . On Board the Sandwich and Others of His Majesty's Ships at the Nore, in May 1797* (London, 1797); William Jackson, *The Newgate Calendar*, VI (London, 1818), 497–508; the logbook of HMS *L'Espion*, and various captains' letters; J. R. Hutchinson, *The Press Gang, Afloat and Ashore* (London, 1913), 273–79; and Charles Cunningham, *A Narrative of the Mutiny at the Nore* (Chatham, 1829). Captain Cunningham was commander of HMS *Clyde*, which

was stationed at the Nore at the time of the mutiny. His *Narrative* is a day-by-day account of the course of events.

2. According to Captain Cunningham, "Parker was said to be the son of a tradesman at Exeter, and in the year 1786 was a midshipman on board the *Culloden* from which ship he was discharged in consequence of his immoral conduct, the Captain considering him a bad example for the younger gentlemen. He was afterwards in the *Leander,* and was discharged from her for the same reason." No indication is given of what his immoral conduct might have been. See Cunningham, 87.

3. *Trial and Defence of Richard Parker.*

4. The captain's log of *L'Espion* for Friday, June 30, notes, "Winds easterly variable," and by 8:00 A.M., "Fresh Breezes and Cloudy."

5. In his letters of July 17 and August 5, 1800, Isaac Coffin, commissioner of the navy at Sheerness, complained about the constant disorderly conduct of the common prostitutes in the shipyard. See *The Mariner's Mirror,* January 1950, 92–93.

6. The certificate is quoted in full in the report in Jackson's *Newgate Calendar,* 508:

> London, July 4 1797
>
> I, Ann Parker, wife of the late Richard Parker, deceased, do hereby certify, that, at my particular request, I have this day seen the body of my late husband, in the Burying Vault of St. Mary, Whitechapel, by permission of the Rector, and Church-Warden of the said Parish; that the burial service was duly performed over him; and that I am perfectly satisfied with the mode of his interment, and the indulgence that I have received from the minister and officers of the said parish. (Signed) Ann Parker.

7. Quoted by Hutchinson, 279.

8. The letter is printed in full in Peter Kemp, *The British Sailor: A Social History of the Lower Deck* (London, 1970), 186.

9. The story of Margaret Dickson is taken from Jackson, *The Newgate Calendar,* II (London, 1818), 153–56.

4. Female Sailors: Fact and Fiction

1. The details of Louisa Baker's life are taken from *The Female Marine and Related Works: Narratives of Cross-Dressing and Urban Vice in America's Early Republic,* edited and with an introduction by Daniel A. Cohen (Boston, Mass., 1997). This invaluable and scholarly book prints the full text of the three parts of the story of Miss Lucy Brewer (also called Louisa Baker and Mrs. Lucy West), as well as *A Brief Reply to the Late Writings of Louisa Baker,* by Rachel Sperry, and *The Surprising Adventures of Almira Paul.* Of the numerous editions of the story of Lucy Brewer, Cohen has selected the text of the tenth edition of 1816 as being the most complete.

2. Cohen, 65.

3. Ibid., 69.

4. Ibid., 72.

5. Ibid., 81.

6. Deborah Sampson Gannet joined the American army in 1778 and served three years as a soldier: See Linda Grant de Pauw, *Founding Mothers: Women in America in the*

Revolutionary Era (Boston, 1975). Other examples include *The Female Volunteer; or the Life, and Wonderful Adventures of Miss Eliza Allen* (Cincinnati, Ohio, 1851); and Loreta Janeta Velazquez, *The Woman in Battle: A Narrative of the Exploits, Adventures, and Travels,* ed. C. J. Worthington (1876, reprint New York, 1972). For a fascinating discussion of the role of army wives, see Paul E. Kopperman, "The British High Command and Soldiers' Wives in America, 1755–1783," in *Journal of the Society for Army Historical Research,* 60, 14–34.

7. They include Hannah Snell (first published in 1750), Mary Anne Talbot (first published in 1804), and Mary Lacy (first published in 1773).

8. Suzanne J. Stark, *Female Tars: Women Aboard Ship in the Age of Sail* (London, 1996).

9. Ibid., 87.

10. ADM 37/5680.

11. Much of the original text of the story of Mary Lacy is quoted in Stark, 123–66. Stark has checked the facts of the story against ships' muster books and other British Admiralty papers and provides detailed documentation to show that Lacy's account of her remarkable life is true in all essential respects.

12. ADM 3/79. Quoted by Stark, 164–65.

13. *Edinburgh Evening Courant,* Thursday, December 31, 1835, 4.

14. *Bell's Weekly Messenger* (London), no. 1941, Sunday, June 16, 1833, 185.

15. *Edinburgh Evening Courant,* Monday, December 30, 1839.

16. *Carlisle Journal,* no. 2642, Friday, September 7, 1849, 4.

17. See Julie Wheelwright, *Amazons and Military Maids: Women Who Dressed as Men in Pursuit of Life, Liberty and Happiness* (London, 1989; cited paperback edition, 1990), 25; Stark, 89.

18. Quoted by Stark, 112.

19. *National Police Gazette* (New York), May 1, 1847.

20. *Bell's Weekly Messenger* (London), no. 1910, Sunday, September 9, 1832.

21. *The Morning Chronicle* (London), Thursday, September 2, 1813.

5. Hannah Snell, Mary Anne Talbot, and the Female Pirates

1. The details of Hannah Snell's life have been take from: Robert Walker, *The Female Soldier; Or, The Surprising Life and Adventures of Hannah Snell* (London, 1750); Matthew Stephens, *Hannah Snell: The Secret Life of a Female Marine* (London, 1997); Suzanne Stark, *Female Tars: Women Aboard Ship in the Age of Sail* (London, 1996); Julie Wheelwright, *Amazons and Military Maids* (London, 1989, cited paperback edition, 1990).

2. Walker, 165.

3. Ibid., 172.

4. Matthew Stephens has tracked down the records of the two marriages of Hannah's father in the Worcester Record Office. The first marriage bond, December 2, 1702, records the marriage of Samuel Snell, dyer, aged twenty-two, and Elizabeth Marston, aged about twenty (Worcester Record Office, document no. BA2036/21b). The second marriage bond, June 30, 1709, records the marriage of Samuel Snell, widower, aged twenty-nine years, and Mary Williams, aged twenty-five (Worcester Record Office, document no. BA2036/28a).

5. According to the Land Tax Assessments for Wapping, James Gray began paying taxes for the house on Ship Street in 1744 (Guildhall Library, document no. MS6016/1630).

6. Walker, 24, 141.

7. The muster book of the sloop *Swallow* (ADM 36/3472) notes that James Gray joined the ship on October 24, 1747.

8. Stark, 188, quotes the entry in the muster book of HMS *Eltham* (ADM 36/1035), "Jae. Gray [released] Cudelore Hopl. 2 Aug 1749, rec'd [into the *Eltham*] from *Tartar* 13 Oct. 1749."

9. Walker, 142.

10. The muster book of HMS *Eltham* (ADM 36/1035) records that Jae. Gray was discharged at Spithead on May 25, 1750.

11. Walker, 104.

12. Chelsea Hospital admission book, 1746–54 (document no. WO 116/4).

13. Several accounts of the life of Christian Davies were published, including *The Life and Adventures of Mrs. Christian Davies, the British Amazon, Commonly Call'd Mother Ross . . .* (London, 1740); and *Women Adventurers: The Adventure Series,* ed. Menie Muriel Dowie (London, 1893), vol. 15. See also many references in Julie Wheelwright, *Amazons and Military Maids.*

14. Stephens, 47.

15. *The Universal Chronicle,* November 3 to November 10, 1759, 359.

16. Stephens provides detailed references for the two later marriages of Hannah Snell and for the life of her son George.

17. The Reverend James Woodforde, *The Diary of a Country Parson,* ed. John Beresford (Oxford, 1924; edition cited, 1981), 224.

18. Stephens quotes the following text from a cutting from an unknown publication of September 14, 1791, found in the British Library (Biographical Adversaria, Add. Man. 5723): "This veteran heroine, who distinguished herself very highly many years ago, by repeated acts of valour, and who served in the navy under the virile habit, is still alive; but it is with regret we inform our readers that she was last week admitted into Bethlem Hospital, being at present a victim of the most deplorable infirmity that can afflict human nature."

19. Bethlem Royal Hospital Archives: Admission Register and Weekly Committee book for February 11, 1792.

20. Dowie, 139–95.

21. Ibid., 167.

22. Stark has checked out the key events of Mary Anne Talbot's life against army records and Admiralty documents and provides a fully documented account in her book, *Female Tars,* 107–10, 190–91. For Talbot's life in the Royal Navy she has examined the muster book of the *Crown,* transport, March–May 1792 (ADM 36/11014); the muster book of the *Brunswick,* March–July 1794 (ADM 36/11176); the muster book of the *Vesuvius,* 1793–95 (ADM 36/12698); and the muster book of Haslar Hospital, June–July 1794 (ADM 102/274).

23. The transcript of the trial was printed in Jamaica by Robert Baldwin in 1721. It was entitled *The Tryals of Captain John Rackam, and Other Pirates.* There are two copies bound into the Colonial Office documents relating to Jamaica in the Public Record Office, Kew (CO 137/12).

24. Captain Charles Johnson, *A General History of the Robberies and Murders of the Most Notorious Pyrates, and Also Their Policies, Discipline and Government, from Their First Rise and Settlement in the Island of Providence, . . . With the Remarkable Actions and Adventures of the Two Female Pyrates, Mary Read and Anne Bonny* (London, 1724). The 1726 edition was enlarged to include more pirates and was printed in two volumes; the full text of this, the most complete edition, is contained in Daniel Defoe,

A General History of the Pyrates, ed. Manuel Schonhorn (London, 1972). For a commentary on the identity of Captain Johnson and a reprint of the 1725 edition, see Captain Charles Johnson, *A General History of the Robberies and Murders of the Most Notorious Pyrates,* ed. David Cordingly (London, 1998).

25. See David Cordingly, *Under the Black Flag: The Romance and Reality of Life Among the Pirates* (New York, 1995; published in England under the title *Life among the Pirates,* London, 1995); and Marcus Rediker, *Between the Devil and the Deep Blue Sea: Merchant Seamen, Pirates, and the Anglo-American Maritime World, 1700–1750* (Cambridge, 1987). Rediker provides further insights into the lives of the female pirates in "Liberty beneath the Jolly Roger; the lives of Anne Bonny and Mary Read, Pirates," in *Iron Men, Wooden Women: Gender and Seafaring in the Atlantic World, 1700–1920,* ed. Margaret S. Creighton and Lisa Norling (Baltimore and London, 1996), 1–33.

26. The full text of the royal proclamation containing the King's pardon was issued by the governor of Bermuda and will be found among the Colonial Office papers in the Public Record Office (CO 37/10, no. 7 (i).).

27. *The Boston Gazette,* October 10–17, 1720.

28. *The Tryals of John Rackam,* 17.

29. Ibid., 19.

30. CO 137/12, no. 78 (i–v), ff. 231–35.

31. *The Tryals of John Rackam,* 19.

32. Clinton V. Black, *Pirates of the West Indies* (Cambridge, 1989), 117.

33. Family papers in the collection of descendants.

34. *Calendar of State Papers, Colonial Series, America and the West Indies* 32 (London, HMSO, 1933), 335.

35. *The Boston Gazette,* February 6–13, 1721.

6. *Wives in Warships*

1. *The Boston Gazette,* October 7, 1811.

2. J. Worth Estes, *Naval Surgeon: Life and Death at Sea in the Age of Sail* (Canton, Mass., 1998), 118–20.

3. Ibid., 145.

4. Harold D. Langley, *A History of Medicine in the Early U.S. Navy* (Baltimore and London, 1995), 190–92.

5. Captain's Orders, HMS *Amazon,* 1799, quoted from *Shipboard Life and Organisation, 1731–1815,* ed. B. Lavery (Navy Records Society, Aldershot, U.K., 1998), 160.

6. Ibid., 14.

7. Ibid., 46.

8. Ibid., 58.

9. The Duke of York issued the order on October 29, 1800. *Collection of Regulations and Miscellaneous Orders, 1760–1807,* quoted by Colonel Noel T. St. John Williams, *Judy O'Grady and the Colonel's Lady: The Army Wife and Camp Follower Since 1660* (London, 1988), 17.

10. Ibid., 19.

11. Ibid., 18.

12. For further information on army wives of this period, see Veronica Bamfield, *On the Strength: The Story of the British Army Wife* (London, 1974); George Bell, *Soldier's Glory: Being Rough Notes of an Old Soldier* (London, 1956), 61, 74–75; William

Tomkinson, *Diary of a Cavalry Officer in the Peninsular and Waterloo Campaign, 1809–1815* (1971); Lady de Lancey, *A Week at Waterloo in June 1815* (London, 1906).

13. Lieutenant William Gratton, *Adventures with the Connaught Rangers, 1809–1814* (London, 1902), 276.

14. ADM 101/102/4, entry for December 8, 1787.

15. ADM 101/102/6, entry for February 5, 1789.

16. ADM 36/11060.

17. Richardson, 139.

18. Ibid., 169.

19. Ibid., 173.

20. ADM 1/5295.

21. ADM 1/5294.

22. ADM 1/5302.

23. ADM 1/5348.

24. Most of the details for this summary of the mutiny on the *Hermione* are taken from Dudley Pope, *The Black Ship* (London, 1963), a fascinating and fully documented account of the events leading up to the mutiny and the subsequent fate of the ship and the mutineers.

25. ADM 6/332, 216–17, minutes of the meeting on August 2, 1803.

26. Henry Baynham, *From the Lower Deck: The Old Navy, 1780–1840* (London, 1969), 27–28.

27. Ibid., 28.

28. ADM 36/14817, muster book of HMS *Goliath*, August 3 to November 30, 1798.

29. Commander W. B. Rowbotham, "The Naval General Service Medal, 1793–1840," *The Mariner's Mirror*, 23 (London, 1937), 366.

30. Daniel McKenzie's name appears in two of the muster books of HMS *Tremendous* for the period covering the Battle of the Glorious First of June. In ADM 36/11658, his name is listed in the muster tables for February, March, and April 1794, as "Daniel McKenzie / Ab," and again in the muster tables for June 12 to August 2, 1794. In ADM 36/11660, his name appears in the muster table for May 1 to June 30, 1794, with the additional information that he was twenty-seven when he joined the ship and was born in Plymouth.

31. Rowbotham, 366.

32. David Howarth, *Trafalgar: The Nelson Touch* (London, 1969; edition cited, 1972), 219; William Robinson, *Jack Nastyface: Memoirs of a Seaman* (Annapolis, Md., 1973), 57–61.

33. Baynham, 160.

34. Captain W. N. Glascock, *Tales of a Tar* (London, 1836).

35. Thomas Cochrane, tenth Earl of Dundonald, Admiral of the Red, *The Autobiography of a Seaman*, ed. Douglas Cochrane (London, 1890), 365.

36. Ibid., 482.

37. See J. H. Hubback and Edith C. Hubback, *Jane Austen's Sailor Brothers: Being the Adventures of Sir Frances Austen, GCB, Admiral of the Fleet and Rear-Admiral Charles Austen* (London, 1906).

7. Seafaring Heroines

1. Most of the details for the story of Mary Patten are taken from Barbara Jagielski, "Mary Patten: Heroine of the High Seas," in *Sea Classics*, August 1992, 65–71.

2. From an interview with Mary Patten published in the *New York Daily Tribune*, February 18, 1857, quoted in Jagielski, 70.

3. Jagielski, 70.
4. Letter from the Union Mutual Insurance Company, New York, February 18, 1857, quoted by Jagielski, 70.
5. Joan Druett, *Hen Frigates: Wives of Merchant Captains Under Sail* (New York, 1998), and "Those Female Journals," in *The Log of Mystic Seaport*, Winter 1989, 115–25.
6. See Phillis Zauner, "Petticoats on the Poop Deck: Those Courageous Bluewater Women," in *The Compass: The Magazine of the Sea and Air* LXV, 1995, 7; and Druett, *Hen Frigates*, 190–91.
7. Druett, *Hen Frigates*, 184.
8. Ibid., 39.

8. Whaling Wives

1. Letter from Nantucket dated September, 19, 1808, Nantucket Historical Society.
2. *The Captain's Best Mate: The Journal of Mary Chipman Lawrence on the Whaler Addison 1856–1860*, ed. Stanton Garner (Hanover and London, 1966), xvi.
3. Ibid., xvi.
4. *The Honolulu Friend*, February 1, 1853.
5. Garner, 3.
6. Ibid., 25.
7. Ibid., 209.
8. Quoted by Haskell Springer, "The Captain's Wife at Sea," in *Iron Men, Wooden Women: Gender and Seafaring in the Atlantic World, 1700–1920*, ed. Margaret S. Creighton and Lisa Norling (Baltimore and London, 1996), 95.
9. *She Was a Sister Sailor: The Whaling Journal of Mary Brewster, 1845–1851*, ed. Joan Druett (Mystic, Conn., 1992), 18.
10. Joan Druett, "Those Female Journals," in *The Log of Mystic Seaport*, Winter 1989, 117.
11. Journal of Henrietta Deblois, November 20, 1856, quoted by Druett, *She Was a Sister Sailor*, 6.
12. Springer, 96.
13. Ibid., 113.
14. Druett, *She Was a Sister Sailor*, 22.
15. Springer, 110.
16. Druett, *She Was a Sister Sailor*, 39.
17. Lisa Norling, "Ahab's Wife: Women and the American Whaling Industry, 1820–1870," in *Iron Men, Wooden Women*, 78.
18. Ibid., 76.
19. Ruth Wallis Herndon, "The Domestic Cost of Seafaring," in *Iron Men, Wooden Women*, 63.
20. Norling, 80.
21. Ibid.
22. Ibid., 82.
23. Letter dated November 5, 1871, Nantucket Historical Society.
24. Letter from Captain George Allen to his sister Hannah Marie Smith, August 29, 1859, Nantucket Historical Society.
25. Margaret S. Creighton, "Women and Men in American Whaling, 1830–1870," in *International Journal of Maritime History* IV, June 1992, 212.
26. Norling, 86.
27. Ibid.

28. Baynham, 89.
29. Norling, 89.

9. *Men Without Women*

1. All the details of the account of the court-martial of George Newton and Thomas Finley are taken from the transcript of the proceedings in ADM 1/5300.
2. ADM 1/5383.
3. ADM 1/5294.
4. ADM 12/086/28.
5. All the courts-martial for 1800 are listed in ADM 12/086/28. This gives the name of the accused, his ship, the charges, and the punishment.
6. *A Selection from the Public and Private Correspondence of Vice-Admiral Lord Colling-wood*, ed. G. L. Newnham Collingwood (London, 1829), 19.
7. Letter written from HMS *Barfleur*, at Torbay, October 4, 1800, in Collingwood, 80.
8. Letter written from HMS *Dreadnought*, off Cádiz, August 21, 1805, in Collingwood, 109.
9. Letter written from HMS *Queen*, off Cartagena, December 16, 1805, in Colling-wood, 165.
10. Letter written from Portsmouth, January 30, 1755, in Spinney, 113.
11. Spinney, 113.
12. Letter dated July 22, 1755, in Spinney, 117.
13. Letter dated July 21, 1748, *Admiral's Wife: Being the Life and Letters of the Hon. Mrs. Edward Boscawen from 1719 to 1761*, ed. Cecil Aspinall-Oglander (London, 1940), 96.
14. Letter written from HMS *Torbay*, at sea, May 3, 1755, "Boscawen's Letters to His Wife, 1755–1756," ed. Peter Kemp, in *The Naval Miscellany* IV (1952), 177.
15. Letter written from HMS *Torbay*, at sea, May 7, 1755, in Kemp, 180.
16. Letter written from HMS *Torbay*, at sea, April 22, 1755, in Kemp, 175.
17. Letter written from HMS *Invincible*, at sea, May 31, 1756, in Kemp, 215.
18. The spelling has been modernized here. The original (quoted by Peter Kemp in his *The British Sailor*, 76) is "i am and so is every Man of us resolved either to lose our lifes or conker our enemys. true british spirit revives and by G-d we will support our King and contry so long as a drap of blood remains."
19. Baynham, 95.
20. Nevens, 81.

10. *Women and Water, Sirens and Mermaids*

1. Letter written from HMS *Ocean*, August 9, 1808. *The Private Correspondence of Admiral Lord Collingwood*, ed. Edward Hughes (Navy Records Society, London, 1957), 251.
2. Linda Greenlaw, *The Hungry Ocean: A Swordboat Captain's Journey* (London, 1999), 137.
3. Nelson to Admiral Jervis, 1801, *Memoirs of Admiral the Right Honourable the Earl of St. Vincent* 2, ed. J. S. Tucker (London, 1844), 120.
4. *The Natural History of Pliny V*, translated with notes by J. Bostock and H. T. Riley (London, 1855), 304.
5. Margarita Russell, *Visions of the Sea: Hendrick C. Vroom and the Origins of Dutch Marine Painting* (Leiden, Netherlands, 1983), 65–68; and Sylvia Rogers, *The Symbolism of Ship Launching in the Royal Navy* (D.Phil. thesis, Oxford), 531–37. There is a copy in the Caird Library, National Maritime Museum, London.

6. *Sigmund Freud: Introductory Lectures on Psychoanalysis,* eds. James Strachey and Angela Richards (London, 1973; edition cited, 1991), 194.

7. Hans Soop, *The Power and the Glory: The Sculptures of the Warship Wasa* (Stockholm, 1986).

8. P. N. Thomas, *British Figurehead and Ship Carvers* (Wolverhampton, U.K., 1995), 66.

9. Thomas, 76.

10. Giancarlo Costa, *Figureheads: Carving on Ships from Ancient Times to the Twentieth Century,* translated from the Italian by Brian Dolley (Lymington, U.K., 1981).

11. Thomas, 40.

12. For a more detailed discussion of the image of Britannia, see Marina Warner, *Monuments and Maidens: The Allegory of the Female Form* (London, 1985; edition cited, 1996), 45–49.

13. Among the books consulted on the subject of sirens and mermaids, the following proved most useful: Angelo S. Rappoport, *Superstitions of Sailors* (London, 1928); F. S. Bassett, *Legends and Superstitions of the Sea and Sailors in All Lands and at All Times* (Chicago and New York, 1885); Helen King, "Half-human Creatures," in *Mythical Beasts,* ed. John Cherry (London, 1995); Gwen Benwell and Arthur Waugh, *Sea Enchantress: The Tale of the Mermaid and Her Kin* (London, 1961); Beatrice Phillpotts, *Mermaids* (London, 1980).

14. Quoted by Benwell and Waugh, 42.

15. Benwell and Waugh, 95.

16. Ibid., 96.

17. Ibid., 97.

18. See Beatrice Phillpotts's book, *Mermaids,* for an excellent selection of paintings, woodcuts, and book illustrations of sirens and mermaids.

11. *A Wife in Every Port*

1. The details of Hervey's life are taken from: M. J. R. Holmes, *Augustus Hervey, a Naval Casanova* (Edinburgh and Cambridge, 1996); *August Hervey's Journal: Being the Intimate Account of the Life of a Captain in the Royal Navy Ashore and Afloat, 1746–1759,* ed. David Erskine (London, 1953); Obituary of Augustus Hervey in the *Gentleman's Magazine* 53 (1783), 1007; and the entries for Hervey and for Elizabeth Chudleigh in the *Dictionary of National Biography* (London).

2. Holmes, 71.

3. Quoted by Erskine in his Introduction to *Augustus Hervey's Journal.*

4. *Hervey's Journal,* 76.

5. Ibid., 101.

6. Ibid., 190.

7. Mrs. Nesbitt's origins are obscure: "This lady, whose origin may be traced to a wheelbarrow, made acquaintance to Mr. Nesbitt, a worthy young gentleman then in partnerships in the banking business. . . ." *Town and Country,* January 1775, 9.

8. Holmes, 238.

9. David Proctor, *Music of the Sea* (London, 1992), 78.

10. PROB 11/960 f. 383.

11. ADM 6/332.

12. See Commander Charles N. Robinson, *The British Tar in Fact and Fiction: The Poetry, Pathos and Humour of the Sailor's Life* (London and New York, 1909). This fascinating book contains a rich selection of illustrations after contemporary woodcuts and engravings, as well as many examples of nautical songs and ballads.

13. *Naval Songs and Ballads,* ed. C. H. Firth (Navy Records Society, London, 1908), 143–44.

14. *Ramblin' Jack: The Journal of Captain John Cremer, 1700–1774,* ed. R. Reynell Bellamy (London, 1936), 131.

15. ADM 101/102/11.

16. Edward Thompson, *A Sailor's Letters, Written to His Select Friends in England During His Voyages and Travels in Europe, Asia, Africa, and America, from the Year 1754 to 1759* 2 (London, 1767), 24.

17. George Robertson, *The Discovery of Tahiti: A Journal of the Second Voyage of HMS Dolphin Round the World . . . Written by Her Master George Robertson,* ed. Hugh Carrington, (London, 1948), 136.

18. Ibid., 166.

19. See J. C. Beaglehole, *The Life of Captain James Cook* (London, 1974), 172.

20. Patrick O'Brian, *Joseph Banks, a Life* (London, 1987; edition cited, Chicago, 1997), 91.

21. Lynne Withey, *Voyages of Discovery: Captain Cook and the Exploration of the Pacific* (London, 1987), 102.

22. David Lewis, *From Maui to Cook: The Discovery and Settlement of the Pacific* (Sydney, 1977), 161.

23. Richard Hough, *Captain Bligh and Mr. Christian: The Men and the Mutiny* (London, 1972; edition cited, London, 1988), 196.

24. Brian W. Scott, "Pitcairn: What Happened," in *Mutiny on the Bounty, 1789–1989* (catalogue of exhibition held at the National Maritime Museum, London, 1989), 131.

12. *Two Naval Heroes and Their Women*

1. The details for the life of John Paul Jones are taken from Samuel Eliot Morison, *John Paul Jones: A Sailor's Biography* (Boston, 1959), which contains a very comprehensive bibliography; William Gilkerson, *The Ships of John Paul Jones* (Annapolis, Md., 1987); and G. W. Allen, *A Naval History of the American Revolution* (Boston, 1913).

2. Morison, 250.

3. Ibid., 280.

4. Ibid., 286. The original letter was written in French.

5. Ibid., 347.

6. Ibid., 376.

7. The details of the lives of Nelson and Lady Hamilton are taken from Flora Fraser, *Beloved Emma* (London, 1986); George P. Naish, *Nelson's Letters to His Wife* (London, 1958); David Howarth, *Trafalgar: The Nelson Touch* (London, 1969); Tom Pocock, *Horatio Nelson* (London, 1987); Tom Pocock, *Nelson's Women* (London, 1999); *Nelson: An Illustrated History,* ed. Pieter van der Merwe (London, 1995); and Oliver Warner, *A Portrait of Lord Nelson* (London, 1958).

8. Fraser, 249.

9. Naish, 353.

10. Pocock, *Horatio Nelson,* 165.

11. Fraser, 220.

12. Warner, 168.

13. Ibid., 268–69.

14. Pocock, *Nelson's Women,* 156.

15. Naish, 586.

16. Pocock, *Nelson's Women,* 193.

17. Ibid., 214.

18. Ibid., 223.
19. Naish, 605–6.
20. Fraser, 326.
21. The friend was Lady Elizabeth Foster; see Pocock, *Nelson's Women*, 227.

13. *The Lighthouse Women*

1. The details for Grace Darling's story are taken from Constance Smedley, *Grace Darling and Her Times* (London, 1932); Richard Armstrong, *Grace Darling, Maid and Myth* (London, 1965); William Darling, *The Journal of William Darling, Grace Darling's Father* (London, 1886); *Grace Darling: Her True Story; from Unpublished Papers in the Possession of Her Family* (London, 1880).
2. Darling, 19–20.
3. From a report in the *Berwick & Kelso Warder*, quoted by Armstrong, 136.
4. Armstrong, 99.
5. Ibid., 112.
6. Smedley, 76.
7. *Grace Darling: Her True Story*, 26.
8. Smedley, 76.
9. Elinor De Wire, *Guardians of the Lights: The Men and Women of the U.S. Lighthouse Service* (Sarasota, Fla., 1953), 189.
10. Mary Louise Clifford and J. Candace Clifford, *Women Who Kept the Lights: An Illustrated History of Female Lighthouse Keepers* (Williamsburg, Va., 1993), 26.
11. Ibid., 29.
12. Ibid., 128.
13. The details of the life of Ida Lewis are taken from Gilson Willets, "Fifty Years a Heroine of the Seas," from an unknown publication of July 1907 in the archives of the Mariners' Museum, Newport News, Va. (Lifesaving at Sea, 1850–1912); and from Elinor de Wire, *Guardians of the Lights;* Clifford and Clifford, *Women Who Kept the Lights*.
14. The journalist was George Brewerton, and his description is quoted in Clifford and Clifford, 91.
15. Ibid., 92.
16. Willets, 42.

14. *The Sailors' Return*

1. Baynham, 93.
2. Ibid., 130.
3. Christopher Lloyd, *The British Seaman, 1200–1860* (London, 1968), 246.
4. Captain Anselm John Griffiths, *Observations on Some Points of Seamanship* (Cheltenham, U.K., 1824), 43–45.
5. ADM 101/90/1.
6. ADM 101/93/2.
7. Richardson, 17–18.
8. Nicholas Blake and Richard Lawrence, *The Illustrated Companion to Nelson's Navy* (London, 2000), 94.
9. There is an excellent chapter on naval diseases with extensive quotations from Turnbull in Dudley Pope, *Life in Nelson's Navy* (first published London 1981; edition cited, 1999), 131–48; see also Christopher Lloyd and Jack Coulter, *Medicine and the Navy, 1200–1900* (Edinburgh and London, 1961).

10. Spavens, 111.
11. ADM 6/332.
12. Oliver Warner, *The Glorious First of June* (London, 1961), 163.
13. Christopher Lloyd, *St. Vincent and Camperdown* (London, 1963), 160.
14. Pope, 80.
15. Letter dated June 9, 1755, Aspinall-Oglander, 179–80.
16. Peter Linebaugh, *The London Hanged: Crime and Civil Society in the Eighteenth Century* (London, 1991; edition cited, 1993), 140.
17. Firth, 140.
18. ADM 1/5125.
19. Spinney, 124.
20. Nantucket Historical Society.
21. Edgar March, *Sailing Drifters* (Newton Abbot, U.K., 1969), 255.
22. Caroline Fox and Francis Greenacre, *Painting in Newlyn, 1830–1930* (catalogue of exhibition at the Barbican Art Gallery, London), 121.

BIBLIOGRAPHY

This is a selected list of books for further reading. References to the books and documents that I have consulted are given in the notes to each chapter.

Armstrong, Richard. *Grace Darling: Maid and Myth* (London, 1965).

Asbury, Herbert. *The Barbary Coast: An Informal History of the San Francisco Underworld* (London, 1934).

Aspinall-Oglander, Cecil, ed. *Admiral's Wife: Being the Life and Letters of The Hon. Mrs. Edward Boscawen from 1719–1761* (London, 1940).

Bamfield, Veronica. *On the Strength: The Story of the British Army Wife* (London, 1974).

Bassett, F. S. *Legends and Superstitions of the Sea and Sailors in All Lands and at All Times* (Chicago and New York, 1885).

Baynham, Henry. *From the Lower Deck: The Old Navy, 1780–1840* (London, 1969).

Beaglehole, J. C. *The Life of Captain James Cook* (London, 1974).

Bell, George. *Soldier's Glory: Being Rough Notes of an Old Soldier* (London, 1956).

Benwell, Gwen, and Arthur Waugh. *Sea Enchantress: The Tale of the Mermaid and Her Kin* (London, 1961).

Berckman, Evelyn. *The Hidden Navy* (London, 1973).

Blake, Nicholas, and Richard Lawrence. *The Illustrated Companion to Nelson's Navy* (London, 2000).

Burford, E. J., and Joy Wotton. *Private Vices—Public Virtues: Bawdry in London from Elizabethan Times to the Regency* (London, 1955).

Cherry, John, ed. *Mythical Beasts* (London, 1995).

Clark, Peter. *The English Alehouse: A Social History, 1200–1830* (London, 1983).

Clifford, M. L., and J. C. Clifford. *Women Who Kept the Lights* (Williamsburg, Va., 1993).

Cochrane, Thomas. *The Autobiography of a Seaman,* Douglas Cochrane, ed. (London, 1890).

Cohen, Daniel A. *The Female Marine and Related Works: Narratives of Cross-Dressing and Urban Vice in America's Early Republic* (Boston, 1997).

Collingwood, G. L. Newnham. *A Selection from the Public and Private Correspondence of Vice-Admiral Lord Collingwood* (London, 1829).

Cordingly, David. *Under the Black Flag: The Romance and Reality of Life Among the Pirates* (New York, 1995).

Costa, Giancarlo. *Figureheads: Carving on Ships from Ancient Times to the Twentieth Century* (Lymington, U.K., 1981).

Creighton, Margaret S., and Lisa Norling, eds. *Iron Men, Wooden Women: Gender and Seafaring in the Atlantic World, 1700–1920* (Baltimore and London, 1996).

Cremer, John. *Ramblin' Jack: The Journal of Captain John Cremer, 1700–1774*, R. Reynell Bellamy, ed. (London, 1936).

Cunningham, Charles. *A Narrative of the Mutiny at the Nore* (Chatham, U.K., 1829).

de Pauw, Linda Grant. *Seafaring Women* (Boston, 1982).

De Wire, Elinor. *Guardians of the Lights: The Men and Women of the U.S. Lighthouse Service* (Sarasota, Fla., 1953).

Diamant, Lincoln, ed. *Revolutionary Women in the War for American Independence* (Westport, Conn., and London).

Dowie, Menie Muriel, ed. *Women Adventurers* (London, 1893).

Druett, Joan. *Hen Frigates: Wives of Merchant Captains Under Sail* (New York, 1998).

————. *She Captains: Heroines and Hellions of the Sea* (New York, 2000).

Druett, Joan, ed. *She Was a Sister Sailor: The Whaling Journal of Mary Brewster, 1845–1851* (Mystic, Conn., 1992).

Dugaw, Dianne. *Warrior Women and Popular Balladry, 1650–1850* (Chicago and London, 1989).

Erskine, David. *Augustus Hervey's Journal: Being the Intimate Account of the Life of a Captain in the Royal Navy Ashore and Afloat, 1746–1759* (London, 1953).

Estes, J. Worth. *Naval Surgeon: Life and Death at Sea in the Age of Sail* (Canton, Mass., 1998).

Firth, C. H. *Naval Songs and Ballads* (Navy Records Society, London, 1908).

Fraser, Antonia. *The Weaker Vessel: A Woman's Lot in Seventeenth-Century England* (London, 1984).

Fraser, Flora. *Beloved Emma: The Life of Emma Lady Hamilton* (London, 1986).

Garner, Stan, ed. *The Captain's Best Mate: The Journal of Mary Chipman Lawrence on the Whaler Addison, 1856–1860* (Hanover and London, 1966).

Gilfoyle, Timothy. *City of Eros: New York City, Prostitution and the Commercialization of Sex, 1790–1920* (New York, 1992).

Gilkerson, William. *The Ships of John Paul Jones* (Annapolis, Md., 1987).

Glascock, Captain W. N. *Tales of a Tar* (London, 1836).

Greenlaw, Linda. *The Hungry Ocean: A Swordboat Captain's Journey* (London, 1999).

Hibbert, Christopher. *Nelson: A Personal History* (London, 1994).

Hill, Marilynn Wood. *Their Sisters' Keepers: Prostitution in New York City, 1830–1870* (Berkeley, Los Angeles, and London, 1992).

Holmes, M.J.R. *Augustus Hervey, a Naval Casanova* (Edinburgh and Cambridge, 1996).

Hough, Richard. *Captain Bligh and Mr. Christian: The Men and the Mutiny* (London, 1972).

Hubback, J. H., and Edith C. Hubback. *Jane Austen's Sailor Brothers: Being the Adventures of Sir Frances Austen, GCB, Admiral of the Fleet and Rear-Admiral Charles Austen* (London, 1906).

Hughes, Edward, ed. *The Private Correspondence of Admiral Lord Collingwood* (Navy Records Society, London, 1957).

Hugill, Stan. *Sailortown* (London, 1967).

Hutchinson, J. R. *The Press-gang Afloat and Ashore* (London, 1913).

Inwood, Stephen. *A History of London* (London, 1998).

Johnson, Captain Charles. *A General History of the Robberies and Murders of the Most Notorious Pyrates* (London, 1724).

Kemp, Peter. *The British Sailor: A Social History of the Lower Deck* (London, 1970).

Lancey, Lady de. *A Week at Waterloo in June 1815* (London, 1906).

Langley, Harold D. *A History of Medicine in the Early U.S. Navy* (Baltimore and London, 1995).

Lavery, Brian. *Nelson's Navy: The Ships, Men and Organisation, 1793–1815* (London, 1989).

Lloyd, Christopher. *The British Seaman, 1200–1860* (London, 1968).

Lloyd, Christopher, and Jack Coulter. *Medicine and the Navy, 1200–1900* (Edinburgh and London, 1961).

Mayhew, Henry. *London Labour and the London Poor* (London, 1851).

Merrick, Reverend G. P. *Work Among the Fallen, as Seen in the Prison Cell* (London, New York, and Melbourne, 1891).

Morison, Samuel Eliot. *John Paul Jones: A Sailor's Biography* (Boston, 1959).

Naish, George, ed. *Nelson's Letters to His Wife* (London, 1958).

Nevens, William. *Forty Years at Sea* (Portland, Maine, 1850).

Phillpotts, Beatrice. *Mermaids* (London, 1980).

Pocock, Tom. *Nelson's Women* (London, 1999).

———. *Horatio Nelson* (London, 1987).

Pope, Dudley. *Life in Nelson's Navy* (London, 1981).

———. *The Black Ship* (London, 1963, and New York, 1998).

Pudney, John. *London's Docks* (London, 1975).

Rappoport, Angelo S. *Superstitions of Sailors* (London, 1928).

Rediker, Marcus. *Between the Devil and the Deep Blue Sea: Merchant Seamen, Pirates, and the Anglo-American Maritime World* (Cambridge, U.K., 1987).

Richardson, William. *A Mariner of England: An Account of the Career of William Richardson from Cabin Boy in the Merchant Service to Warrant Officer in the Royal Navy As Told By Himself* (London, 1908).

Robertson, George. *The Discovery of Tahiti*, Hugh Carrington, ed. (London, 1948).

Robinson, Captain Charles N. *The British Tar in Fact and Fiction: The Poetry, Pathos and Humour of the Sailor's Life* (London and New York, 1909).

Robinson, William. *Jack Nastyface: Memoirs of a Seaman* (Annapolis, Md., 1973).

Rodger, N.A.M. *The Wooden World: An Anatomy of the Georgian Navy* (London, 1986).

Sanger, William. *The History of Prostitution: Its Extent, Causes and Effects Throughout the World* (New York, 1858).

Smedley, Constance. *Grace Darling and Her Times* (London, 1932).

Soop, Hans. *The Power and the Glory: The Sculptures of the Warship Wasa* (Stockholm, 1986).

Spavens, William. *The Narrative of William Spavens, a Chatham Pensioner, written by himself* (Louth, U.K., 1796).

Spinney, David. *Rodney* (London, 1969).

Stanley, Jo. *Bold in Her Breeches: Women Pirates Across the Ages* (London, 1995).

Stark, Suzanne J. *Female Tars: Women Aboard Ship in the Age of Sail* (London, 1996).

Stephens, Matthew. *Hannah Snell: The Secret Life of a Female Marine* (London, 1997).

Stone, Lawrence. *The Family, Sex and Marriage in England, 1500–1800* (London, 1977).

Thomas, P. N. *British Figurehead and Ship Carvers* (Wolverhampton, U.K., 1995).

Tucker, J. S., ed. *Memoirs of the Admiral the Right Honourable the Earl of St. Vincent* (London, 1844).

Walker, Robert. *The Female Soldier; Or, The Surprising Life and Adventures of Hannah Snell* (London, 1750).

Walkowitz, Judith R. *Prostitution and Victorian Society: Women, Class and the State* (London and New York, 1980).

Ward, Ned. *The London Spy* (first published 1703; edition published by Folio Society, London, 1955).

Warner, Marina. *Monuments and Maidens: The Allegory of the Female Form* (London, 1985).

Warner, Oliver. *A Portrait of Lord Nelson* (London, 1958).

Wheelwright, Julie. *Amazons and Military Maids: Women Who Dressed as Men in Pursuit of Life, Liberty and Happiness* (London, 1989).

Williams, Noel T. St. John. *Judy O'Grady and the Colonel's Lady: The Army Wife and Camp Follower Since 1660* (London, 1988).

Withey, Lynne. *Voyages of Discovery: Captain Cook and the Exploration of the Pacific* (London, 1987).

ACKNOWLEDGMENTS

This has been a surprisingly difficult book to write. My first forays in libraries revealed masses of material about mermaids but very little about real women who went to sea. There were plenty of journals and memoirs written by seamen, but there seemed to be remarkably few written by seafaring women. The biographies of the few well-known women sailors were all written by men and contain a great deal of undocumented and dubious material. And then I came across Suzanne Stark's book, *Female Tars,* which uncovered and analyzed the facts about women in the Royal Navy. This confirmed my suspicions about some of the stories of female sailors but also preempted much of what I had intended to write about.

I therefore decided to change tack and to look beyond the stories of women sailors to the relationships between seafarers and their women, afloat and ashore. It soon became apparent that several volumes would be required to do justice to such a fascinating subject, so I limited myself to the Anglo-American maritime world in the eighteenth and nineteenth centuries, and selected a number of representative characters and areas within that period. I am acutely aware that I have only scraped the surface and that there is much more material waiting to be unearthed.

In some chapters, I have made several references to popular prints and paintings of the period because these not only provide useful information on the appearance of seafaring men and women, their clothes, their houses, the streets they lived on, and their harbors and ships, they also reflect contemporary attitudes to sailors and their women. Because of production costs and high reproduction fees, only a selection of these pictures appear in this book, but many of these images will be shown in exhibitions that are being planned, notably the exhibit at the Mariners' Museum in Newport News, Virginia, which is entitled *Women at Sea* and opens in March 2001.

The staff at the Mariners' Museum have been endlessly helpful during the preparation of this book, and I would like to acknowledge the financial assistance they have given me as guest curator. In particular, I would like to thank the following: John Hightower, the president of the museum; Claudia Pennington, the former director (now executive director of the Key West Museum of Art and History); Bill Cogar, chief curator and vice president; Karen Shackelford, who has been largely responsible for the preparation of the exhibition; Benjamin H. Trask, who supplied me with a constant stream of information; and the staffs of the library and the education department.

I would also like to thank Suzanne Gluck, my agent in New York, and Gillian Coleridge, my English agent, for their constant support, and to thank the editorial staff of my publishers at Random House, New York, and at Macmillan in London for their good advice and sympathetic editing. Tanya Stobbs, Becky Lindsay, and Nicholas Blake were particularly helpful. I would also like to record my thanks to David Moore, Stephen Jaffe, Pieter van der Merwe, Peter and Mary Neill, Elisabeth Shure, Jo Stanley, and Pamela Tudor-Craig, as well as to the staff at the Library of Congress, the British Library, the London Library, and the Public Record Office, and my former colleagues at the National Maritime Museum, London.

The Notes and Bibliography indicate the sources that I have used in writing this book, but I would like to record my debt to four writers in particular. The first is Antonia Fraser, whose biographies are legendary and who encouragingly wrote in her preface to *The Weaker Vessel*, "After all, to write about women it is not necessary to be a woman, merely to have a sense of justice and sympathy." The second is Linda Grant de Pauw, whose pioneering work, *Seafaring Women*, I vividly recall reading and enjoying during one of my visits to the Library of Congress. The third is Suzanne Stark, whose *Female Tars* I have already mentioned. And the fourth is Joan Druett, another pioneer in the study of seafaring women, who has published a succession of fine books on the subject. Her most recent book, *She Captains*, fortunately appeared after I had completed work on this book. Otherwise, I might have been tempted to abandon it and go back to the drawing board.

Finally, I would like to thank my daughter, Rebecca, who kept me on track when sometimes I could not see the forest for the trees; and my wife, Shirley, who helped me the most and to whom this book is affectionately dedicated.

D.C.

Brighton, Sussex

September 2000

About the Author

DAVID CORDINGLY was for twelve years on the staff of the National Maritime Museum in Greenwich, England, where he was curator of paintings and then head of exhibitions. His book *Under the Black Flag: The Romance and the Reality of Life Among the Pirates* is considered the definitive account of the great age of piracy. He is a graduate of Oxford and received his doctorate from the University of Sussex. Cordingly now works as a writer, and lives with his wife and family by the sea in Sussex.

About the Type

This book is set in Fournier, a typeface named for Pierre Simon Fournier, the youngest son of a French printing family. He started out engraving woodblocks and large capitals, then moved on to fonts of type. In 1736 he began his own foundry and made several important contributions in the field of type design; he is said to have cut 147 alphabets of his own creation. Fournier is probably best remembered as the designer of St. Augustine Ordinaire, a face that served as the model for Monotype's Fournier, which was released in 1925.

24.95

910.45   Cordingly, David.
C
         Women sailors and
           sailors' women.

DATE			
	WITHDRAWN		

BAKER & TAYLOR